TQM
AMERICA

TQM
AMERICA

How America's most successful companies profit from Total Quality Management

Eric E. Anschutz

McGuinn & McGuire
PUBLISHING, INC.
Bradenton, Florida

Library of Congress Cataloging-in-Publication Data

Anschutz, Eric E., 1929-
    TQM America : how America's most successful companies
profit from total quality management / Eric E. Anschutz.
        p.   cm.
    Includes bibliographical references and index.
    ISBN 1-881117-13-8 (acid-free paper : pbk.)
    1. Total quality management. 2. Total quality management –
United State. I. Title.
    HD62.15.A57   1995
    658.5'62 – dc20   95-4163

Printed in the United States of America

Preface

The title for this book, *TQM America*, was inspired by a perceptive and prescient statement made more than 200 years ago by America's first President, George Washington. As cited in Vice President Al Gore's 1993 "Report of the National Performance Review," President Washington said:

> Take two managers and give each the same number of laborers and let those laborers be equal in all aspects. Let both managers rise equally early, and go equally late to rest, be equally active, sober, and industrious, and yet, in the course of the year, one of them, without pushing the hands that are under him more than the other, shall have performed infinitely more work.

Washington's implied message, which was that management *methods* make an important difference, is as true in contemporary America as it was in the earliest days of our nation. Our continuing search for effective management methods has led us to Total Quality Management: TQM is *the* right management method for our time; it makes the important difference that President Washington saw the need for.

Our TQM has evolved in ways that suit it perfectly to the rich American tradition of social mobility, egalitarianism, and open frontiers that are such an important part of our cultural heritage.

In this book, the reader is presented with leading-edge TQM concepts as practiced by the most successful American companies. You will find these "world-class" concepts readily usable in the renewal of your organization because they are supported with benchmark examples drawn from the best practices of American companies, many of whom are winners of the prestigious Baldrige Award. The fundamentals of general management are discussed in the context of TQM principles; theory is always related to practice.

The book is easy to read. On page after page, top-level executives and managers in organizations of every kind will recognize the issues with which they deal on a daily basis, and will profit from the collection of cutting-edge management ideas, all cross-linked and mutually reinforcing. *TQM America* will also be useful to university students interested in the study of management.

TQM America is a *how-to* book, intended for those who want to make a benchmark comparison of their TQM strategy with the best practices of Baldrige winners and other successful organizations. TQM practitioners will find the book rich with ideas on how to make things happen. It reflects the author's strong view that TQM has a single purpose: to improve the performance of your business. TQM is *a means* to that end; it is not an end in itself.

Foreword

Why another book about TQM? The subject is no longer new. Most executives and managers know about it, and an estimated 67% of American organizations have embraced a quality strategy of some sort. Countless articles and numerous books have been written on the subject. Total quality management consultants abound and not a month goes by without still another TQM seminar or conference. Yet, some of the most important elements of TQM remain unstated.

The purpose of this book is to offer interesting, useful, and, in some cases, new perspectives about TQM. It is above all intended as a book for practitioners, a "how to" book, rich with ideas on how to make things happen. It reflects my strong view that TQM must not be allowed to become merely another set of things to do, an added layer of bureaucracy. TQM has a single purpose: to improve the performance of *your* business. It is a means to that end, not an end in itself.

Since my 1950 graduation in engineering management from MIT, I have been seeking an integrated management strategy that combined the simplicity of common sense with the sophistication necessary to deal effectively and efficiently with the complexities of multifaceted programs. TQM, which I first learned about in the early 1980's, is such a management strategy. The simplicity of TQM might be likened to the "simplicity" of the Golden Rule. "Doing unto others . . .," while simple, is endlessly profound and challenging, and filled with the possibility of a better future when practiced. TQM, too, is simple, but nonetheless profound and challenging, and there is an abundance of evidence that things improve for those who practice it.

This book brings together all I have learned in my decade-long TQM journey. My goal in writing it has been to bring to the reader new insights into such TQM-bedrock topics as involvement, empowerment, leadership, teamwork, training, reward systems, decentralization, supplier integration, process improvement, reengineering, customer focus, kansei, and strategic planning using Hoshin Kanri methods. I have sought throughout the book always to supplement TQM theory with illustrative benchmarks and with *actionable* ideas on how to bring about the cultural transformation essential for TQM success.

The intended audience for this book is executives and managers, both those new to TQM and those who have been on the TQM track but want to pause to reflect on whether some of their efforts might be strengthened by redirection. TQM and this book are applicable to organizations of all kinds: manufacturing, service, small, large, educational, private sector, and public sector including federal agencies, states, and municipalities.

The material presented in this book has evolved from my early experiences as a public sector TQM practitioner and my still ongoing experience as a TQM consultant and teacher. As Technical Director of Naval Air engineering and flight test centers during the mid-1980's, I was closely associated with development and implementation of the Navair TQM strategy which won the 1989 Presidential Award for Quality and Productivity Improvement. In 1989, I founded a TQM consulting practice divided equally between the private and public sectors, and since then have also been on the faculty of The George Washington University Center for Organizational Effectiveness teaching TQM-related courses and seminars.

While some of the ideas offered here are original with me, much is of course derived from the work of others. The originating giant in this business is Dr. W. Edwards Deming. Chapter 2 is devoted to a discussion of Deming and his famous Fourteen Points. Another whose prolific work has especially enriched my ideas is Peter Drucker. TQM practitioners whose writings about their implementation experiences have been important to my still-growing understanding include David Kearns, former CEO of Xerox, Don Petersen former CEO of Ford, and Jack Welch, CEO of General Electric.

The Malcolm Baldrige criteria are another vital centerpiece to all of us in the TQM field. The seven Baldrige categories have become the common language of TQM practitioners. Companies in completely different businesses can "benchmark" one another and share "best practice" experiences in each of the seven categories (24 criteria). Chapter 16 contains a summary of each of the seven categories, together with a listing of best practices for each of the categories provided by recent winners of the Baldrige Award.

I owe a debt of gratitude to the continuing avalanche of informative articles from journals, magazines and newspapers. Among those most important to me have been the *MIT Sloan Review,* the *MIT Executive, The Harvard Business Review, Business Week, Inc., Fortune,* and the business sections of *The New York Times and The Washington Post.* A complete bibliography, listed by chapter, is included at the end of the book.

I owe many thanks to the Director and staff of The George Washington University Center for Organizational Effectiveness for their support of my University sponsored TQM courses and seminars over the years. My gratitude goes also to the numerous colleagues, clients, and students whose shared experiences, insights, and penetrating questions have broadened, illuminated, and refined my thinking over the decade of my involvement with TQM.

Special thanks go to my brother, Bob, who did much to sustain my own work by the example of his unstinting efforts to help shape this into a more interesting, more readable, and, I hope, more useful contribution to TQM lore. Deep appreciation goes to my wife, Sidsel, for her love and support during the many late nights and lost weekends devoted to this writing. The ever-growing list of accomplishments of my three adult children, Chris, Kari, and Eric, serve as an endless source of pride to nourish my life and my work. And, finally, we all owe much to our Oma, who continues to show us what love, intelligence, and work are all about.

Eric E. Anschutz
Bethesda, Maryland

Contents

1. TQM Overview   **1**
Purpose, Focus and Simplicity   1
The Four Components of TQM   2
Report of the MIT Commission   4
The Ford Task Force   5
Zero Sum and the Cost of Quality   6
Universality   9
The Malcolm Baldrige National Quality Award   9
The Presidential Award for Quality   11
Traps   12
Baldrige Award Stock Market Plays   14

2. Deming and His Fourteen Points   **15**
Deming in Japan   15
The Fourteen Points   17
The Seven Deadly Diseases   28

3. Listening is the First Step   **31**
Why Didn't They Ask Us?   31
Matsushita: We Got the Message!   32
More Like Us   33
Cultural Transformation   35
Valuing   36
Easing Into Empowerment   36

4. Empowerment: How to Make It Happen   **41**
Open-Book Management   41
We-They Relationships and Egalitarianism   45

Discretionary Effort   46
Job Enrichment   48
Horizontal Management   50
Span of Control   52
Two-Track Promotion   52
Involvement with Customers and Suppliers   53
Work Force Role in Selection of New Employees   53
Trust   54
Economic Value Added   54

5. Teaming   59
What is a Team?   59
How to Bring About Team Behavior   59
The Four Stages of Team Development   63
Team Building   65
"Outward-Bound"-Type Teambuilding   67
Diversity as a Positive Factor in Team Composition   68
Unions and Teams   68
Teams at Saturn   71
Teams at Ford   72
Teams at AT&T Credit   73
Teams in a Bank   74
Teams in the Classroom   75
Suppliers Are Part of the Corporate Team   76
Reducing the Number of Suppliers   77
The JUSE Code of Standards   78
Supplier Teams at Semco S/A   79
Teams are Not New   80
CEO Pay and its Effect on the Corporate Team   81

6. TQM Reward Systems   83
How Do TQM Reward Systems Differ from Traditional Ones?   83
Numerical Goals and Management by Objectives   83
Performance Appraisal   85
Appraisal as a Feedback Mechanism   87
TQM Appraisal Factors   87
Evaluation of Supervisors by Employees   88
Gain Sharing   88
Two-Track Promotion   91
Skill-Based Pay   92
Non-Monetary Rewards   93

Quality of Work Life   94

7. Training and Education   **95**
   Purpose   95
   How Much is Enough?   96
   What Kind of Training Should be Provided?   98
   Training Payoff: Some Case Studies   99
   Orientation Training for New Employees   103
   TQM Training   104
   Training in Small Companies   106
   TQM in Academia   108
   Apprentice Programs   108
   Disposing of a Red Herring   109

8. Leadership in an Empowered Organization   **111**
   Leadership Characteristics   111
   The Role of Leaders   115
   Micro-Management Is Not Leadership   117
   Leadership Requires Trust   117
   Sam Walton's Leadership Rules   118
   The Deming Prize Leadership Audit   119
   Leadership From Desert Storm   120

9. TQM Management Infrastructure   **121**
   You Already Have It   121
   The Quality Council   121
   Quality Management Boards   123
   Process Improvement Teams   124

10. Kaizen and Reengineering   **127**
   Process is King   127
   The Red Bead Experiment   128
   Kaizen   130
   Reengineering   131
   Balance   139

11. Process Improvement Methods   **141**
   Benchmarking   141
   Getting Started with Benchmarking   144
   The Plan-Do-Check-Act Process Improvement Cycle 145
   GE Workout   148

Responsibility for Process Improvement 148

12. SPC, Six-Sigma, and All That 151
Statistical Process Control 151
Process Capability 154
Six-Sigma Quality 155
Taguchi Loss Function 156

13. Customer Obsession 159
CARE: Customers Are Really Everything 159
Customer Expectations: Current and Future 161
Customer Relationship Management 164
Commitment to Customers 166
Customer Satisfaction Determination 166
Customer Satisfaction Comparison 168
Kansei 169
Finding and Filling a Niche 170
Internal Customers 171

14. The Public Sector Challenge 173
Contrast 173
Reinventing Government 174
The Importance of Vision 176

15. ISO: The Link With International Trade 181
What is ISO? 181
Overview of ISO Content 182

16. The Hoshin Planning Process 183
Hoshin Kanri Planning: Features 183
Hoshin Kanri Planning: Method 184
Hoshin Policy Deployment 186
The Corporate Vision 187

17. Strategic Planning 191
Overview 191
Baldrige as a Basis for Planning 191
Correlation of Planning With Performance 192
Outline for a Corporate Strategic Plan Based on
    the Seven Baldrige Categories 193
Benchmarks for the Seven Baldrige Categories 199

Leadership   199
Information and Analysis   200
Strategic Planning   201
Human Resource Development and Management   203
Management of Process Quality and
      Quality and Operational Results   204
Customer Focus and Satisfaction   206
The von Moltke Rule   207

18. Some Concluding Thoughts   **209**

Notes   **215**

Recommended Reading   **223**

Index   **225**

1

TQM Overview

Purpose, Focus, and Simplicity

Total quality management has but a single purpose: to improve the performance of your business. It is a means to that end, not an end in itself.

TQM should lead to better products; delighted customers; a more interested, involved, and dedicated work force; leaner and more focused management; more efficient use of resources; more effective and responsive suppliers; improved quality and productivity; greater market share; and higher profits.

It must not be allowed to become merely another set of things to do, an added layer of bureaucracy, another set of reports to prepare, another endless round of meetings to attend.

TQM requires a cultural transformation. Managers must change from authoritarian and remote to participative and accessible. Supervisors must change from bosses to coaches. Staff support people must change from monitors and approvers to facilitators and advisors. Workers must change from 9 to 5 employees to full-time partners. And everyone must become obsessed with quality and with customers.

TQM is simple. Its four components are already practiced in one form or another by virtually every manager, even those that have never heard of TQM. The elements of TQM are so central to good management practice that we might designate them as Management 101, a four-topic curriculum for all aspiring managers.

- Work Force Empowerment
- Process Improvement
- Customer Obsession
- Strategic Planning

There is nothing new about any of these four components. Enlightened managers have always sought to motivate workers, satisfy customers, improve processes, and plan for the future. What is new about TQM is the *laser-like* focus that it brings to the four components, their integration and interaction, and the set of methods by which each of the four can be strengthened.

The Four Components of TQM

We will later develop in some detail each of the four components of TQM, but at this early juncture, it is useful to describe each in brief.

Empowerment: Since the beginning of organized endeavor, managers have sought to motivate workers. Motivational methods have varied over the years, and vary still from one culture to another. The authoritarian methods used in our early industrial sweatshops gave way to the paternalism of only 25 years ago.

Today, our most successful organizations are those that achieve a partnership between workers and managers. That partnership is achieved by work force involvement and empowerment. Traditional organizations have vertical schisms based on where people stand in the corporate hierarchy, and horizontal schisms based on their departmental boundaries.

TQM seeks to build bridges across hierarchical and departmental moats, forming a seamless web of corporate partnerships. This is discussed in chapters 3 through 8. The TQM corporate partnership extends to include supplier organizations, and, in the best of cases, even customers.

Process Improvement: Workers generally want to do a good job. Most would wish to succeed, to earn the esteem of their peers, and to feel good about their personal contribution. Most want their organization to succeed, if only to ensure job security, promotion opportunities, and increasing pay. The most frequent barrier to good performance is not those popular whipping boys: unions, lack of work ethic, or poor training. It is *badly designed processes.*

Processes that result in a high rate of defects must be redesigned so that defects are *prevented* by the structure of the process. Processes that are slow need to be redesigned to improve flow, eliminate needless steps, or employ automation. TQM seeks continuous improvement of processes.

Perhaps the biggest payoff of all is to examine every step of every process to ask whether we need to be doing it at all. Much of what we do could be eliminated with no adverse consequence. This is particularly true for administrative processes. General Electric has coined the word "administrivia" to describe "the cramping artifacts that pile up in the dusty attics of century-old companies: the reports, meetings, rituals, approvals, controls and forests of paper that often seem necessary until they are removed."[1]

Process improvements of 10-20% are relatively easy to achieve through fine tuning. Quantum (order of magnitude) improvements are possible using the principles of "reengineering" prescribed by Michael Hammer and James Champy in their important book, *Reengineering the Corporation.*[2] Process improvement concepts and methods are covered in chapters 10 through 12.

Customer Obsession: Every business succeeds only to the extent that it meets the needs of its customers. Customer satisfaction has always been the goal of every enlightened business manager. Yet, too often, customers are taken for granted, with more resources devoted to seeking and winning new ones than to serving and keeping those we already have.

The term "customer obsession" was made popular by Xerox. David Kearns, former CEO of Xerox, and David Nadler, Xerox's quality consultant, in their excellent book, *Prophets in the Dark*, wrote: "People commonly think that customers buy a physical product . . . . They really don't. They buy a total experience – the nomenclature, the software, the instruction booklet . . . . If any part of the offering is wanting . . . you don't have quality."[3]

The Japanese word "kansei" means "to take to completion." "Kansei engineering" is the process used to gain a *profound* understanding of customer requirements and expectations, and to provide a product or service that exceeds mere satisfaction of those requirements to achieve customer delight and excitement. This focus on customer satisfaction is reviewed in chapter 13.

Strategic Planning: All would agree that a well-considered and widely-shared vision of the corporate future, and a strategy for getting there, are important for any organization. Yet, too many managers, driven by a variety of factors to focus on the short-term, give less thought than they should to where they would like the organization to be in three to five years or more.

Effective TQM implementation requires development of a long-term (three to five year) corporate vision and strategy, and a short-term (one year) operating plan. A planning method known as *Hoshin Kanri* yields both long- and short-term plans, and involves all responsible parts of the organization to ensure realism, widespread consensus, and knowledgeable support. Hoshin planning is done on a consensus basis involving both managers and affected subordinates and is discussed in chapter 16.

Report of the MIT Commission

Improving organizational performance should start with studying the "best-practices" of companies already known for their excellence. The MIT Commission on Industrial Productivity, assembled in 1986 to identify factors leading to the decline in U.S. industrial competitiveness, took such an approach. The Commission examined the operations of "best practice" companies with the intention of finding a set of management practices common to outstanding organizations.

The Commission's findings, reported in an excellent book titled *Made in America,* are based on analysis of organizations of every kind, from old-line manufacturing firms to new high-tech, both large and small, both union and non-union.[4] Despite their diversity, six key similarities were found among best-practice firms:

> (1) a focus on simultaneous improvement,
> (2) close links to customers,
> (3) close relationships with suppliers,
> (4) effective use of technology,
> (5) less hierarchy and less compartmentalization than usual, and
> (6) human-resource policies that promote continuous learning, teamwork, participation, and flexibility.

Concerning these six characteristics, the Commission added an important observation:

> The six responses are mutually reinforcing. Indeed, they form a single integrating strategy. The specific changes in business aims and methods, internal organization, and supplier relations that characterize best industrial practice cannot be treated as individual items on a list from which firms can pick and choose at will.

The findings of the MIT study provide striking support for the principles of TQM. Though the work of the MIT Commission was done without reference to TQM, the six characteristics of best practice organizations found by the MIT study are contained in the four elements of TQM: workforce empowerment, process improvement, customer obsession, and strategic planning. This represents a strong and independent corroboration of the legitimacy and historical effectiveness of TQM principles.

The Ford Task Force

During the early 1980's, Ford faced an increasing threat of Japanese competition.[5] To find out why Japanese car manufacturers were outperforming their American counterparts, hundreds of Ford people, from all parts and levels of the organization, were sent to Japan to study Japanese methods. Don Petersen, former CEO of Ford, reports in his 1991 book, *A Better Idea,* that these studies led to the conclusion that efficiency was greater in every part of Japanese organizations, not just in manufacturing. Ford's study of the financial activities of Japanese car companies, for instance, disclosed that its own financial staff was needlessly bloated.

The secret of Japanese efficiency, Ford discovered, was in how the people worked together: their empowerment and teamwork. Based on this insight, Ford appointed a task force to identify methods used by U.S. organizations which had achieved the highest reputations for excellence in "people management." Six firms were selected: IBM, TRW, 3M, General Electric, Dana, and Hewlett-Packard.

Petersen reports that, when the project was completed, the six benchmark companies were found to share the following ten characteristics:

1) To broaden communication, each firm circulated a statement of corporate goals. In addition, executives spent 50 to 80 percent of their time outside the office, communicating ideas to employees.

2) All of the firms emphasized the importance of people and respect for every individual. They shared the belief that, while the latest equipment and technology can be purchased by any company, the workforce can provide a true competitive edge.

3) They substituted trust for strict rules and controls.

4) Each firm stressed that it was customer-driven.

5) All the firms emphasized teamwork and used cross-functional project teams.

6) Each of the firms tried to eliminate layers of management and to drive down authority to lower levels.

7) The firms emphasized free and open communications, including "Management by Wandering Around," a concept made popular by Tom Peters, and widely known as MBWA.[6]

8) Managers relied on peers and occasionally on subordinates to evaluate other managers. Team players were promoted over individualists.

9) All of the firms offered sophisticated training for both managers and the workforce.

10) Managers made a habit of asking their people, "What do you think?"

Again, just as with the findings of the MIT Commission, the findings of the Ford Task Force serve as independent confirmation of TQM principles. The things that TQM prescribes are the very things that well-managed companies have been doing all along.

As was noted earlier, TQM is nothing more than good management. There is little about TQM, or about the MIT list of six characteristics common to best practice organizations, or about the ten benchmark practices identified by the Ford Task Force that we don't already know. TQM performs the important function of integrating these (and some other) good management practices into a single coherent TOTAL management philosophy.

Zero Sum and the Cost of Quality

Managers of an earlier time often tolerated marginal quality out of concern that the cost of improvements to quality would cause their product's prices to become noncompetitive. We now know this notion is misleading, and often false.

Game theory, a branch of mathematics, employs the term "zero sum" to describe the relationship between independent variables that add up to a constant quantity. An example of a zero sum relationship might be the elements of a fixed budget for corporate expenses. Any increase in one of the expense items must be offset by a comparable decrease in another part of the budget because the total is fixed. The sum must remain constant: zero change to the sum.

Quality and productivity are generally thought to have a zero sum relationship to one another. We tend to assume that any increase in quality must be offset by a comparable decrease in productivity (increased cost per unit). To increase quality, we might use higher cost labor, higher cost materials, work more carefully and slowly, or do some of each. Each of these would seem to add to the cost per unit, and the apparent zero sum relationship between quality and productivity would appear to have been maintained.

But this apparent reality overlooks important results of improved quality: less rework, less scrap, lower warranty and guarantee costs, and, often, decreased costs of inspection. Thus, *quality improvement generally leads to lower costs per unit of output, not higher.* Quality and productivity bear a nonzero sum relationship to one another.

To take this logic a step farther, the TQM ethic holds that improved quality is in fact often the very best route to lower costs. One of the largest expenses (often overlooked) in any organization is that associated with detecting, reworking, or redoing things done wrong the first time. This expense is known as the "Cost of Quality", COQ.

Chrysler, in 1987, estimated its Cost of Quality: "Defects, both in-house and by parts suppliers, cost the firm about four billion dollars per year, or nearly 25% of sales revenue."[7] A major electronics company found that 20% of its revenues, 24% of its assets, 25% of its people, 40% of its space, and 70% of its inventory were devoted to coping with defective components or products.

The Cost of Quality is often on the order of 25% of revenues, even for otherwise well-run organizations. Even this high percentage does not take into account the cost resulting from loss of customers due to a reputation for poor quality. Nor does it include the cost of uphill marketing when the product or service has a reputation for poor quality. Adding these costs, unknowable but certainly large, raises the incentive to improve quality to a level where failure to do so constitutes management negligence if not malpractice.

To reiterate, the surest way to lower costs is to increase quality and thereby reduce rework and scrap. The other (more traditional) way to reduce costs is by a frontal assault on deferrable expenses.

We have all either received or sent a memorandum, addressed to all departments, along the following lines:

> All departments are directed to reduce costs by 15% within the next six months. Departments will forward their plans for meeting this directive within one week. Actions to be taken

will include, but not necessarily be limited to: a ban on all non-urgent travel, a hiring freeze, a pay freeze, a reduction in purchasing, a ban on nonessential training, deferral of non-essential maintenance, and reduction in staff.

It is possible – indeed likely – that actions taken in response to such a directive (and every manager will recognize it as something sent or received on roughly an annual basis) will have the perverse effect of helping to undermine its intent. Thus, compliance with such a directive will soon *increase* costs rather than decrease them.

• Bans on travel can adversely affect communication with customers, suppliers, and other departments of the organization.

• Hiring freezes can result in skill imbalance.

• Pay freezes can weaken the motivation or hasten the departure of the most productive people – the very ones who would otherwise have been rewarded with raises in pay.

• Buying limits can lead to deferral of automation and other improvements, and to shortages of tools, parts, and materials.

• Limits on training can keep people at less productive skill levels.

• Deferred maintenance can lead to lower quality and decreased production, to accelerated deterioration of facilities and equipment, and, ultimately, to higher maintenance costs.

• Reduction in staff can weaken morale across the entire organization. As a result, cooperation between staff members might be replaced by competition, and looking good might become more important than doing well.

In view of these effects, the cumulative result of the directive to cut costs might well be opposite to the one intended. Such a result would mean, even in the relatively short-term, a decline in productivity and increased overall costs. Long-run consequences, however, would be even more dire. Customers would be lost, corporate revenues would shrink, and another directive to cut costs would be handed down. Such a disaster might be described in several ways: a downward spiral, a slippery slope, a treadmill to corporate oblivion.

What it points to, however, can be summed up in a single word: *mismanagement*. And what is called for, instead, is adherence to the common-sense principles of TQM, with the resultant increase in quality *and* productivity.

Universality

TQM purposes and its four elements have applicability to organizations of all kinds: private and public, manufacturing and service, large and small, union and non-union.

Because of its use of (rudimentary) statistical principles, managers sometimes perceive that TQM applies only to manufacturing organizations, or that, because of its focus on customers, it applies only to private sector organizations.

The stunning results of TQM application to large manufacturing enterprises (Ford, Chrysler, Motorola, Xerox, Milliken, to name just a few) have been well publicized. Less is known about its equally great success when applied to small companies (Granite Rock, Marlow Industries), service organizations (AT&T Universal Card, Federal Express) and to federal government agencies (Air Force Logistics Command, Naval Air Systems Command, Internal Revenue Service Center in Ogden, Utah). TQM is used with success by a number of municipal governments (Hampton, Virginia, and Madison, Wisconsin, to name just two) and state governments (Oregon, Vermont, Florida, and others). It has been applied successfully to the operations of a small financial/property management organization (Eastern Realty Investments, Washington, D.C.), to universities (University of Wisconsin, The George Washington University, and the MIT Sloan School of Management), and even to an elementary school (Sarah MacAuliffe Elementary, Prince William County, Virginia).[8]

While it is true that TQM principles must be adapted to each organization, organizations of *every* kind seek quality and productivity, a dedicated and motivated work force, greater satisfaction of customers (taxpayers are customers, too), improved processes, and consensus plans for the future. And these are the very things that TQM is all about.

The Malcolm Baldrige National Quality Award

The Baldrige Award is given annually, since 1988, to U.S. companies that excel in quality management and quality achievement. Up to two awards may be given in each of three eligibility categories: manufacturing companies, service companies, and small businesses. Though there can be a total of six winners in any one year, there have never been more than five (1992), and there have been as few as two (1989 and 1993).

Only for-profit U.S. companies are eligible to win the Malcolm Baldridge award. It is not available to not-for-profit organizations; to non-U.S. companies; or to federal, state, or municipal government organizations. It was authorized by a 1987 Act of Congress (H.R. 812-2). Some of the more pertinent paragraphs of the Act follow:

(1) the leadership of the United States in product and process quality has been challenged strongly (and sometimes successfully) by foreign competition, and our nation's productivity growth has improved less than our competitors over the last two decades;

(2) American business and industry are beginning to understand that poor quality costs companies as much as 20% of sales revenues nationally, and that improved quality of goods and services goes hand in hand with improved productivity, lower costs, and increased profitability . . .

(8) a national quality award program . . . in the United States would help improve quality and productivity by –

(A) helping to stimulate American companies to improve quality and productivity . . .,

(B) recognizing the achievements of those companies which can improve the quality of their goods and services and providing an example to others,

(C) establishing guidelines and criteria that can be used by business, industrial , governmental, and other organizations in evaluating their own quality improvement efforts, and

(D) providing specific guidance for other American organizations that wish to learn how to manage for high quality by making available detailed information on how winning organizations were able to change their cultures and achieve eminence.

Purpose – It is the purpose of this Act to provide for the establishment and conduct of a national quality improvement program under which (1) awards are given to selected companies and other organizations in the United States that practice effective quality management and as a result make significant improvements in the quality of their goods and services, and (2) information is disseminated about the successful strategies and programs.

The Baldrige award is traditionally presented by the President of the United States at special ceremonies in Washington, D.C. The number of applicants has varied from a low of 40 companies in 1989 to a high of 106 companies in 1991. Applicants, whether they win or lose, appear to be unanimous in their belief that the most valuable result of the Baldrige application experience is the audit that they receive of their quality strategy. The audit for each entrant provides a point score, together with a detailed statement of what the organization might do to improve its strategy.

The importance of the award can hardly be overstated. Administered by the National Institute for Standards and Technology, an agency of the U.S. Department of Commerce, the seven Baldrige categories have become the *lingua franca* of the U.S. quality movement. These seven categories, discussed in later chapters of this text and extensively detailed in Baldrige documentation, have provided not only a common language for quality practitioners, but a basis for sharing best-practice ideas, or "benchmarking," to use the TQM term of art. They have become a focal point for the quality strategies of many, if not most, U.S. organizations.

Baldrige documentation states that "Award recipients are expected to share information about their successful quality strategies with other U.S. organizations." The enthusiasm with which the winners do share information, and participate in the well-attended quality conferences that take place almost monthly under various auspices, make it possible for newcomers to the quality movement to devise quality strategies appropriate to their organizations, and for practitioners to adjust their strategies in response to new information from the most successful companies.

Chapter 17 provides a description of each of the seven Baldrige categories. For each category, successful strategies provided by recent Baldrige winners are summarized.

The Presidential Award for Quality

The United States federal government has created a quality award available exclusively to agencies of the federal government. Known as the Presidential Award for Quality, the award is administered by the Federal

Quality Institute, an arm of the United States Office of Personnel Management.

First given in 1989, the Presidential Award is now based on exactly the same seven categories used for the Baldrige Award. Until 1993, the Presidential Award categories were eight in number, and the criteria, though similar to the Baldrige criteria, were not identical. Adoption by the Presidential Award documentation of the seven Baldrige categories and Baldrige criteria is welcome, because it simplifies the process of cross-benchmarking between public sector and private sector organizations.

Public sector agencies have, on the whole, been less aggressive and less successful than private sector organizations in implementation of quality strategies. The reasons for this, and some thoughts on how public sector organizations can overcome the lag, are discussed in Chapter 14.

Traps

There are several traps to which the TQM practitioner must be alert.

The first is that TQM can be perceived as the current "buzz" word. Just as zero defects, staff-based management, zero-based budgeting, and management by objectives became fashionable for a time, some see in TQM an idea destined to fade in the not-too-distant future. Because that kind of thinking leads to cynicism and a consequent unwillingness to commit to an ongoing effort, it must be acknowledged and dealt with.

TQM differs from the above-listed and other earlier management concepts because, as we saw previously, it does not purport to be anything new. TQM is a restatement and a refocusing of what every manager has done since the beginning of organized endeavor. It is an integration of the four facets of management into a coherent entity, bound together by an obsession with quality and customer delight. Its purpose is to energize management and the workforce, replace we-they relationships with a corporate partnership, improve products and processes, simplify operations, and plan for the future. TQM is more than a philosophy or a slogan. It brings to these purposes a set of methods by which they may be achieved.

The second possible trap is that it takes a while for TQM results to become apparent. This needs to be understood and accepted from the onset of implementation to avoid disillusion after only a few months of effort.

As was earlier noted, the TQM cultural transformation requires fundamental changes in attitudes and behavior of both managers and employees. It requires changes in the corporate attitude to customers and suppliers. It also requires new thinking about products and processes, about quality, and about intracorporate relationships.

None of this happens quickly, and none of it happens without some turmoil. Because of the growing body of experience, it takes less time and is less disruptive than before. The chapters that follow will help you chart a course for the smoothest and swiftest transformation possible. Positive results should become evident within a year from the start of implementation, and massive corporate-wide improvement should be apparent on a continuing basis in about three years.

A third possible trap is that TQM can become a "program," demanding its own managing and implementing infrastructure, its own army of support personnel, its own body of meetings, its own set of reports. Some implementing organizations have reported that, "TQM takes so much of our time and resources that it interferes with performance of our assigned task."

TQM is *not* a program. It is a *strategy,* a way of doing business, a way of managing, a way of looking at the organization and its activities. Though TQM requires a managing infrastructure, that infrastructure is the current business management infrastructure. The business managers are the TQM managers.

Taking time at staff meetings to consider the four components of TQM cannot be viewed as a new burden. These are the very topics to which enlightened and effective managers already devote time and resources. Staff meetings are too often devoted exclusively to "fire fighting," to dealing with day-to-day problems.

TQM, by providing a coherent and integrated set of management methods, and with its focus on people, customers, products, processes, and plans, ensures that managers invest some of their time on business fundamentals. By so doing, the day-to-day problems are dealt with in fundamental ways, not merely superficially. To put it in fundamental terms, managers must still put out fires, but with TQM they attend to the root cause of the fire to insure it doesn't happen again.

Because TQM is a management strategy and not a program, its most relevant measurement of success is improvement in the fundamentals of your business, not the details of the TQM effort itself. General Electric spoke eloquently to this point in its 1990 Annual Report:

> Some people are uncomfortable with this soft stuff and press us to quantify it, to measure its progress. It would be easy to quote numbers of Work-Out sessions, best practice teams, suggestions implemented, money spent on training,

and the like; but we've resisted because the last thing this effort needs is its own bureaucracy and measurement systems. But we can tell you it is working. We see it in people's faces and we hear it in the confidence in their voices. And we are beginning to see its results in . . . working capital turnover, operating margins and, above all, productivity growth.[9]

Baldrige Award Stock Market Plays

Since 1988, according to *Business Week*, winners of the Baldrige Award have outperformed the Standard and Poor's 500 by nearly three to one.[10] $1,000 was invested, hypothetically, in each publicly-traded Baldrige winner at the time of the award. Excluding dividends, "Baldie-playing" resulted in a cumulative 87% gain. The same amounts invested in the S&P 500 stock index yielded 33%.

This is further evidence that dedicated implementation of a TQM strategy pays. On average, companies that empower employees, improve processes, become obsessive about customers, and plan for the longer term perform better than those that do not.

2

Deming and His Fourteen Points

Though there were other important contributors, both American and Japanese, Dr. W. Edwards Deming is widely acknowledged as the founding father of what we now call TQM.[1, 2] Dr. Deming was born in 1900, and died in December 1993, having been active until the end of his life. This chapter is a tribute to his early and formative contributions. It includes a summary of Deming's early work in Japan, and a brief analysis of his famous Fourteen Points.

Deming in Japan

Recent (1993-94) travails of the Japanese economy notwithstanding, Japanese industry has in the decades since World War II become a benchmark of excellence. In industries ranging from automobiles to electronics, from wristwatches to pianos, Japan has achieved renown for the quality of its products and services, its ability to anticipate and meet consumer requirements, and its cost-effective operations.

Contrary to our initial belief, Japanese industrial success is not entirely a cultural phenomenon, attributable to a strong work ethic and good education. We need only to recall the low repute in which Japanese industry was held in the time prior to World War II. Western consumers in those years thought of the Japanese invidiously as makers of trinkets. Indeed, "Made in Japan" was in the years prior to the 1950's a synonym for junk.

Unlike Germany, Japan of the immediate postwar years had no tradition of industrial strength or effectiveness. War-inflicted damage to Japan's economic and societal infrastructure further reduced its industrial potential.

Yet, by the 1970's, Japanese industry was beginning to claim important markets from the United States and Europe, and by the 1980's, Japanese industry was a threat to our industrial competitiveness. American business and industrial managers by the hundreds were trooping to Japan to seek understanding of how they had done it. What was their secret?

One by one, American managers returned to report that the real secret was that there was no secret. The Japanese were simply paying attention to the fundamentals of good management practice.

Ex-Ford CEO Don Petersen put it this way in A *Better Idea,* his book about the implementation of TQM at Ford:

> Before those visits [of Ford managers to Japan] many of the people at Ford believed that the Japanese were succeeding because they used highly sophisticated machinery. Others thought their industry was orchestrated by Japan's government . . . . [We discovered, however] that the real secret was how the people worked together . . . . Somehow or other, they had managed to hold on to a fundamental simplicity of human enterprise, while we built layers of bureaucracy.[3]

U.S. industry had emerged from World War II as the world's dominant supplier. European and Asian industries had suffered war-inflicted damage, while ours remained not only unscathed but greatly strengthened by war-nourished growth. The abundant worldwide demand for products provided ready markets for all we could make.

During these "good" years of the 1950's, 60's, and 70's, when American industry was the envy of the world, some of our managers were forgetting the simple fundamentals of quality, customer focus, lean organizations, efficient operations, work force motivation, and planning. These fundamentals, which were the basis for Japan's postwar industrial success, were taught to the Japanese, ironically enough, by the American statistician, Dr. W. Edwards Deming.

Deming's postwar lectures to Japanese engineers and managers presented ideas that were new to them, and caused widespread and even passionate interest. Deming soon became a revered figure to the Japanese, who saw in his methods the means for their industrial transformation. His lectures went beyond statistical process control and process improvement to embrace the concepts of customer focus, workforce empowerment, and planning.

The Japanese gave Deming's philosophy a name: Total Quality Control. And they further honored him by establishing a national annual quality award in his name. Known as the Deming Prize, the award is administered by the Japanese Union of Scientists and Engineers. It remains to this day the highest honor to which Japanese companies can aspire; the annual award ceremony is nationally televised.

In 1980, the National Broadcasting Company aired an NBC White Paper, called "If Japan Can, Why Can't We?". The program, which sought to identify the reasons for Japan's postwar industrial success, concluded that the teachings of Dr. Deming and Japanese adherence to them were the primary reason.

While Deming was not wholly unknown in the United States, his native country, he was not an important influence on U.S. managers until as late as 1980. The NBC program provided the springboard to a wider and far more receptive U.S. audience for Deming's ideas. Ford, among others, was stimulated to begin its TQM journey, in part, as a result of the program. From 1980 onward, TQM strategies spread rapidly through the U.S. business community, in both private and public sectors.

The Fourteen Points

Deming had summarized his quality management philosophy into fourteen points.

Deming's Point Number 1: Create constancy of purpose toward improvement of product and service, with the aim to become competitive, stay in business, and provide jobs.

The message in Deming's first point is twofold: customer obsession and strategic planning. In the late 1940's, Deming was teaching the Japanese to reach out to customers, conduct surveys, understand customer requirements, and do everything necessary to satisfy them. He observed that unless this obsession with customers is a constant feature of management and workforce attention, the business is destined to fail.

Constancy of purpose requires strategic planning. One cannot maintain a successful business strategy without planning for and committing to a set of agreed goals and a means for their achievement.

Deming added another important admonition: ". . . aim to become competitive, stay in business, and provide jobs." It is the manager's responsibility to become (and stay) competitive; the alternative may be corporate demise.

To take Deming's advice a step farther, the health and strength of business is, in today's world, inextricably linked with national and international economic and societal well-being. Viewed in this wider context, the obligation of businesses, especially large ones, transcends responsibility to stockholders for profits and growth. Business has responsibilities to society in return for its use of communal resources: people, capital, environment, and municipal and federal services. While profit and growth are vital to business health and strength, to new products, and to expansion of job opportunities, their pursuit in the name of social good is a more compelling and more inspiring motivation than the fattening of corporate wallets. So viewed, corporate growth is society's affirmation of the worth of a company's activities.

Deming had noted in another context that the "system of business" includes competition. Every company must accept the fact that competition is a normal component of business. Efforts aimed at taking business away from competitors will lead to short-term advantages, but will suboptimize the system to the longer-term detriment of all parties. Taking this view into account, Deming held that companies are best served by efforts to expand their markets rather than by efforts aimed at beating the competition. The goal of market expansion is met by gaining profound insights into customer requirements and expectations, and offering new and better products and services at prices the customer will pay. When the market is expanded, Deming asserted, the system of business will have been improved, and everyone will gain.

Deming's Point Number 2: Adopt the new quality philosophy. We are in a new economic age.

The old philosophy, the one that led numbers of U.S. organizations into a decade-long competitive downturn, seemed to embrace the following concepts:

• Profits are the single most important purpose of business activity.

• Undue emphasis on quality will make a business noncompetitive because unnecessary improvements in quality will add to cost.

• Employees are a cost burden; the goal must be to pay as little as possible, and to down-size whenever business volume falls off.

• Unions are the natural enemy of management and of corporate well-being.

• Long-term investment is by definition a loser for management because results don't appear until our successors are in place.

• Customers don't know what they want. With effective marketing and advertising, we will condition their requirements and desires to conform to the products and services that we as product experts know will best serve their needs.

• Top management must project an image of corporate wealth and success. Executive dining rooms, reserved parking spaces, plush office decor, big salaries, even bigger bonuses, and tailored three-piece suits are essential to that purpose.

The *new* quality philosophy, advocated by Deming, and central to the TQM ethic, stands in stark contrast. It has the following tenets:

• Quality is the single most important factor in corporate success. Quality leads to productivity, to satisfied customers, and, hence, to competitiveness, market share, return on investment, and profitability.

When near-term profit is deemed more important than quality, actions are often taken that are counterproductive in the long term. Three examples include:

"Ship it, the customer won't know the difference."

"We can't afford to provide that feature; our profits are too low already."

"We've got to let those people go or we'll show a loss in the next quarter."

• Employees are partners with management. Upper management should consult with them on corporate decisions whenever feasible. Experience has shown that employee involvement often leads to better decisions because of the diversity of input, and it always leads to greater support for decisions once made.

• Improvement in quality will reduce rework and scrap, and will lessen the costs of warranties and guarantees. The result will be lower overall costs and increased competitiveness.

• During times of economic downturn, management will consult with employees to chart a course of action. When reduction of staff costs becomes essential to corporate health, management will join with its workforce partners to identify ways to share the burden equally. The search for an equitable strategy to reduce labor costs will include consideration of such things as reduction of management salaries, reduction of staff salaries, a reduced work week, and bringing in-house some of the work currently contracted out to suppliers.

The goal, insofar as possible, is to preserve and build upon the existing work force. There are major costs inherent to downsizing: they include immediate costs associated with early-outs and layoffs, and future costs associated with recruiting and training replacement workers when business turns up. Collectively, these costs often add up to an amount greater than the cost of riding out the storm with the existing workforce. Perhaps even more important, companies with a reputation for workforce retention during bad times sustain higher morale, as well as worker good will and identification with corporate well-being.

• Long-term investment is important, not only for the organization, but for current managers. Though there are demands for near-term profitability, the financial community is also looking for future prospects. This is demonstrated by the higher price-to-earnings ratios of growth-company equities. The basis for future growth is enhanced by long-term investment in the development of improved products, services, equipment, and processes. One culprit forestalling long-term investment is executive bonus systems which are keyed to near-term profit. Linking them, at least in part, to longer-term results would increase incentives for more aggressive investment in the organization's future strength and growth.

• Customers know what they want; indeed, customers define quality. What the supplier thinks is quality is not unless the customer agrees. A fundamental obligation of the corporate manager is to reach out to customers, and to seek and understand their requirements and expectations. The objective must be to provide the customer with a reason to buy from you rather than from your competition.

• Corporate egalitarianism is increasing in popularity. Organizations all over the United States are closing executive dining rooms (one has converted that anachronistic white elephant into a day-care center for the children of employees). Executive parking areas are being closed. Managers who want a good place to park can get it in only one way: by arriving early. Some U.S. organizations are even banning suits and neckties, requiring everyone to wear a khaki uniform; others are abandoning honorifics, insisting that even senior executives be called by their first name.

Egalitarianism has its advantages, but an important caveat is prompted by a cartoon that appeared some time ago in the *New Yorker.* The cartoon, which pictured a plush office, door wide open, with a pompous-looking executive sitting behind an imposing desk, was captioned: "Behind every open door sits a closed mind." The message is vital to any corporate effort at increased egalitarianism: you must mean it!

Deming's Point Number 3: Cease dependence on mass inspection.

This point may at first seem to be in conflict with Deming's earlier admonition to adopt a quality philosophy. How can we achieve increased quality without recourse to increased inspection? The answer is that no amount of inspection will reduce the *rate* of defects. Inspection will only limit (but not eliminate) the risk that defects will reach the customer. The only way to produce fewer defects is to change the process by which the work is being done.

It is important to note that Deming was not really telling manufacturers to cease inspection. He was telling them to *cease dependence* on inspection, which is quite another thing. Depending on inspection to improve quality is a trap that has misled many. Even fully successful inspection, where all defects are found, would not affect the level of waste associated with processes that yield a high rate of defects. Deming preached that business should *prevent* defects through process improvement, rather than through relying on inspection for their detection.

A story told in the early days of TQM in the U.S. sheds some light on the issue. It seems that an American company was specifying the then widely-prevalent three-sigma quality level (approximately three defects per thousand) to its Japanese supplier. One thousand good parts were delivered, and separately wrapped in the same box were three defective parts. In an accompanying note, the supplier stated that it was puzzled by the quality specification of three defects per thousand!

Deming and TQM philosophy have turned the quality requirements full-circle. No sector of our economy has remained untouched. Restaurants, department stores, manufacturers, service companies, and even government agencies have felt the impact of the tidal change in quality emphasis. Quality standards in the U.S. have risen to a point where, increasingly, nothing less than "world-class" quality levels are acceptable.

Just think about it. Late-model cars rarely break down. Television sets never break down. Service is more timely and more courteous. Inspection did not bring this about. Contemporary quality levels are the result of a determined effort over the last decade to improve the processes we employ to make things and to provide services.

To improve quality and, thereby, produce fewer defects, we must identify the root cause of defects through analysis, and then change the production process until the defect rate is low enough to be acceptable. The prevailing quality standard for many U.S. organizations is six-sigma quality – about three defects per million – a level that would have been unthinkable for most manufacturers only five years ago. Once that level is reached, and the process is stable, inspection can indeed be reduced, or eliminated altogether. Much more about all of this is provided in chapters 10 through 12.

Deming's Point Number 4: Cease selecting suppliers on the basis of price alone.

Paying twice as much for supplies can be wise if the higher priced product lasts four times as long, or is vastly less costly to maintain, or is of greater value in some other way. The idea is to minimize lifecycle costs, not merely to minimize initial cost.

We all know these things, yet in our managerial (and private) capacities we often overlook the simple rule set forth in Deming's fourth point. There is the oft-told joke of the astronaut who, about to be launched, recalls with trepidation the fact that every part in his massive system was supplied by the low-cost bidder!

Building on Deming's point, TQM has gone on to prescribe a set of principles to guide the selection of suppliers and their relationship with the customer organization. See chapter 5 for more on supplier relationships.

Deming's Point Number 5: Improve constantly and forever.

Our search for quality, productivity, better products and services, customer satisfaction, better management, more involved and dedicated employees, more responsive suppliers, an expanded market for our products and services, and higher profits will succeed only if the organization takes steps leading to improvement. The search for better ways to do everything must become a continuing focus of everyone in the organization. Since Deming's fifth point might be said to be what TQM is all about, ways to realize constant improvement will be the subject of virtually every chapter of this book.

Our consideration of Deming's Point Number 5 is closely linked to the preceding discussion of Point Number 3. We have seen that improvement of the processes used to do our work is the essential basis for the elimination of defects. Process improvement is just as important to every other aspect of corporate strengthening. We cannot shorten product development cycles without improving the product development process. We cannot bring better people into the organization unless we improve our recruitment process. We cannot lower employee turnover unless we improve our human resource policies and processes. We cannot improve our understanding of customer requirements unless we improve our marketing processes. And so on and on. Process improvement is key to corporate strengthening. This is self-evidently true for manufacturing processes. It is at least equally, and perhaps especially, true for business processes. It is in the support areas, such as accounting, marketing, human resources, purchasing, etc., that many of our organizations have become especially wasteful, sluggish, and obese. See chapter 10.

Constant improvement in the TQM context once implied a focus on small increments of improvement to existing processes. The Japanese word "kaizen" was understood to mean just that. Recently, however, a new term, process *reengineering,* has gained prominence, and we are seeing a greater emphasis on total process redesign as opposed to the earlier emphasis on small increments of process improvement. The new emphasis on total process redesign is driven in part by the initiative of Michael Hammer and James Champy, and their book, *Reengineering the Corporation.* Again, see chapter 10.

Deming's Point Number 6: Institute training on the job.

Employee training has been of less importance for U.S. organizations than for those in competitive countries. German and Japanese companies, in particular, are noted for their large investments in training, and it is fair to assume that training is an important factor in their relative industrial success. Chapter 7 provides a comprehensive discussion of this subject, with TQM recommendations.

Deming's Point Number 7: Institute leadership.

TQM mandates changes in leadership practices from authoritarian to participative, from directive to facilitative, and from boss to coach. With these changes, management becomes less hierarchical and spans of control are widened, leading to fewer layers of management.

One of the chief benefits of workforce empowerment is that managers .are relieved of the need to "micro-manage;" their attention can shift from a vertical focus (downward to employees and upward to superiors) to a horizontal focus (laterally to adjacent managers, suppliers, customers, business issues, and strategic planning). Horizontal management facilitates true leadership by virtue of its focus on the larger issues of business instead of the narrower issues of individual employee activity.

The value of CEO-level involvement is demonstrated by such exemplary leaders as Robert Galvin of Motorola, Jack Welch from General Electric, David Kearns of Xerox, and Don Petersen of Ford, who personally led the TQM transformations. These men became involved in the details, and gained a profound understanding of TQM principles. They led, they pushed, they inspired, they expected, and, as a consequence, they *achieved* a corporate transformation. See chapter 8 for a discussion of leadership in a TQM organization.

Deming's Point Number 8: Drive out fear.

Deming was absolutely right: fear is costly to organizations. Fear keeps people from speaking out on matters that might run against the conventional wisdom. Fear inhibits risk-taking, and we know that risk attends change and change is necessary for improvement. Fear inspires me-tooism, a search for bureaucratic safety; makes looking good more important than doing well; and gives priority to short-term over long-term results.

Yet, it is clear that fear can never be completely removed from organizations. As long as an employee's level of pay and promotability are linked to the good will of an organizational superior, he or she will strive to "look good" for the boss, to avoid confrontation, and to defer. While these actions may not always be fear-based, they remain factors that can distort fully honest interactions between organizational subordinates and superiors.

Recognizing the reality of fear in organizations is important, and working to mitigate and minimize fear is essential, even when we accept our inability to eliminate it fully. Workforce empowerment and its counterpart, participative management, are central components of TQM and powerful mechanisms for achieving relaxed, honest, forthright, and egalitarian-based relationships between levels of the organization. Chapters 3, 4, 6, and 8 each have something to say on this important subject.

Deming's Point Number 9: Break down barriers between departments.

The term "stove-pipe" has become a popular way to describe organizations with department-level functions that are at times more inwardly than corporately focused. Examples might be an engineering department that develops designs without regard to producability, or a sales department that promises customers a product feature, a price, or a delivery schedule without first checking its feasibility with the engineering and manufacturing departments.

A major impediment to getting things done quickly is the queuing and transit-time delays associated with work that passes serially from one "specialist" function to another. Processes based on this heritage from Adam Smith and Frederick Taylor need to be wholly reengineered to consolidate the entire task in the hands of one person or one co-located cross-functional team. Chapters 4 (empowerment and job enrichment) and 10 (process improvement and reengineering) address these ideas in some depth.

In traditional organizations, barriers between departments are more the rule than the exception. They arise, in part, because employees tend to stay with the functions into which they were hired. As a result, their loyalties are to the function rather than to the wider organization. This narrowed loyalty is strengthened when pay and promotion are linked to local ratings to the exclusion of corporate ones; moreover, people gain an inflated view of the importance of their function relative to others. Job rotation and the use of cross-functional teams are among the TQM answers to this dilemma.

Deming's Point Number 10: Eliminate slogans, exhortations and targets.

Most would agree that placards on the factory walls or along the office corridors urging safety, or quality, or whatever, are at best a waste of paper and wall space, and at worst an insult to the intelligence of employees.

Communication to the work force of corporate ideas, information, and purposes is vital, but the use of slogans and exhortations is like junk mail and relentless commercials: people tune out. More about "Open Book" management in chapter 4.

Deming's Point Number 11: Eliminate numerical goals, including MBO.

Deming's first argument here was that when standards are set, people work to meet them, but then relax and make no further effort to go beyond. Deming's second point was that basing pay (or other rewards) on output compared to a standard or goal ignores the variability inherent in all processes. When the goal is exceeded, we have no way of knowing whether the good outcome was the result of special effort by the employee, of random variation, or of some other factor in the system unrelated to the employee's effort.

For Deming, Management by Objectives (MBO) was especially ineffectual. An objective is without value unless it is supported by a strategy, (or plan, or means) for achieving it. Suppose that the objective is to increase market share by 8% during the coming performance period, or to reduce the defect rate by 25%, or to reduce overhead by 10%. The employee's success or failure in meeting these or any other goals is only partly the result of effort and intelligence; other factors outside the employee's control can influence the outcome, up or down.

TQM does not quarrel with setting objectives, but it insists that they be supplemented by development of a strategy for achieving it. Thus, the goal of an 8% increase in market share may be perfectly sensible, but it needs to be supported by a strategy: how do we propose to meet that objective?

Any true measure of employee performance needs to be made against the strategy (developed jointly by the manager and the employee) for achieving it. Did the employee do everything called for in the strategy? Was implementation of the strategy carried out imaginatively? Did the employee make effective changes to the strategy as new information became available? Using this approach, the manager rates the employee on overall effectiveness, rather than on whether objectives were met. The employee focuses on intelligent action and on effective management of the process over which he or she has control, rather than on outcome over which there is less control. See chapters 16 and 17 for a discussion of Strategic Planning.

Deming's Point Number 12: Remove barriers to worker pride. This includes abolishment of annual performance appraisal.

For any job, there are numerous factors that influence the worker's performance and yet are outside the worker's control. When the process (generally put in place by management) is poorly designed, performance is inevitably less than it might otherwise be. Job performance is also degraded when training is less than it should be, when supervision is intrusive rather than facilitative, when there is competition between co-workers rather than teamwork, and when workplace physical conditions are unsafe or needlessly uncomfortable. Deming's twelfth point states that these barriers to high performance, all outside the worker's control, must be removed if we are to achieve good results.

Damage to worker pride results when, despite his or her best efforts, the worker is not able to perform effectively. Damaged pride leads, in turn, to reduced enthusiasm and a downward spiral to ever-poorer performance.

Performance appraisal, widely used in "white collar" operations, is done for the purpose of providing guidance to workers, and as a basis for setting salary increases. But the considerable damage done by performance appraisal leads to the question of whether we shouldn't find other ways to provide guidance (such as periodic off-the-record counseling) and other ways of setting salary increases (such as letting the market determine an employee's worth by asking: "If this person were being hired today, what would we need to pay to attract him or her?").

The ways in which performance appraisals are counterproductive include: fostering competition between workers in lieu of mutual support; causing workers to focus more on looking good than on doing well; and inhibiting willingness to take risks. See chapter 6.

Deming's Point Number 13: Institute a program of education and self-improvement.

TQM brings change to organizations: work is arranged in new ways; cross-functional work teams are formed; empowerment leads to reductions in the management hierarchy; workers make more decisions and assume greater responsibility for processes and output; process improvement leads to workforce reduction; and elimination of "administrivia" results in less support personnel.

Because a TQM organization is a changing organization, its members, both managers and workers, must be prepared for lateral changes in position. A program of education and self-improvement will facilitate change.

Organizations implementing TQM must make it clear from the beginning that, while TQM can lead to some workers being assigned to different or expanded functions, no one will lose work or pay because of new efficiencies. Absent such assurances, TOM will be sabotaged from within. No worker will support actions that could lead to the loss of work and income.

To provide such assurance, the TQM organization must institute a program of education and self-improvement designed to qualify displaced workers for new and more challenging jobs than before.

Even without TQM, the worker who stays with a single employer for his or her entire career can, on average, expect to change jobs within the organization no less than eight times. Change is inherent in a free-enterprise economy; indeed, it is the greatest source of its vitality and strength. While accepting and lauding the flexibility inherent in our economic system, we must also recognize the importance to employees, including managers, of employment stability. Senior managers have a responsibility to facilitate employment stability for the changing organization. A rich program of training and education is vital to that purpose.

See chapter 7 for a discussion of training and education in a TQM organization.

Deming's Point Number 14: Put everybody to work to accomplish the transformation.

The corporate transformation required for successful implementation of TQM requires understanding, active involvement, and support from every function and every level in the organization. Though TQM must be led and inspired from the top, Deming was right in his assertion that everybody needs to be put to work to accomplish the transformation. Indeed, the most important TQM contributions to quality and productivity, product integrity, and customer satisfaction come from workers, not managers. The basic ability and willingness of the lower levels of the work force to contribute to improvement of the organization's fortunes may be one of the least appreciated features of TQM.

At successful TQM organizations, everyone is involved in the corporate transformation. Partnership breeds involvement, and involvement breeds partnership. Once the cycle begins, it becomes self-sustaining. But the initial impetus must come from the leader; only he or she can get the cycle started.

The Seven Deadly Diseases

Dr. Deming had complemented the positive suggestions set forth in his fourteen points with a statement of seven obstacles that need to be overcome. Known as the Seven Deadly Diseases, each is listed below.

1. Lack of constancy of purpose. This "disease," essentially the reciprocal of Deming's Point Number 1 (create constancy of purpose), warns that, unless we identify our purpose and then pursue it with relentless determination, the goal of improved products and services, competitiveness, staying-power, and job provision will elude the best-intentioned manager.

Implementation of TQM is not something that can be done by the well-meaning but easily distracted. It requires development of an internally consistent vision, goals and strategy, integration of TQM with everyday business management, and the purposeful and steady application of TQM principles in pursuit of improvement, competitiveness, staying power, and job provision.

2. Emphasis on short-term profits. With his second disease, Deming warned that it is at our peril if we ignore or postpone investment in such things as research, training, maintenance, customer surveys, and improvement of products, services, and processes.

Every executive understands the value of such investments. The problem is that they absorb resources immediately, but don't pay off until some time in the future. Because of the alleged demand by stockholders and financial institutions for immediate profits, and because the payoff won't be seen until later (when possibly a new management team will be in place to reap the benefits), even the wisest and most conscientious executives can be tempted to defer such investments.

The fact is, however, that failure to invest in the future on a disciplined and timely basis is a disease that can rapidly become terminal.

3. Evaluation by performance, merit rating, or annual review of performance. This third disease is the reciprocal of Deming's Point No. 12, in which we were admonished to abolish annual performance appraisal. Deming's warning, here, was that organizations that continue to evaluate and reward people solely on the basis of individual performance will destroy teamwork and build fear. See chapter 6 for a discussion of TQM reward system alternatives.

4. Mobility of management. Deming warns about the increasing penchant to look upon management as a skill easily transported from one organization to the next. Of special concern is the movement of executives between organizations in entirely different technologies. Deming held that, without a considerable amount of time spent in their organizations, executives cannot develop the requisite deep understanding of its problems, possibilities, culture, and people. Nor will they be there long enough to follow through on their initiatives. See chapter 8 for a discussion of leadership in a TQM organization.

5. Running a company on visible figures alone. Deming asserted that the most important figures are unknown and unknowable. As an example, he pointed to the cost of an unhappy customer, one who defects to the competition, or to the "multiplier" effect of happy employees and delighted customers. Such figures are, indeed, unknown and unknowable; yet, they are among the most important to any organization. Executives who focus on balance sheets, to the exclusion (or the detriment) of these unquantifiable figures, will fail.

6. Excessive medical costs for employee health care, which increase the final costs of goods and services. With this sixth disease, Deming was campaigning for changes to the American system of health care. Escalating health care costs are a major burden to American business and threaten our international competitiveness. The health-care debate begun in 1993-94 can lead to development of a political consensus on how to deal with this issue.

7. Excessive costs of warranty, fueled by lawyers who work on the basis of a contingency fee. Warranty costs are linked to quality. When improvements in quality are realized through the application of TQM, warranty costs will decline.

3

Listening is the First Step

Why Didn't They Ask Us?

Workers generally have stories to tell about actions taken by their management that were detrimental to corporate well-being. "Had they asked us, we could have told them this wouldn't work." They might be talking about the wrong material, the wrong machine, the wrong software, the wrong supplier, or the wrong process. Of course, the workers might not have had full information, and the manager's decision might very well have been the right one. But then again, perhaps not. What is important here is two things: first, making the best possible decision requires bringing all relevant perspectives to bear on the question, and second, employees become disgruntled when some of those affected by the decision are not part of making it.

David Kearns, former CEO of Xerox, relates a powerful story concerning his meeting with a group of employees. One of the things discussed was a new copier: despite a major investment in design, the copier had failed in the marketplace. An employee got up and said he had a question: "David, why didn't you ask us what we thought about it?[1] We could have told you it was a piece of junk." Kearns goes on to remark: "Of course he was absolutely right. Why didn't I ask the employees? I was stupid. We were not using our people in a way that would make a difference."

I can offer a similar anecdote from my own experience with a client that owns and operates hotels and shopping centers. A group of maintenance employees told me of a costly energy management system bought by their managers that had proved to be the wrong choice. They posed the same question: "Why didn't they ask us? We knew from the start that the system was the wrong one for that application."

Bringing workers into the decision process requires simply that managers undertake consultation with empowered subordinates, seek consensus, and act accordingly. A word of caution, however: *empowerment of the workforce does not imply abrogation of managerial responsibility.*

The manager remains the manager. Following discussion of a corporate issue between the manager and affected subordinates, should the manager's view differ from the consensus, the manager's judgment must prevail. Such an outcome is unlikely when the manager is an active and informed party to the discussion; generally, he will persuade the workforce to his view, or will be persuaded to theirs. When the manager's view does remain contrary to the work force consensus, my experience shows that the workforce cheerfully accepts that outcome. The important thing is that the workers will have been consulted, and during the dialogue will have learned the reasons for the manager's position.

Matsushita: We Got the Message!

Kosusuke Matsushita, founder of the Japanese company Matsushita Electric (owners of the Panasonic trade name, among others) made a challenging statement some years ago concerning the need for managers to consult on corporate issues with affected members of the workforce:

> We [Japanese industry] will win, and you [the industrial west] will lose. You cannot do anything about it because your failure is an internal disease . . . . You firmly believe that sound management means executives on one side and workers on the other, on one side men who think and on the other side men who can only work. For you, management is the art of smoothly transferring the executives' ideas to the workers' hands . . . . For us, management is the entire work force's intellectual commitment at the service of the company . . . without self-imposed functional or class barriers . . . . We know that the intelligence of a few technocrats – even very bright ones – has become totally inadequate to face [today's] challenges. Only the intellects of all employees can permit a company to live with the ups and downs and the requirements of its new environment. Yes, we will win and you will lose . . . .[2]

Whatever we may think of the tone of Matsushita's remark, its accusations accurately reflect American pre-TQM management practices. Matsushita was wrong, however, in his prediction that the industrial west is going to lose. Organizations all across America have understood the need for transformation to a corporate culture of empowerment, and *are* now listening to their people:

• General Electric, in its 1993 Annual Report, said, "We believe the only way to gain more output from less input – to grow and win – is to engage **every** mind within our businesses – exciting, energizing, involving and rewarding **everyone**."[3] (Emphasis in the original text.)

• General James Maier, former Chief of Staff of the U.S. Army, wrote, "Delegate, don't fear mistakes . . . hold people accountable, don't micro manage . . . management's role is mainly to set priorities, provide resources, and remove roadblocks."

• Executives at AT&T have been quoted as saying, "Empowerment means that employees can perform their work without turning to an overprotective boss or an all-encompassing rulebook."

More Like Us

James Fallows' celebrated book *More Like Us* (published in 1989, and validated in the several years since) states that America can regain its economic and political preeminence, not by becoming more like the Japanese, but by becoming *more like us* – that is, more in step with the traditions of social mobility and open frontiers that helped make America great in the first place.[4]

As groundwork for this thesis, Fallows compares the very different American and Japanese cultures in terms of their ability to meet two standards that are essential to any successful society: a wide radius of trust, and a belief on the part of individuals that they control their own destiny.

Japanese society is successful, Fallows suggests, because Japanese culture effectively meets the first of these standards through racial homogeneity, and the second through a belief (constantly vindicated) that effort will be its own reward – that doing one's part for one's corporation, for example, will ensure the reciprocity of lifelong security. On the basis of what Fallows terms its *talent for order,* Japan is able to get the most out of ordinary people by organizing them to adapt and succeed.

By contrast, American culture must satisfy the two criteria of a successful society in ways that reflect a unique openness to social change (in Fallows' words, *a talent for disorder*). Given America's ethnic heterogeneity, high mobility, and broad exposure to disruption, the desired wide radius of trust must necessarily be based on a single cultural value: the belief that everyone in the society is playing by the same set of rules.

Fallows points out, further, that the randomness and fast pace of change experienced by Americans encourage them to adapt to change as individuals rather than as a group. This means, he says, that the second criterion for a successful society – the sense on the part of individuals that they control their own destiny – must be met in America by a culture that offers individuals "the constant prospect of changing their fortunes, their identities, their roles in life. Americans are most likely to try hard, adapt and succeed when they believe that they can improve their luck, that the rules of competition are more or less fair, and that if they take a risk and fail, they won't be totally destroyed." When these conditions are met, America is able "to get surprising results from average people by putting them in situations where old rules and limits don't apply."

Fallows summarizes his important message:

> To put the point yet another way, Japan is strong because each person knows his place. America is strong when people do not know their proper places and are free to invent new roles for themselves. Therefore, if Americans lose their sense of possibility and instead believe that they belong in predictable, limited roles, the United States will have lost what makes it special. It will have a harder time prevailing in economic and military competition, and it will no longer offer the freedom to start over that people have always come to America to find.

If the values Fallows presents as instrumental to American success sound familiar, there's a reason: they are entirely consistent with TQM principles of participative management and workforce empowerment.

Several connections between TQM and Fallows' American values are immediately suggested. For example, the TQM opportunity to participate in decision-making surely gives workers the chance to "change their role in life" and to meet the challenge of "situations where old rules and limits don't apply." The same is true of rotating work assignments or membership on various project teams. Important, too, is the new value that TQM places on worker contributions with respect to the success of the entire organization. This goes a long way toward creating a community of interest in which "everyone is playing by the same set of rules" and risks can be taken without undue fear of failure.

Cultural Transformation

For organizations that are structured and managed along traditional pyramidal lines, creating empowerment requires a cultural transformation.

Employees in traditional organizations are accustomed to having little information about the company's business plans or prospects, no contact with customers or suppliers, no knowledge of competitive pressures, no control over how their work is organized, and, often, a passive or (in the worst cases) active hostility toward management.

The separation of our organizations into "management" functions and "worker" functions is wrongheaded from two points of view. First, it keeps the work force from knowing about and identifying with corporate issues, and, by doing so, denies to workers a crucial sense of partnership in the corporate enterprise. Second, it denies to management the workforce perspective on corporate issues that would, in many cases, improve decisions, and the wider participation that would, in all cases, improve support for decisions.

For management, transformation to a culture of empowerment requires full acceptance of the notion that intelligence and corporate dedication are not the sole province of managers.

I am always impressed by the wisdom and insight that people at the bottom of the organizational totem pole bring to my TQM workshops when we deal with such "management" topics as improvement of customer satisfaction, identifying and eliminating corporate waste, and development of a corporate vision and strategy.

Given the same information, employees at the lowest levels of the organization generally deliver ideas equal in value to those generated by their managers. Indeed, because working-level people are not prisoners of corporate conventional wisdom, and because their perspective about products, processes, and customers often differs from those held by managers, their workshop offerings sometimes contain unorthodox notions that can be the beginning of a genuinely new insight.

Transformation from traditional management to empowerment does not endow the workforce with the right to decide to relax its efforts. Nor is this even a temptation. To the contrary, empowered workers become more conscientious than before. When the transformation from employee to partner takes place, people seek added responsibility, look for ways to improve, and develop a stronger understanding of customer requirements and the need to satisfy them if they and the company are to prosper.

Empowerment is not for everyone. To make this crystal clear, consider the case of a child requiring neurosurgery; no parent would empower an untrained stranger to perform it. We would seek someone with the proper training, experience, motivation, and a demonstrated history of successful performance; only to such people would empowerment be granted in matters important to us personally.

It is no different in the workplace. Empowerment is conferred only on those proven able and willing to do the job. People with insufficient training or experience, or not properly motivated, need to be raised to the requisite standard before they are elevated to the level of full partnership and granted full empowerment. Doing so is the job of the manager.

Valuing

Midwest Medical, a Duluth, Minnesota, supplier of home-care medical equipment, conducts a "valuing" session at every staff meeting. A different staff member is designated before the staff meeting as the person to be valued, and all staff members come prepared to speak about what they value in that person. No negative comments are allowed.

The designated person is different at each staff meeting. Managers are included in turn. When every member has been the beneficiary of valuing, rotation among staff members begins anew. In this way, every person is the recipient of valuing once every few months.

The company's managers are convinced that valuing is a source of strength for the organization. Because people are obliged periodically to search their minds for what it is that they value in one another, bonding between members attains levels greater than one generally sees in businesses. The notion of a business "family" has become a reality at Midwest, and valuing has made a major contribution to the cultural transformation needed as a base for TQM implementation.

Easing Into Empowerment

Moving directly from an authoritarian management environment to full empowerment can invite chaos. Neither manager nor worker is comfortable with an overnight transition; indeed, neither one will fully understand their new role. Confusion and uncertainty will be the almost certain result, as well as mutual disenchantment with the concept of empowerment.

When moving to empowerment, the first requirement is a dialogue between managers and workers. They need to agree among themselves as to what empowerment should mean in their particular environment. What specific things are there for which instructions, or permission, or monitoring, or review are now provided? How might we restructure so that these management interventions can be reduced or eliminated altogether? Will it be necessary to provide training before empowerment can be granted?

The opportunity for misunderstanding abounds. I often encounter managers who firmly believe that empowerment is their natural management style ("I've always empowered my subordinates."), and whose subordinates just as firmly view them as authoritarian. Just as often, I encounter workers who ask to be empowered in some aspect of their work, only to be told by the boss that they have always been so empowered. "You're not using the power you've always had."

The importance of dialogue between worker and manager cannot be overstated. Each needs to seek an understanding of the other's view of empowerment, not in vague philosophical terms, but in the specific context of the work situation.

Some managers find it difficult to surrender the authority they worked for so many years to win. Others find it difficult to trust subordinates. Because managers are ultimately responsible for their unit's output, some believe that only continued close monitoring of the work force can ensure sustained quality and productivity.

Such managers need to be persuaded by the logic inherent in Peter Drucker's observation: "To give up power is to gain power." Implicit in this seeming paradox is the notion that, when the manager of a unit gives up power to the work force, the newly empowered workers will become more proficient, the unit's output will improve, and the manager will thereby gain in power.

Easing into empowerment might be facilitated by identification of the several stages of empowerment. Workers and managers, in jointly developing a plan to undertake greater empowerment, can benefit from reviewing and discussing the stages of empowerment. They can determine which stage they've already attained, and move forward gradually, one stage at a time. For example:

• Stage Zero is the stage where the organization's management culture is entirely autocratic and authoritarian. As has been noted, few, if any, organizations are at the stage of zero empowerment in the contemporary United States. In contemporary America, most pre-TQM organizations are at Stage 1 or 2. TQM should take them successively through the higher stages until they reach Stage 4.

• Stage 1 is the stage where management sets guidelines and the worker is authorized to perform work without close monitoring, but must seek guidance on how to deal with unexpected situations and must submit completed work to management for inspection or review.

• Stage 2 is the stage where the manager and worker jointly establish guidelines, the worker is empowered to work independently as long as activity remains within the guidelines, and where completed work does not need to be inspected or reviewed if the worker determines that it meets established standards.

• Stage 3 is the stage where the worker is fully empowered to work without supervision, to set guidelines, and to inspect or review completed projects without supervisory input, but is required to report periodically on progress and/or problems.

• Stage 4 is where the workers are chartered to run a mini-business within the business. As "captains of their game," they would be required only to report periodically on the kinds of things an autonomous division might be expected to communicate to company headquarters: work status, quality and productivity levels, customer comment, profit and loss, market projections, etc.

Ralph Stayer, CEO of Johnsville Foods, has written on the difficulty he had bringing empowerment to his company. Frustrated after two years of trying to bring about empowerment, Stayer recognized the need for a new intervention. The key, he decided, was to remove management from any responsibility for checking the product; as long as management retained that responsibility, they would implicitly remain responsible for quality and performance. To encourage people to become responsible for their own performance, line workers were informed that, henceforth, quality would be *their* responsibility. The resulting change was rapid and dramatic. People accepted their new ownership with enthusiasm. They asked for information about costs and customer reactions, collected relevant data, formed teams and held daily discussions to resolve problems, imposed sanctions when workers failed to meet standards, and undertook selection and training of new workers. Stayer was able to reduce the number of management layers from six to three.[5]

Let me add a word of advice on the undertaking of empowerment. Once there is agreement that empowerment will be practiced, each party needs to hold the other's feet to the fire. I say this because old habits are often hard to break. Thus, should an empowered worker ask his or her manager "How many widgets should I order?" after it has been agreed that widget ordering is entirely within the prerogative of the empowered worker, the manager must refuse to be drawn into the decision. Instead, he must gently remind the worker that the decision is his or hers to make.

By the same token, should a manager revert to old ways and direct the empowered worker to order 27 widgets from a particular supplier by tomorrow, the worker should courteously but firmly remind the manager that the decision on whether, from whom, and when to order widgets is now entirely within his or her authority.

In closing this discussion on the necessity for easing into empowerment, I need to give emphasis to the advice we got from David Kearns (Xerox) in the opening paragraphs of this chapter: *ask the people what they think.* Empowerment cannot be mandated, or given, or taken for granted. It must be discussed between the empowerers and the empowerees, and in their discussion they need to reach agreement about two things: what empowerment means in the context of their particular organization and the job at hand, and how best to bring it about. Only then will there be a smooth transition.

4

Empowerment: How to Make It Happen

Our purpose in this chapter is to provide TQM implementers with a list of actions that collectively will move a workforce toward involvement and empowerment. The reader is invited to view the ideas presented as a checklist, a descriptor of things that might be done. Not every item will necessarily be practical for every implementing organization, but each one is worthy of your consideration. If you decide that some of the particulars are not relevant to your needs, you should replace them with more applicable alternatives.

While some of the items overlap, attention is needed to each of them to achieve a true partnership between workers and managers, to ensure that every person in the organization fully understands and supports corporate purposes, and to bring about enthusiastic and sustained efforts toward their achievement.

Open-Book Management

Don Petersen, former CEO of Ford, has suggested ways (in his book, *A Better Idea*) to bring about involvement. His first suggestion is to "open up the books." Let everyone know all you can about the company.

Robert Galvin, the now-retired Chairman of Motorola and 1989 winner of the Baldrige Award, has spoken about the importance of being informed. As the son of the founder of Motorola, Galvin had joined the company as a young engineer. Because he was the founder's son, people from all departments of the company came to him with information. They reported their concerns, their accomplishments, and their ideas. Galvin believes that as a consequence of all this information, he was able to perform more effectively than otherwise. Having this in mind, he has made information availability the centerpiece of his management style. To this day, one of the factors leading to Motorola's success is the steady availability of information to everyone in the organization.

Steve Jobs, CEO of Next Computer, has said that for Next to be competitive, his employees must "contain the company's DNA and therefore must be privy to crucial information like sales, profits, and strategic plans."[1] Indeed, Next takes openness a step farther: everyone can find out about everyone else's salary and stock holdings simply by asking. Next's director of manufacturing and engineering believes sharing pay information helps morale: "The availability of salaries ensures that most inequities in the system get resolved."

President Clinton, moderating a panel at the Conference on the Future of the American Workplace, July 26, 1993, remarked:

> And the phrase . . . that made the biggest impression on me here was "open-book management . . . ." If we could do nothing other than convince people that somehow the only way to get everybody on the same team is to give them the same information, the same capacity to evaluate the information . . . I think that would be a terrific thing.

In sharing information with employees, managers will recognize the difficulty for meaningful dialogue presented by large, formal meetings. For a variety of reasons, people are often inhibited from making statements or asking questions in large group settings. Managers need to be sensitive to that reality, and be prepared to go the extra mile to create the kind of trust and interest that will bring about a real exchange.

Managers need to bring to these sessions the information that they find useful in managing the company: What is selling well? What are customers saying? What are the quality trends? What are the cost and profitability trends? What is the competition up to? Are there any plans for changes or improvements to products or services? Which suppliers are serving us well, and which ones are in need of improvement? Which of our processes need review and improvement? What are our alternatives for the future?

Above all, the manager must ask that all-important question: What do you think? To prompt the necessary dialogue (and to get useful insights) managers need to ask specific questions of employees: What do you think of the change we made to the product or service? Would you think it useful to buy a new computer system? Are our suppliers giving you needed support?

Employees might want to know any number of things.

People in an automobile manufacturing company might like to know how blue cars fare in comparison with red ones, how sedans sell compared with station wagons and trucks, how the company is doing this year compared with last year and compared with various competitors, and how current productivity and quality levels compare with earlier levels and with competitors.

People working for a bank might be interested in learning the demographics of their bank: the number and average value of accounts for various age groups, profiles of commercial account customers, and how their bank compares with competition in profitability. People working for the United States Postal Service might want to know how it compares in various ways with Federal Express and UPS, and with the postal services of Japan and Germany.

These examples are certainly not complete or definitive. They merely illustrate the kind of information that every organization has (or should have) about itself, and which could be a basis for dialogue with employees. Employees who are informed about these and related matters begin to identify with the organization. They move from employeeship to partnership. They become involved.

Shared information falls into two broad categories. One, of which blue cars versus red ones is representative, serves essentially to give employees a sense of proprietorship. The implication of sharing this kind of information with employees is that this is their company, and as partners they deserve to know everything about it. The second category is information crucial to the well-being of the company, such as quality trends. It is provided to raise their awareness about company strengths and weaknesses, and to induce employees to consider their contribution to the corporate effort. When negative trends are reported, or when comparisons with competition show that the company is lagging, employees have some initial facts that might stimulate thinking about how they and their team might work to improve things.

Traditional (non-TQM) organizations rarely make corporate information available to employees. They are even less likely to communicate the corporate vision and strategic plan, which are usually seen only by managers at the top level. Information of this kind should not only be made available to everyone in the organization, but, to the extent feasible, employees should have a voice in developing the corporate vision and plan. Planning methods are discussed at greater length in chapter 16.

As important as it is to make corporate information available to all members, we need to be realistic. Very large organizations cannot involve everyone in developing the corporate vision and strategy. Not only would it take too much time to consult with large numbers of individuals, but achieving a consensus with a population of thousands is impractical, if not impossible. When that is the case, one reaches as far down into, or as far across, the organization as practical.

Organizational decentralization is thus a natural and important corollary to workforce empowerment. Every large TQM organization is in fact reorganized as an integrated collection of smaller ones: mini-businesses under the corporate umbrella. This makes it possible to achieve total employee involvement in dealing with departmental issues and plans which would be impossible for the corporation as a whole. Such mini-organizations can seek departmental consensus on corporate issues, and report them to the corporate level.

There is also the issue of corporate privacy. When premature disclosure would threaten the implementation of a corporate plan, privacy is crucial, and wide dissemination of the plan among employees can be contrary to corporate interests.

The answer to concerns about corporate size and corporate privacy is simply to exercise common sense. "Knowledge is power" is not merely a timeworn cliché. People generally perform more effectively with complete knowledge than with partial knowledge or with none at all. Senior management's goal must be to get as much information to employees as possible, to involve them in discussion in the search for improvement, and to create a sense of corporate partnership. But common sense prevails. One does that which serves the common good of the organization, and refrains from doing that which would damage it.

Company newsletters are another way to involve employees. Their basic purpose is to create a sense of family, which is typically brought about with news about company bowling and softball teams, employee marriages, births, new hires, and retirements. A second purpose is to motivate high levels of achievement by conferring honor and local fame on excellent performers. To that end, newsletters often contain articles about people and teams that have made notable contributions to the corporate effort. All of that is good, and should continue.

There is a third potential function of newsletters that is not always served: communicating corporate information. People want to know what is going on, and the newsletter is a good place to inform them. The kinds of information people might want to know about (red cars versus blue ones) were discussed earlier, and each organization will need to decide for itself the kind of corporate information that would interest its employees. The corporate newsletter is a good vehicle for communicating information about such things as the company's plans, prospects, problems, new products or services, technological trends, and even profiles of important customers or suppliers. It is also a good forum for the discussion of alternative courses of corporate action, and for posing that all important question to employees: What do you think?

We–They Relationships and Egalitarianism

The easy path for any organization is to permit "natural" groupings and alliances to form. Every organization has numbers of we-they relationships. Blue collar–white collar, union–non-union, engineering–manufacturing, men–women, product A team–product B team, salaried–hourly, headquarters–field, management–non-management, office–factory. The we–they list is as lengthy as one cares to make it. The we's do not associate closely with the they's. The they's snub the we's. Information remains unconveyed. Invisible fences are built between departments, between functions, and between product lines. Resentments flourish and important tasks fail to get done because of lack of communication. Tasks are performed serially rather than in parallel; products are developed for which there is no market because engineering and marketing pursue their work independently rather than jointly; and products are developed that cannot be built without redesign because engineering failed to consult manufacturing.

As a young engineer, my first job was with a large electronics organization that separated employees into "first-class" and "second-class." Our badges proclaimed our status, or lack of it, to all who gazed upon them. Second-class employees were hourly wage earners, and first-class applied to salaried people. The distinction remains etched in my mind after these many years because – you guessed it – junior engineers, my entry-level position, were designated second-class employees. To make sure that everyone knew their place, supervisors wore badges with markings that indicated their rank.

Today, we are more enlightened. Few organizations outside the military would so blatantly distinguish status by badge type, and none that I know of would confer the onerous status of "second-class" on any group of employees. Yet, many organizations, even those that consider themselves enlightened, continue to segregate employee parking areas into zones based on rank, and to provide plush (and subsidized) dining privileges to executives while lesser employees must make do with a cafeteria or, worse yet, vending machines standing alongside picnic tables set on the shop floor.

The common justification for preferred parking is that senior people must frequently come and go during the work day, and close-in parking saves time and money. Executive dining facilities are said to provide seniors with an opportunity to interact with their peers, and to provide a means for impressing VIP guests.

Andrew Grove, CEO of Intel, announced some years ago the elimination of preferred parking based on rank, stating that if managers want a good parking spot they will henceforth need to get to work early! To further drive home the point about egalitarianism, Grove has elected to run the company from a personal office which is a cubbyhole comparable in size and decor to what one might expect for a first-level supervisor in the purchasing department of a cardboard-box factory.[2] Though senior managers at Intel "rough it" compared with their peers in traditional organizations, Intel's continued success suggests that egalitarianism is not a barrier to corporate achievement. To the contrary, people at Intel and comparable superior organizations believe that egalitarianism contributes to the creation of widely inclusive corporate partnerships that bring out the best in every member of the organization.

Nucor Corporation, one of America's most innovative and successful steel manufacturers, has no company plane, no executive dining room, and no preferred parking; moreover its executives are expected to answer their own phone. Out of 5500 employees (22 plants), only 20 (including secretaries and the CEO) are at headquarters, which is located next to a shopping center in Charlotte, North Carolina. Nucor prides itself at having fewer than one employee at headquarters for every plant in the corporation – almost certainly a record low!

Discretionary Effort

Max DePree, CEO of Herman Miller Furniture Company, in his superb book, *Leadership is an Art*, relates the story of the millwright at Herman Miller. One day, the millwright died. The manager visited the millwright's bereaved family, and was asked by the widow if she might read from the millwright's poetry. The manager was so impressed by its beauty that he asked himself whether this person had been a poet who worked as a millwright, or a millwright who wrote poetry?[3]

DePree's message is that most people have hidden talents, finding dignity away from the workplace in accomplishments that few outside their family will even know about. Some repair old cars or build cabinetry, some cook gourmet meals or do exquisite needlepoint, and still others play the violin or master an ancient language. The point is that most people have ability far beyond those they deliver to the workplace.

Every person who works for another knows what it takes to satisfy the employer. There is always some minimum amount of work that must be done to stay out of trouble, to stay employed and in good graces with the boss. But that threshold is generally far below what almost anyone is capable of. The difference between what we must do to stay employed and what we are capable of doing is discretionary effort. It is at our discretion whether we deliver effort beyond the minimum that it takes to stay employed. The fraction of work which is discretionary is smaller on the assembly line than it is in the executive suite, but some fraction of our output (or lack of it) is up to us, no matter where we work.

The millwright was an excellent workman, but the sensitivity of soul and the artistic ability apparent in his poetry suggest that the he might also have been able to make a contribution to furniture design, to devising innovative marketing strategies, and to writing creative advertising copy.

I am not suggesting that everybody in the organization should be invited to take part in everything. That, of course, would lead to chaos. Organizations need specialties and assignments, and, with such a focus, there will be limits on the ability of even the most talented and energetic worker to contribute in spheres outside his or her assigned area.

TQM organizations can and must make it possible for people to work to the limits (or at least closer to the limits than now) of their capacity and interest. Ways to bring this about include job enrichment, job rotation, and cross-functional teaming. Each of these can widen the horizon of employees, and give them an opportunity to learn about and involve themselves in areas of endeavor outside their assigned responsibilities.

As earlier discussed, another factor in broadening employee horizons is information: the more each employee learns about the organization's purposes and activities, the greater the likelihood that he or she will be stimulated to contribute discretionary effort.

It probably goes without saying that the principle of discretionary effort applies within areas of assigned responsibility. To go back to the millwright, it is reasonable to assume that a person with the intelligence to write poetry could apply that intelligence to his work as a millwright. Every person of intelligence, properly motivated, can think of ways to perform assigned functions at a higher level of quality and productivity. All such persons can think of ways to improve the product or the service they are paid to produce. But again, such contributions are at the worker's discretion. No one can prove that a worker can in fact do his or her job better. Workers themselves must make the effort, and they will do so only if they feel included in the local (departmental) and corporate partnership.

Job Enrichment

We all remain the heirs of Frederick Taylor, the turn-of-the-century industrial engineer who is considered by many to be the father of the American assembly line. Stopwatch in hand, Taylor timed jobs, and sought to divide functions so that each job was as short as possible. The idea was that, because short jobs can be easily and quickly taught, people with few or no skills (and often with little or no ability in English) could be hired to perform most production line functions at very low pay. Employee turnover was not a problem. Because replacements could be trained in minutes, workers were thought of as replaceable parts.

The Taylor approach contrasted with our pre-industrial period, when people thought of themselves as craftsmen. Individual cobblers built whole shoes, individual clock makers created timepieces that often were works of art, and individual seamstresses made clothing on order. The assembly line was seen as a way to free industry from the slow pace, relatively high cost, and rugged independence of individual craftsmen.

Assembly lines were successful, albeit often at substantial initial cost to the dignity of working people. Though wages came down, prices came down even more, and after some decades of tension between unions and management, most would agree that industrialization has raised the living standard for most people.

Taylor's ideas were important to the success of industry in those early days. Industry grew at such a pace that workers were recruited not primarily from the ranks of displaced skilled craftsmen, but from the ranks of generally unskilled farmers and immigrants. The short job, narrow skill requirements, and ease and rapidity of training suited the low skill level and the often limited language ability of the workforce of our early industrial age.

Work during this period was often boring and monotonous, and the 70-hour work weeks, low wages, and sweat shop conditions were inhumane by current standards. But the Taylor precepts made possible a leap into the industrial age that may not otherwise have been so quickly achieved.

Though Taylor's principles were right for his time, they are not right for today. It is true that we continue to have problems with inadequate education and language skills, but those affected are generally not part of the industrial work force. They are, in most cases, either unemployed or in low-skill service jobs. To be sure, this represents a social problem that needs to be dealt with, but it is not a current threat to industrial competitiveness. Indeed, we now have a surplus of skilled and willing workers, not a shortage. What we do have a shortage of is effective managers knowledgeable in TQM concepts and practices.

Henry Levin, a Stanford University economics professor who has studied work force skill needs, suggests that our top CEO's have used work force skill levels as a convenient excuse for a decade of abysmal management practices: "The easiest way to take the pressure off themselves for producing a lousy product with too many middle managers, too high executive salaries, and too little creativity is to say, 'How can we do it? We have a lousy work force!' This is basically an excuse for a lousy management process."[4]

According to a study by the Japan Labor Ministry, reported in 1992, American workers, by some measures, out-produce their Japanese counterparts.[5, 6] The ministry divided the 1989 gross domestic product for each country by the number of workers and found that American workers produce 1.62 times more than the Japanese, when the value of their work is calculated according to purchasing power. When productivity is calculated without considering purchasing power, using only the currency rate of exchange to compare national output, American workers produce 1.09 times as much as their Japanese counterparts.

U.S. workers are ready, willing, and able to accept wider and deeper responsibilities, which can be achieved by both "vertical" and "horizontal" job enrichment. Vertical job enrichment means greater operational involvement, such as responsibility for building an entire unit rather than just parts (entire chairs as opposed to chair legs, or arms, or backs, or seats). Horizontal job enrichment is brought about by assigning support activities to operations personnel, so the chair maker will be responsible for buying wood, screws, glue, and varnish (formerly bought by the purchasing department). He or she would also be responsible for interviewing and selecting new teammates (formerly done by the human resources department), etc.

Dedication to the principle of job enrichment is illustrated by Kodak's R & D Center in Japan.[7] The Center's Japanese director reports that, when his researchers visit Kodak headquarters in Rochester, New York, for orientation, they are strongly impressed by the fact that their American counterparts are backed by a team of technicians who perform the hands-on laboratory work. However, says the director, when his researchers request the same technical support, "We tell them, 'Absolutely not.' The essence of research in Japan is to put your best people in the laboratory, where they can see the unexpected first-hand."

In addition to accepting this broadened vertical involvement, the Japanese researchers must also extend themselves horizontally. Says the R & D director, "We want them visiting customers all the time, so they can see what the market needs."

The logic behind the use of technicians (and marketing people) to support researchers is, of course that highly-salaried researchers are thereby freed from the tedium of hands-on laboratory work and marketing activity done by lower-salaried technicians and marketers. While that logic has merit, it is also true that researchers who avoid real-world application of their ideas lose something thereby that no amount of additional theorizing will provide.

The principles of job enrichment would argue that the effectiveness of researchers is increased as a consequence of hands-on laboratory and customer involvement. Thus, the "efficiencies" achieved by shielding them from the laboratory and field environments can, in the broader sense, be seen as counterproductive. They become less effective by not knowing firsthand the realities of the laboratory and the marketplace.

In many cases, the same thinking applies to managers who type their own correspondence and answer and place their own telephone calls. In this era of word-processors and voice-mail, personal involvement with the mechanics of correspondence and telephone communications gets more work done, with fewer mistakes, and with less ambiguity than our traditional recourse to secretarial transcription of dictation or handwritten drafts. "Displaced" secretaries can be converted to greater productivity as administrative assistants or transferred to line responsibilities.

The purpose behind deepening and widening jobs is to make it possible for workers or teams to think of themselves as a small business and as meaningful contributors to, and partners in, the collective corporate enterprise. By controlling as much of their work as possible, workers are motivated to assume responsibility for improvements in product quality, productivity, and design.

Horizontal Management

Most managers will, at one time or another, have said or thought, "I'm so busy putting out fires that I don't have time to plan for the future." This may be rather like the airplane pilot who says, "I'm so busy avoiding bumpy air and monitoring distribution of soft drinks and peanuts that I don't have time to plan for our landing."

To put it generically, most managers in traditional organizations have a vertical focus. They are either looking downward to be sure their subordinates are doing the right things, or they are looking upward to provide information to and/or to receive micro-management from their downward looking bosses. There is neither time nor energy nor inclination to look horizontally, and to attend to the many things (planning is only one of them) that only the manager is equipped (by virtue of knowledge and rank) to attend to.

Numerous things are wrong here. By "micro-managing," the downward-looking manager is insulting the dignity of subordinates and slowing them down. Subordinates are denied the opportunity to assume responsibility and to become accountable for their own performance. Jack Welch, CEO of General Electric, insists that all GE employees be given the opportunity to be "captains of their game." Supervisors defining for employees how work must be done, hovering over employees while work is underway, and insisting on the right to review output before work advances to the next station or to the customer are doing a major disservice to the subordinate, the organization, and themselves.

From his experience as CEO of Ford, Don Petersen has written, " 'Check with me' may be among the most counterproductive words a manager can utter." I would guess that every manager is guilty of using that counterproductive phrase, probably often. But think of what it implies: that the manager hasn't formulated the task clearly enough, or that the employee is not considered trustworthy. In either case, dignity is affronted, time is lost, accountability is left vague, and the vertically preoccupied manager is distracted from horizontal management.

By looking outward, by managing horizontally, the manager finds a set of tasks that only he or she, at whatever level, can do effectively. Depending on the particulars of the manager's position, such tasks might include planning, working with customers, working with suppliers, working with adjacent departments, thinking about how the product or service might be improved, analyzing competitive positions, considering how market share might be improved, evaluating the possible impact of geopolitical events, and so forth. Support specialists may attend to some or all of these tasks, but managers disengage from them *at their peril.*

It is entirely natural that managers should focus vertically. After all, most of them, especially at the lower levels of supervision, became managers because they were good at their functions. Their history as successful performers motivates them to monitor the performance of their subordinates; it does not motivate or prepare them for their entirely new and vastly more important function, which is to lead people and manage resources.

Preparation and motivation of managers for horizontal management, and cessation of vertical management, is one of the great challenges of the TQM cultural transformation. But unless senior managers understand this challenge and deal with it for themselves as well as for subordinate managers, the corporate-wide magic that can come with successful TQM implementation will remain less than fully realized.

Span of Control

It is difficult to bring about empowerment when only 2 or 3, or even 5 or 7 people report to a supervisor. When the span of control is small, the temptation to micro-manage the work of subordinates is great. On the other hand, when a manager supervises large numbers of people, say 20, or 50, or 100, there is no time to micro-manage the work of any one individual.

TQM organizations seek to reduce the management hierarchy not only because it makes empowerment more achievable, but because the overhead costs of excess supervision are a needless expense. For any given business, from the factory floor all the way up to the Corporate Executive Office, there are opportunities for minimizing levels of management and increasing the span of control.

Guided by these precepts, Ford, for example, has eliminated the position of first-level foreman. Former foremen are now coaches and facilitators. They are there to support their former subordinates, not to give them orders. Lincoln Electric has an average of 100 people reporting to a supervisor. Westinghouse Baltimore went from 14 layers of management to four. General Electric has gone from nine levels of management to as few as four.

Two-Track Promotion

Bringing about a wider span of control will of course result in a corresponding reduction in the number of supervisory positions.

The resulting reduction in opportunities for promotion to management positions can be offset by simultaneous introduction of a two-track promotion system: a professional track and a managerial track, with parallel and equal levels into which outstanding performers can be promoted. More will be said about this in chapter 6, which discusses Reward Systems.

Involvement With Customers and Suppliers

Generally, members of the work force see little of external customers and suppliers. Putting aside obvious exceptions, such as sales people and purchasing agents whose job it is to deal with customers and suppliers, more generalized contacts outside the organization are exclusively the province of managers. This must change if we are to raise everyone in the organization to the status of full partner.

To the extent that it is practical, management should seek to create conditions whereby every worker, at least from time to time, sees and talks with real customers, with actual users of the company's product or service. Depending on circumstances, this might be done by bringing customers to the organization or by taking workers to the customers. Concurrently, workers should be kept apprised of customer satisfaction surveys and the results of customer focus groups.

These proposed meetings between workers and customers provide benefits in several ways. First, and perhaps foremost, workers develop the pride in product and company that comes from playing a representational role. Second, the firsthand insights into customer requirements can result in product improvement ideas and in greater dedication to quality. Third, greater customer appreciation for the people who make the product could lead to increased product loyalty.

Ordinary employees should also be given the opportunity to develop relationships with external suppliers. Whether the supplier provides raw materials, parts, or support of any other kind, employees need to develop the feeling that the supplier is responsible to them. For example, when the supply is late or deficient in quality, the workers who depend on supply should, as corporate partners, be given a role dealing directly with the supplier that let them down. They should be involved in deciding how the supply problem needs to be corrected.

Work Force Role in Selection of New Employees

Selection of new employees is generally done entirely by managers, assisted by the human resources unit. Bringing employees into this activity can be a powerful contribution to empowerment. After all, if the prospective employee is to work with Smith and Jones, why shouldn't Smith and Jones have a voice in who their new partner will be?

Three benefits result. First, a better selection is made. Because workers often have a different perspective on the characteristics and abilities that the new worker candidate should possess, their insights, when combined with that of the supervisor, can lead to selection of a stronger candidate. A second benefit is greater buy-in. When workers are part of the selection process they will have a stronger motivation to help the new person succeed. A third benefit is an increased sense of partnership that comes about when ordinary workers participate in the new employee selection process, a function normally associated with senior status in the organization.

One of the arguments made against involving ordinary workers in the selection of new employees is the host of rules, regulations, and even laws that attend the hiring process. Employees insensitive to them could, for example, leave the organization open to charges of discrimination. The answer to this is simple: educate the employees that are brought into the hiring interview. They are partners, so they should know the rules of the game. As a second, though far less desirable alternative, one can conduct interviews where supervisors, human resource specialists, and workers are all in attendance.

Trust

Empowerment requires trust. Managers may have an intellectual understanding of empowerment and fully accept its merits, but still be reluctant to confer meaningful empowerment because of lingering doubt about whether the worker can really be trusted to do things "right" (generally defined as the way the manager would do it!).

In such cases, the manager's logic often goes something like this: "This is my department, I am accountable for its output, and, until that changes, it would be irresponsible of me to let subordinates make decisions that I am paid to make, and for which I am the only one with sufficient experience and training."

Unless managers overcome the trust barrier, real empowerment cannot happen. There is no silver bullet to bring it about. Training, discussion, persuasion, heart-to-heart talks with subordinates, and benchmarking with successful empowerers are helpful.

But in the final analysis, the reluctant manager needs to take a leap of faith. Empowerment rarely fails because empowered workers fail to rise to their new level of responsibility. Always keep in mind that, like all human beings, they, too, are strongly motivated to avoid failure.

Economic Value Added

A new financial management tool has emerged during the past few years that fits well with TQM empowerment precepts. The tool, known as Economic Value Added, or EVA, enables managers and performers to see at a glance whether the work unit for which they are responsible is increasing or decreasing in value. This kind of feedback, at the performing level, provides empowered workers and unit managers with the kind of information needed to manage their corner of the business effectively.[8]

Developed by financial consultants G. Bennett Stewart and Joel M. Stern, and as reported in *Fortune* magazine, EVA is used by increasing numbers of America's most successful organizations. Coca-Cola, AT&T, Quaker Oats, Briggs & Stratton, and CSX Intermodal are only a few among the many companies who testify to the powerful effect the tool has on corporate performance.

The EVA system determines an operation's profitability (Economic Value Added) by subtracting the cost of capital from net operating profit. Thus, EVA = NOP - COC. The net operating profit is the gross profit minus taxes. The cost of capital includes two factors: (1) the cost of borrowed capital, which is the interest payments adjusted for tax deductibility; and, (2) the cost of equity capital, which is set by estimating the annual percentage gain your shareholders might expect to be getting if they had invested in companies similar to yours in promise and risk. When computing the cost of capital for small units of a larger organization, it is the prorated cost with which EVA is concerned.

Amazingly, until the advent of the EVA methodology, few companies (and even fewer subunits of large companies) paid much attention to the cost of equity capital. After all, the company isn't obligated to pay interest on equity capital, and dividends are paid only when profits were made. But, on reflection, we know that there is a cost to equity capital.

One need only to think of the company as a sole proprietorship to see the point. Money needed by a sole proprietorship for additional facilities, resources, machinery, or whatever needs to be taken from the owners bank account or from the sale of other investments. Unless equity invested in the sole proprietorship promises to yield more than can be obtained from other investments, the owner would soon be disinclined to put additional funds into the company.

Outside investors are even less tolerant of low return on equity. When they have reason to believe that the return on equity invested in a company is less than they might get elsewhere, they will promptly shift their funds to the place with greater promise and/or less risk. When this happens repeatedly, the company will pay for equity capital with increasingly higher amounts of equity for each dollar of capital; share price will decline. Ultimately, the profitless company will be unable to raise capital for any amount of equity.

As I said earlier, EVA is usable for small units of large organizations. Remember: EVA = NOP - COC. We need only determine two things for each small operating unit: (1) the net operating profit for that unit (profit center), and (2) the cost of capital (borrowed or equity) invested in that unit. The amount invested in a unit includes the prorated and amortized cost of such things as desks, machines, real estate, vehicles, *and* R & D and training. Balance sheets generally treat R & D and training as expenses rather than investments, but EVA deals with them more realistically as investments that pay off over a period of years.

The power of EVA is that it focuses the attention of both managers and performers, as never before, on the need to justify every dollar invested in equipment, property, training, etc. When unit managers are shielded from the harsh reality of the cost of capital and the need to achieve increased economic value, they can become careless about "investments" in equipment or facilities that might be nice to have, but which may not contribute to increasing the unit's economic value.

When the unit's EVA is negative, the unit's managers and people know that failure to raise it to positive levels will raise questions about the unit's future viability. The company will not invest for long in a unit that continues to lose economic value.

The *Fortune* article about EVA provides a number of examples to demonstrate its usefulness. The example of CSX Intermodal is particularly instructive. CSX, which invests in a fleet of locomotives, containers, and rail cars to transport freight to trucks or cargo ships, had a negative EVA (in 1988) of $70 million. Managers, trained in the EVA concept, were told to raise EVA to positive levels, or face sale of the unit. With the cost of capital principle now firmly understood, managers realized that the portion of the company's 18,000 containers allowed to sit idle between runs represented wasted capital. Accordingly, processes were changed to reduce turnaround time between runs from two weeks to five days, thereby bringing about a reduction in the number of costly containers to 14,000. At the same time, freight volume went up by 25%.

CSX also reduced its costly locomotive fleet from 150 to 100 units, a $70 million reduction in capital. Four locomotives had been used to power trains at 28 m.p.h. over the New Orleans to Jacksonville route, causing their arrival at midnight, hours before crews could unload them onto trucks and freighters. With EVA principles in mind, managers began to operate the trains with three locomotives, at 25 m.p.h., arriving three hours later, still well ahead of the unloading that began at 4 or 5 A.M.

CSX Intermodal's EVA had risen to plus $10 million in 1992, and was expected to triple in 1993. Its stock value increased from $28 per share before EVA was introduced, to $75 in August 1993.

The several examples noted in the *Fortune* article share a common theme. Each company trained its people in the EVA concept, each held people accountable for improving EVA, each empowered people to take actions to improve EVA, and each provided them with the EVA data. The people took it from there, changing processes in ways that caused capital to be invested both more intelligently and more productively, and that resulted in increased Economic Value Added.

5

Teaming

What Is a Team?

Teams might be defined as groups of people bound together by a common objective. Typical characteristics include: agreement on a strategy for achieving the objective, interdependency, a sense of shared destiny and shared reward, and loyalty to one another. Teams must also collectively possess the set of skills needed to perform their assigned function.

Teams can be ad hoc in nature: brought together to perform a specific task and disbanded when the task is completed. Or they can be permanent: put together to perform a continuing task.

Ad hoc teams are useful because they can be assembled to perform specific, short-term tasks, and disbanded with no trauma to the permanent organization from which their members came. Such teams might be formed to develop a corporate policy, to make a decision on a costly new item of capital equipment, or to improve a particular product or process.

Permanent teams are assembled to perform work that is expected to continue. Examples include teams that assemble car doors, build houses, and process insurance claims. Although the work of such teams is of a continuing nature, nothing in business is truly permanent. Thus, the composition of such teams will change as people leave and new people join. The team will evolve in size and capability as their task changes in scope and nature.

How To Bring About Team Behavior

Countless studies have been done to identify the factors that contribute to team effectiveness. A synthesis of study results and my own experience suggest that the following are most important:

Clear charter - The team must have a good sense of what it has been assembled to accomplish. Ambiguity about charters leads to hesitancy and confusion; clarity creates focused effort and helps to bring about acceptance of responsibility for outcome.

The team's charter, in addition to a clear statement of the assigned task, should include a sense of urgency, a sense of challenge and importance, and a description of applicable metrics (quantification of satisfactory outcomes). Team members should have a major role in establishing the charter; their strong involvement will help to assure that the task is doable, will serve to bring about team "buy-in," and will be an important first step in creating the bond of shared commitment.

Commitment - The team members must be committed both to the objectives of the team and to each other. Deep commitment to objectives and to fellow team members is crucial to good team performance. These two aspects of commitment combine to motivate the high level of effort needed for success and the synergistic mutual support that distinguishes teams from a mere grouping of individuals.

Ownership or autonomy - Teams need to believe they are in control of their destiny. They need to feel that their success or failure will result primarily from their own ability and effort. When teams are "second-guessed" by managers, or when they need to ask permission to take "ordinary" actions (extraordinary actions may be a different matter), or when others represent the team to customers and suppliers, the sense of ownership and self-reliance is compromised.

Potency - Teams need to believe that what they are doing truly matters, and that they have the resources to succeed. They should have the sense that the organization has a real stake in the outcome of their efforts. When members perceive their assignment to have important corporate and/or social consequence, and conclude that no one is better qualified than the team to carry it out, the prospects for success are strong.

Interdependence - Team members need to understand that their personal success cannot be realized without cooperation from other team members. When personal "stardom" is possible through independent action, competition between members will displace cooperation and mutual support. Maximum task interdependence requires that tasks be designed so that team members must interact frequently to do their work. Soccer and football teams epitomize task interdependency. For those who may regret the downplaying of individual achievement, it might be observed that personal stardom remains possible on the sports field, but *only* as a result of mutual support between team members. The same is true for places of business.

Loyalty - Mature teams build strong (even fraternal) loyalty among members. While loyalty within the team is good because it results in strong team performance, it can become counterproductive when it causes teams to shield weak performance, or when it results in information hoarding, strident demands for resources, or mindless competition with other teams or corporate functions. Management response to these conditions can include such things as: creation of interteam councils, establishment of corporate goals to supplement team goals, or redesign of the reward system to motivate interteam cooperation and corporate loyalty.

Team-based reward - Though reward (pay, recognition, promotion) should continue to be based in some part on individual performance (perhaps even in large part, depending on the job), some portion of a person's reward must be based on the performance of the team of which the person is a part. Only then will the reward system motivate cooperation between team members. Reward based exclusively on individual performance inspires competition between members at the expense of mutual cooperation and support.

Recognition - Though recognition is a part of the reward considerations just discussed, emphasis is warranted. Recognition may be one of the most important features of effective management. People need to be told that what they are doing is important and valued. Recognition is needed not only for ego-building, but as feedback to promote continuous and smooth reconciliation of goals and effort.

Self-confidence - Teams, like individuals, are stronger when possessed of self-confidence and pride, and when convinced that their output is important to the organization as a whole. Successful teams frequently adopt team names, hold team social and recreational events, and adopt team insignia such as T-shirts, pins, or coffee mugs. However achieved and displayed, successful teams develop an "identity." Management sponsors of successful teams reinforce the requisite *esprit* by conveying to the team a strong sense of its importance to the corporate whole.

Wide responsibility - Permanent and mature teams should be encouraged to take on responsibility for control, and administrative and support tasks (such as designing the team's processes, determining job assignments, scheduling vacations, and procuring needed supplies and equipment). Teams also need to be responsible for continuous improvement of processes and products, and for development of their members.

Self-direction - Teams must be allowed to discipline themselves, perform necessary liaison with external customers and suppliers, interact with other teams and functions in the corporation, and elect their own leaders. Teams should be trusted to work out for themselves ways of doing these things, although management assistance and counseling (not direction) can be helpful. To the extent that it is sensible to do so (and this will vary with the organization and the team's maturity), a team should be viewed by the rest of the corporation as a resident subcontractor, responsible for its piece of the business.

Note: Team leadership is usually rotated among the members. Team leaders are generally elected for a specified period. One to three months is not unusual, though some teams rotate leadership daily to give everyone experience in that role, and to avoid creating a leadership dependency or a leader mentality. Teams sometimes develop several *de facto* leaders for different functions, such as social, technical, and representational.

Information - To be effective, with a sense of self-direction and self-confidence, the team needs to be informed. It needs to know enough about corporate policies, values, vision, and strategies to make sensible decisions, to develop plans, to interact intelligently with external customers and suppliers, and to procure and manage resources wisely. To put it simply, because successful teams manage their own affairs, they must be given the kind of information managers get.

Hiring - Teams must be allowed to have a primary role in the selection of new teammates.

Training - Training needs to be provided both for supervisors displaced by the creation of self-directing teams, and for team members.

Training of displaced supervisors must be designed to facilitate their transition from supervisor to coach, internal consultant, or senior performer. Displacement of supervisors is one of the most difficult aspects of TQM. These people became supervisors because they were top performers, and it is greatly to the advantage of the organization to retain them for their experience and expertise. Training and counseling of displaced supervisors must be done with sensitivity in order to preserve (or restore) self-confidence. Though there is no magic formula, these proven performers need to be persuaded that the transition from supervisor to coach or consultant is not a step down, but a lateral move that is in their own long term interest, as well as essential to the corporate interest.

Three kinds of team member training need to be provided: technical, administrative, and team building.

Technical training is initially focused on the team member's assigned task, but then broadens to include other team tasks; when team members learn one another's jobs, they can take up tasks other than their own when that becomes necessary to balance output. Another important benefit of cross-training is the development of people; wider skills lead to broader outlooks, increased confidence, and eligibility for higher pay.

Administrative training is needed to enable team members to assume responsibility for routine administrative and support activities formerly provided by functional specialists. For example, certain Human Resource activities (such as interviewing and hiring, and maintenance of attendance records) are often taken over by self-directed work teams. Other support and control activities often assigned to self-directed work teams are purchasing, shipping and receiving, quality control, and inventory management.

Team building training will be discussed later in this chapter.

Size - Though teams can and do range in size from two members to any larger number, team size in the range of about four to twenty members is most workable. A minimum of about four members is generally needed to achieve the dynamic interaction and variety of perspectives that enrich team performance. On the other hand, when team size is larger than twenty members, communication and interaction become more difficult. My own experience suggests that the optimal team size is eight to ten members.

Reference is often made to corporate "teams" of hundreds or thousands. Such large groupings may share general corporate aspirations, but they clearly lack in any semblance of the intense loyalty, focused purpose, interdependence, partnership, and close interaction that are characteristic of successful small teams. Teams larger than twenty or so tend (properly) to subdivide into an appropriate number of smaller teams.

The Four Stages of Team Development

Teams go through an evolutionary process. They begin with some uncertainty, and gradually work their way to full performance. The several stages of team development have been profiled by a number of analysts. The simplest and perhaps the most widely used profile is Allan Drexler's. It describes four stages of team development:

Stage 1: The "forming" stage. Here, team members go through the necessary process of defining their collective task, agreeing on individual roles and responsibilities, and generally settling in and getting to know one another. Managers often play an important start-up role during stage one. In many cases, they define or help to define the team's collective task, help with the assignment of member's roles, facilitate team relationships with customers and suppliers, and provide training in requisite functional skills and team building.

Stage 2: The "storming" stage. In this stage, there is some jousting for position, a test of wills to see which plan of action or process will prevail, and perhaps some forming of cliques or alliances within the team.

Stage 3: The "norming" stage. Here, things begin to settle down and stabilize. The collective task, individual roles, and the team's plan of action have been agreed upon. Members are working smoothly and harmoniously together, and opposing coalitions are disbanding. Managers withdraw from active involvement, while the team assumes responsibility for appropriate administrative, control, and support tasks, and becomes self-directing. Teams also begin to manage their own relationships with adjacent teams and other corporate functions.

Stage 4: The "performing" stage. At this stage, team maturity has been reached. Team members have strong loyalty to the team and to one another, performance is of a high order, and members are striving for continuous improvement. The members are thinking of themselves as partners in a mini-business, perceiving team goals as their personal goals.

Motorola, a 1989 Baldrige Award winner and a world-class TQM practitioner, has defined seven stages of team development:

• Stage 1: Supervisor assigns all work. All support functions are external.

• Stage 2: Operators determine their own training needs, and provide on-the-job training to others.

• Stage 3: Supervisor presents problems and asks for input. Operators take individual responsibility for quality and productivity.

• Stage 4: Teams take ownership of departmental performance, employ team problem solving and goal setting, and track their own progress.

• Stage 5: Teams organize their own work, interface with other teams, suppliers, and customers. Teams prepare and present reports, plans, and metrics.

• Stage 6: Teams are fluid, highly skilled, and multifunctional. They take on administrative work formerly done by supervisors with minimal management supervision. Boundaries between hourly and professional employees diffuse.

• Stage 7: Teams have become the responsible business unit, focused on the customer. Team structure is flat and operates horizontally. Teams are empowered to place responsibility and decision-making authority where the work is being done. Management sets the vision, teams take part in setting strategy, goals, tactics, and policies of implementation.

The usefulness of taking note of the stages of team development is that we are thereby better able to facilitate team evolution from one stage to the next. An awareness that all teams evolve through a number of stages enables us to set more realistic timetables for achieving the full performance stage (Drexler's "performing" stage or Motorola's Stage 7), and to provide counseling and training that will facilitate rapid evolution to full performance.

Team Building

Team building is little more than reminding people of what it takes to get along in group settings. Though every thinking adult knows the difference between constructive and destructive social behavior, there is often a difference between what we know intellectually, and what we practice in our daily interactions with others. Teams that have been given team building training are unanimous in proclaiming its benefits. Team building training is routinely provided at such successful TQM organizations as Motorola, Xerox, and General Electric.[1]

Some of the standard components set forth in team building training are:

• only one person speaks at a time;

• special efforts must be made to involve everyone in group discussion and decision-making, including shy and junior people;

• avoid "put-downs" of unconventional ideas, because they may, after discussion, lead to breakthrough thinking;

• listen with care;

• acknowledge and applaud achievements;

• share information;

• keep agreements;

• arrive on time for meetings;

• have an agreed upon meeting agenda and stick to it;

• come to meetings prepared;

• make decisions by consensus;

• learn and practice the methods of conflict management (avoidance, accommodation, compromise, collaboration, and confrontation);

• encourage risk-taking, and forgive mistakes rapidly.

The art of listening warrants some amplification. True listening is a kind of tribute from listener to speaker. It is a sign of recognition. Careless or inattentive listening is a put-down, a denial of the speaker. True listening, on the other hand, is a sign of recognition and respect, and strengthens the relationship between listener and speaker. It creates the possibility for a meaningful dialogue, because the speaker, having been listened to, now "owes" an attentive ear to the response from the former listener.

True listening must include an honest attempt at understanding. The true listener is obligated to avoid judgment, criticism, or ridicule. Response and even objection may be in order, but they will be effective only if given in the spirit of meaningful dialogue.

Consensus decision-making warrants further comment. Of numerous methods for achieving it, one that is both simple and effective is known as value-voting. Faced with numerous alternatives, each participant is given five votes that may be distributed any way he or she wishes. For example, all five votes may be awarded to a single option, or split, say three votes for one alternative and two for another. After voting, results are tallied and the alternatives with the fewest votes are eliminated. Additional rounds of voting are done as necessary, with each participant getting only three votes each time, until the consensus is established.

"Outward Bound"-Type Teambuilding [2, 3]

"Outward Bound"-type teambuilding methods have received much attention in recent years. Though many "graduates" of these shared-experience courses believe strongly in their teambuilding effectiveness, there are two studies that raise questions.

To improve teamwork, the Naval Weapons Support Center sent its civilian employees to "outdoor challenge training," where the idea was to do difficult things together, such as climbing high ropes and bridging wide chasms. To test the effectiveness of such training, the NWSC did some psychological testing before and after. What they discovered was surprising:

• Trust among co-workers who trained together actually deteriorated.

• All-male groups did not get as much out of the training as mixed groups.

• Managers who trained without the people with whom they normally worked learned little about teambuilding.

Additional results come from a study of "Outward-Bound"-type training done by Richard Wagner at the University of Wisconsin.

• The training has no impact on individual attributes, such as self-esteem.

• The quality of the facilitator is a make or break factor.

• Managers who participate without their subordinates are no better at teambuilding than those who don't go at all.

• Work groups feel better if their bosses are with them, but learn just as much without them.

• People who go voluntarily get no more out of it than people who are required to attend.

• All-male and all-female groups had more trouble solving problems than mixed-gender groups.

Diversity as a Positive Factor in Team Composition

The conclusion reported above from both the Navy and the University of Wisconsin studies to the effect that all-male and all-female groups were less effective in problem solving than mixed-gender groups warrants brief amplification. Other experiments, replicated at a number of organizations, corroborate that conclusion, and also report the more general finding that groups (teams) with a diverse composition (mix of genders, races, ages, and national origins) are generally more creative and innovative than homogeneous groups.

In each experiment, the finding was reached in a similar way. The same problem was assigned to both homogeneous and diverse groups, otherwise equal in experience and education. In almost every case, the homogeneous groups came back with "centrist" positions and "conventional wisdom," while diverse groups delivered innovative and creative solutions.

This positive correlation between diversity and creativity should not be surprising. Diversity generates different points of view, and brings to bear a richer collective experience. Greater creativity and innovativeness are to be expected.

Unions and Teams

There has been some anxiety among TQM companies about a December 1992 ruling by the National Labor Relations Board (NLRB). The NLRB case resulted from a challenge to the legality of employee teams brought by the Teamsters Union against Electromation, Inc., an electrical parts manufacturer in Elkhart, Indiana. Electromation had established five committees, each with up to six employees and one or two managers, whose role it was to deal with worker-related issues such as pay scales. The Teamsters, which had been seeking to unionize Electromation workers, took the case to the NLRB charging that the teams violated the NLRB Act of 1935. That law states that employee groups which perform functions normally performed by unions, but under management control, are sham unions and therefore illegal. Accordingly, the NLRB found Electromation's employee teams in violation of the law, ruling that they dealt with traditional bargaining issues (which made them "labor organizations") and were also "dominated" by management.[4, 5, 6]

Several NLRB members have pointed out that the NLRB Electromation decision does not rule out teams categorically. They can be in conformity with the 1935 law when three conditions are met:

• First, employee teams must be precluded from dealing with issues affecting employees that are not members of the team. Team members in that case do not "represent" other employees.

• Second, employee teams must focus primarily (better yet, exclusively) on work-related issues. Team involvement with such things as products, processes, quality, productivity, and improvement would appear to be wholly within the law. Questions could arise, however, in regard to issues such as pay, grievances, or working hours.

• Third, management involvement with employee teams must not extend to domination. Management retains the right (perhaps even the obligation) to recommend the formation of teams, to help set them up, and to provide needed resources. Managers can also be members of the team, as long as they remain in the minority. In that case, secret ballot voting would seem to ensure team independence of management domination.

In a nutshell, meaningful empowerment of teams seems to be the answer to the legality issue. Companies willing to give their teams wide latitude in deciding what to do and how to do it; to let their teams direct their own affairs without second-guessing; and to deal with them as equal partners in the corporate enterprise have little to fear from the NLRB.

Still, while the issue of compliance with the NLRB Act of 1935 seems not to be a major concern for unionized companies, some local union officials have been less than fully supportive of employee teams. The reasons seem to be several. Teams have been seen by some as a way of getting people to work outside their job description. Others have seen them as a way of extracting more work for no additional pay. Teams have also been seen as a device to circumvent local union officials. This is because team empowerment serves to bridge the gap between, workers and managers, thereby displacing union leaders who have traditionally performed the bridging function.

Donald Petersen, the retired CEO of Ford Motor Company, has addressed the issue of the UAW attitude toward employee involvement in his book about TQM implementation at Ford.

According to *Detroit News* editorial writer Richard E. Burr, Petersen's original galley proof carried the assertion that the UAW presidential heir-apparent, Steve Yokich, tried to end employee involvement at Ford, but that the employees "liked it too much to allow Yokich to kill it." The published version of Petersen's book smoothes over that language and states that Yokich was "wary" of employee involvement but eventually became "more cooperative in his approach to various issues."

During the recent decades of relatively high wages and ready employment opportunities, the U.S. public has developed a generally negative view of unions. Much of this has been brought on by the unions themselves, in part by demanding arguably excessive wages and fringe benefits, sometimes by unwisely resisting technological progress to keep their people employed, and at other times by imposing needlessly narrow skill profiles that prohibit members of one craft from doing work "belonging" to another craft.

Some years ago, when railroads made the transition from coal-fired locomotives to diesel and electric, union rules required the railroads to continue carrying firemen aboard diesel and electric locomotives. In a similar vein, carpenters or plumbers may be required by union rules to stand needlessly idle while awaiting the arrival of some other craftsman such as electricians or plasterers to do a simple thing that the carpenter or plumber could easily do himself.

Things have changed greatly, however, for the better. The recent period of economic downturn and the need for U.S. companies to meet international competition have forcibly brought common sense back to the work place. Traditional union-management animosity has increasingly given way to joint acceptance by unions and management that they are inextricable partners in the search for corporate success and job security. Both realize that any animosity is best directed toward their common adversary: the competition.

Just as managers accept and even embrace the need for change in the way business is done, so now do union members and their leaders. Most understand completely that unless their companies remain competitive, corporate viability will decline and individual job security will erode. Even more important, both sides understand that corporate partnerships and continuous improvement are the keys to competitiveness, and that adversarial union-management relationships are destructive.

TQM implementation and teams cannot succeed without union support. When unions are not initially receptive, support must be won by a program of education that demonstrates how TQM and teams support job enrichment and job security. One of the best ways for management to win union support is to identify a role for unions in TQM implementation and team management. The Saturn experience, which follows, is a compelling case in point.

Teams at Saturn [7, 8, 9]

Saturn, the General Motors subsidiary, has found an uncommonly effective means for forging a strong bond between union and management in common pursuit of quality management goals. Symbolic of the union role at Saturn is the co-location of the UAW president and the company president in adjacent offices in the executive suite.

Teams at Saturn, known as Work Units, are supported during the "forming" phase by two Work Unit Advisors, one from the UAW and one from management. Each pair of advisors oversees four to six Work Unit teams. Each Work Unit consists of about 15 people who make decisions by consensus.

At the beginning of the "forming" phase, a "Charter Team Member" is designated by management. The CTM hires the other members of the team, teaches them Saturn's mission and philosophy, and trains members in needed team skills. During the forming phase, the CTM assumes responsibilities normally assigned to supervisors or foremen, and is responsible for interaction with the two external advisors.

During the "storming" phase, team members become increasingly responsible for individual or collective performance. In the "norming" phase, the CTM ceases direct monitoring and supervision of Work Unit team members, but continues to be the focal point for interaction with the two Work Unit Advisors. Finally, in the "performing" phase, the team becomes completely self-directed, members deal directly with the two Work Unit Advisors, and the Charter Team Member becomes an equal team participant.

At Saturn, team transition from the first phase to the fourth phase can take as long as two to three years. When the team experiences major changes in its work responsibilities or composition, it may retreat to the third stage for a time until it can qualify itself again as a self-directed stage-four team.

Saturn's use of teams applies at every level in the corporate hierarchy. The four to six Charter Team Members that "report" to two advisors are in turn collected into a team known as a Decision Circle. Decision Circles generally consist of about six to eight people, and sometimes include resource people (specialists) as advisors, temporary or permanent. Decision Circles are responsible for such things as cost reduction, quality initiatives, job content, and job rotation.

The Work Unit Advisors form another team known as the Business Unit. Saturn's manufacturing center consists of three business units: Powertrain, Body Systems, and Vehicle Systems (assembly). The three business units, in turn, are overseen by the Manufacturing Area Council. There are two other Councils: Engineering and Sales. Each contains its own Work Unit Modules and Business Units. A Strategic Action Council oversees the entire organization and sets strategic direction

Union guidelines on which workers' job descriptions are based are less rigid at Saturn than at comparable organizations. Distinctions between various categories of workers have been blurred. "Blue collar" and "white collar" labels are simply less meaningful when people work across job categories and everyone dresses similarly (coats and ties are not worn by managers). The UAW contract stipulates that everyone is paid on a salaried basis: there are no hourly personnel at Saturn. Bonuses are paid as a percentage of salary, depending on the plant's profitability.

The UAW is deeply involved with Saturn management in strategic decisions. Management and workers have collaborated from the beginning, starting with plant design and technology choices, marketing and advertising strategies, and development of work force recruitment and training programs. The actual design of the Saturn car was determined jointly, and the union insisted on the aggressive (non-negotiable) pricing strategy that has become a Saturn hallmark. The UAW contract states that any party may block a decision but that this party then has the responsibility of providing an alternative. It specifies that problems are to be solved through continuing negotiation, which includes the (never exercised) right to strike.

Teams at Ford [10]

Ford employs teams to support rapid development of new products. Using a method known as "simultaneous engineering," project teams have achieved dramatic reductions in development cycle time.

Suppose a project team is trying to solve the problem of insufficient space behind the instrument panel. A recommended solution might be to change the design of the air-conditioning system, which would produce more space, but also increase the cost of the air conditioner. At this point in the old function-based top-down organization, the climate control department would enter the discussion. However, in the new product-based, cross-functional team structure, the project team itself, free of undue influence by the team leader, decides on the best solution by weighing available options. There are no meetings, no memos, no written studies, no waiting – and, hence, no decline of commitment and enthusiasm. Without asking superiors, the team can make trade-offs within the scope of its charter and the size of its budget.

Multiplied many times, this is the kind of accelerated, improved performance that becomes possible in any organization with empowered cross-functional product/project teams. In the case of Ford, specifically, some parts of the company (most parts of Ford Europe and Ford North America) have entirely abandoned traditional function-based organizations, and have adopted organizations run by product-based cross-functional teams aligned either to particular car or truck models, or to major components such as an all-new engine. At Ford's Romeo, Michigan, engine plant, there are in fact no functional managers at all. Instead, each product area is run by a team and team leader. Team members learn to do every job in the area, and are rotated regularly.

Team leaders at Ford are designated by management. In choosing team leaders, Ford has been careful to avoid over-representation, and hence over-influence, by a single operational function. Accordingly, team leaders are drawn on a rotating basis from design, engineering, sales, and so on through every function in the organization.

In those parts of the company that have preserved function-based organization, cross-functonal teams have been established using an overlay of traditional matrix management. In those areas, however, team leaders are empowered to veto anyone assigned to their team. In addition, all key people work directly for the team leader, not their function (department) manager, for the duration of the team project.

Teams at AT&T Credit[11]

AT&T Credit, the 620-employee financing arm of the American Telephone and Telegraph Company, assembled an employee team to review and redesign the way it conducted its business. Following many months of deliberations, including interviews with fellow workers, managers, customers, and suppliers, the team recommended major organizational and procedural changes, all of which were accepted and implemented. The success of this effort makes the AT&T Credit team a worthy case study. What needs to be examined here are the methods used by the company to create the team and to give it the incentive, the opportunity, and the resources to succeed.

First, appointment to the team was an honor. To make that clear, and simultaneously to enhance the opportunities for success, selection of team members was highly competitive. Sixty employees applied to be on the team. A steering committee of four executives asked each of the applicants to write a short essay on how AT&T Credit should be reorganized. To further test their analytic capabilities, it asked each applicant to read an article on corporate turnaround and to write a short summary of its salient points. The 25 who made it past that first set of hurdles went on to interviews with the committee, which looked for such traits as ability to work with others and to dig for information.

The 10 people finally selected to be on the team were given training in team building and in organizational development, and were asked to spend 50% of their time on the team's work. At that point, the management steering committee stepped completely out of the picture. Even when the redesign process took months longer than expected, there was no management nudging or other intervention. The company's president states that, with the benefit of hindsight, the only thing he would do differently would be to authorize team members to spend 100% of their time on the project.

Team members were given full authority to meet with employees, customers, managers, and suppliers. Their work resulted in far-reaching reorganization of functions and of the work assignments of individuals. Following publication of the team's results, management invited employees to apply for the new job assignments that seemed of interest. It also designated a new cross-functional transition team whose charge was to mete out the new jobs and pick out new furniture!

Team building at AT&T Credit can serve as a model for similar undertakings anywhere. The team was endowed with all of the attributes described earlier in this chapter as essential to team success: a clear charter, potency, commitment, self-direction, interdependence, recognition, wide responsibility, training, and information.

Teams in a Bank

The Universal National Bank and Trust Company, Palo Alto, California, has created mini-banks within the bank. Each mini-bank is headed by a senior vice-president with three to four people on the team. Each team has its own customer list, oversees its own portfolio of loans, and sends out correspondence on its own letterhead.

To avoid competition between the mini-bank teams, they are not considered separate profit centers, and all compensation is tied to the performance of the entire bank. Teams are thereby encouraged to work together, share best practices, and give their ultimate loyalty to the corporate team.

The bank fully empowers teams and individual employees. Its president has said, "What will kill this bank is a bunch of people running around with their noses stuck in rule books and manuals. Tellers, for example, decide for themselves whether or not to honor a check: no need to ask permission from a supervisor."

The notion of a corporate team is reinforced by "Statement Day," held on the first business day of every month. All 200 employees, from chairman to janitor, assemble to prepare each customer's bank statement, and to trade jokes and socialize. The exercise also ensures that each customer's statement will be in the mail on the second business day of the month.

Teams in the Classroom

Business schools all over America are embracing the cross-functional team concept which is increasingly valued by the business community.

• MBA candidates at the University of Tennessee are being divided into teams of ten. Each team will take a 15-credit course revolving around a complex business case-study requiring input from every business function. The course will be team-taught by ten professors who will use just-in-time methods to schedule their lectures. For example, when the team working on its case study is ready to deal with cash-flow problems, the finance professor will be there to instruct.

• In an effort to move students away from narrow functional parochialism, Dartmouth, Northwestern, and Indiana are replacing traditional functional courses in such topics as accounting, marketing, and finance with integrated courses that deal with cross-functonal problems.

Teaching in the functional disciplines is thereby provided in a real-world cross-functional team context as the need for functional information arises.

• Harvard Business School is proposing to revamp its curriculum to focus more on cooperation. Its fabled case-study program of instruction would be de-emphasized. MBA students would complete up to 25% of course work in teams off-campus.[12]

To further encourage collaboration among team members, the Harvard proposal would do away with the grading curve which motivates competition and stymies cooperation.

Numbers of primary and secondary schools are also experimenting with "cooperative learning." Students study in groups and teachers serve as facilitators and guides, rather than as lecturers and policemen. The theory is that students learn more and retain far more when they learn in teams and through active involvement, rather than passive listening.

Team effort is a centerpiece of the new system. At Pomperaug High School in Southbury, Connecticut, for example, a team of 34 sophomores is grouped into clusters and four teachers wander among them to monitor and guide the students. The interdisciplinary curriculum combines English, social studies, and biology. Each student within a cluster has a project. Because no one gets credit for the course unless all the tasks are satisfactorily completed, competition between the students and the usual focus on grades are reduced. They are instead replaced by the more productive values of teamwork and collaborative success.[13]

Suppliers Are Part of the Corporate Team

Motorola

Organizations that undertake TQM implementation will operate under a handicap unless their suppliers do so, also.[14] A company cannot sustain a successful quality strategy if it receives defective parts and services from its suppliers. Recognizing that fact, in 1989, Motorola, a 1988 Baldrige Award winner, challenged its suppliers to compete for the award. It was convinced that application for the award is one of the most significant steps a company could take to focus on quality improvement and customer satisfaction.

Motorola is not concerned that the supplier be a winner. Their belief (widely shared) is that the greatest benefit is not in winning, but in competing, since competing for the Baldrige Award forces a company to develop a quality strategy responsive to the seven Baldrige categories, to benchmark itself against world-class competition, and to undergo an audit of its quality strategy by Baldrige examiners.

Motorola has defined its corporate Quality System as "the collective plans, activities, and events that are provided to assure that products, processes, and service will satisfy given customer needs." The company has established a system of Quality System Reviews (QSRs) to evaluate the ongoing health of its Quality System and to identify opportunities for improvement. Recognizing the impact of suppliers on its own quality, Motorola has extended the opportunity for participation in the Quality System Review Process to its suppliers.

To assist its suppliers further in reaching their quality goals, Motorola has expanded its corporate quality training center (known as Motorola University) to include a Supplier Institute which offers courses on such topics as achieving manufacturing efficiency through quality and cycle time improvement, benchmarking, change, and quality implementation.

While Motorola's Baldrige challenge was the first step toward integrating its suppliers into the corporate quality team, it has continued to plot its corporate quality course, fully recognizing the needs of its quality team mates. It seeks to offer them the opportunity to achieve the same high level of TQM effectiveness that Motorola itself has achieved and continues to pursue.

IBM, Ford, United Technologies, and Others

Pursuing a strategy much like that of Motorola, IBM sent a letter to suppliers (dated April 29, 1989) stating:

> The [Baldrige] program embraces all the elements that IBM and other U.S. enterprises must comply with if we are to meet essential quality objectives. IBM cannot and will not continue to do business with suppliers that fail to meet these objectives.

Ford, United Technologies, and the Department of Defense, among many other organizations, have taken steps similar to those taken by Motorola and IBM. Ford, for example, has created a "Q-1 Supplier" certification which is awarded only to suppliers with a history of high quality and with a strong and successful quality strategy in place. New suppliers applying for Ford's Q-1 certification can get it only by demonstrating their dedication to quality principles, and by proving the success of their quality strategy. Ford now buys exclusively from suppliers to whom its Q-1 certification has been awarded.

Reducing the Number of Suppliers

A collateral action taken by customer companies is to reduce the

ɔir suppliers. Remembering that every supplier is an added
riability, and an added administrative burden, successful
ﱟies have embraced a few select suppliers, and begun to deal
with them as though they were a department of the customer company. In
so doing, they have substituted a close partnership or team relationship for
the earlier more distant customer-supplier relationship.

Ford has reduced its number of suppliers from 22,000 in the early
1980's to 1700 in 1993. Xerox, in the same period, has gone from 6,000
suppliers to 400. The financial operation of Baxter Healthcare has cut its
suppliers from 16 to 6. Toyota has only 300 first-tier suppliers; the rest are
second tier suppliers who work for the first tier, not for Toyota itself.

Each of these companies, and TQM organizations generally, have
replaced the traditional annual competition (to keep prices down) and
multiple-sources (to keep suppliers on their toes) with long-term contractual relationships and single-source arrangements for each end item. The
results are that prices are kept down, quality remains high, and suppliers
do everything possible to maintain the relationship. Suppliers make the
effort not because of the immediate threat of competition (though that
threat is subtly present), but because they value the stability and higher
volume of business.

At Saturn, too, the corporate team extends to include suppliers. Saturn's goal is to establish long-term relationships with one supplier per end
item. Supplier partnerships are based on mutual trust, high quality standards, just-in-time deliveries, and continuous improvement. Saturn has
high standards for supplier selection, and works with the supplier after the
contract is awarded to ensure continuous improvement.

The JUSE Code of Standards

The Japanese Union of Scientists and Engineers, which is the Japanese
society for quality professionals, has developed a Code of Standards,
widely used in Japan, intended to govern the relationship between suppliers and customers. Its seven points apply equally in the United States and
other western countries:

1. Mutual respect and cooperation.

2. Prior contractual understanding.

3. Agreed methods of evaluation.

4. Agreed plans for settling disputes.

5. Exchange of essential information.

6. Supplier responsible for delivery of a good product.

7. Customer's interests are predominant.

Supplier Teams at Semco S/A [15]

Semco S/A, of Sao Paulo, Brazil, a 500-person developer and manufacturer of marine and food service equipment, has successfully undertaken what may be the most radical approach of all to self-directed work teams and supplier relationships. Semco's methods provide an interesting and worthy benchmark.

It all began in the mid-1980's when three Semco engineers proposed they be allowed to form a three-man unit, wholly free from regular assignments, whose role would be to seek to improve existing products and processes, invent new ones, devise new marketing strategies, etc. The unit would be free to set its own agenda and timetable – it would receive no direction from management. Twice a year it would report to management which would decide whether or not to keep it for another six months.

Management accepted the proposal in principle, but countered with its own proposal to reduce sharply the guaranteed pay of the team's members, and to link future pay to a percentage of savings, royalties, and other proceeds of their work. The three engineers accepted the pay idea, and the unit, now named the Nucleus of Technological Innovation (NTI), was promptly established.

It was agreed that NTI, in addition to doing work for Semco, would be free to sell consulting services on the open market. Meanwhile, Semco gave them a cushion against failure and the support of Semco's manufacturing operation. By the time of the first six-month review, NTI had 18 projects underway. Within a few years, NTI's unexpectedly rich cornucopia of inventions, improvements, and ideas brought prosperity to its members, and Semco operations came to rely on its output.

In 1990, Semco moved to introduce the NTI concept throughout the company in an effort to liberate the creativity of its *entire* workforce. Workers were encouraged (it was and remains voluntary) to leave the Semco payroll and start "satellite" companies of their own. Seed money was given in the form of severance pay (very generous as required by Brazilian law). Training was given on such topics as cost control, pricing, inventory management, etc., and was made available to all.

Each satellite company was given assurance of an amount of work from Semco for an initial period, and allowed to use Semco facilities for two years at no cost. After that, they would be expected to compete for Semco work and to pay a nominal cost for use of Semco's facilities. From the beginning, each of the new satellite companies was encouraged to work for outside companies (including Semco competitors) as well as for Semco.

Today, most of Semco's white collar functions are entirely handled by these satellite companies, as is 50% of manufacturing (soon to be 70%). Some satellites now work entirely for outside companies, including, in some cases, Semco competitors. They nonetheless continue to use Semco facilities, paying for the privilege. The company has set aside a large room, known as the "Thinkodrome," with desks and computers for use as a place for the satellite owners to work and to meet with customers.

Semco owner, Roberto Semmler, believes this program is a proven success, both for Semco and for the satellite companies (only one of which has failed).

Semco's unorthodoxy extends to its management methods. The company has only three levels of management. It is managed by six "Counselors," each of whom takes six-month turns as acting CEO. The company's budget cycles are semiannual, beginning in January and July. The six-month CEO cycles begin in March and September. The decoupling of these two cycle periods is deliberate to avoid making a single person responsible for a given budget. Owner Semmler reasons that when one person is responsible for the budget, all the other managers can relax. At Semco, all are responsible, and, as a result, each of the Counselors makes every effort to keep the others informed.

Teams Are Not New

Peter Drucker noted in *Adventures of a Bystander*[16] that, during World War II, General Motors grouped untrained workers, many new to industry, into self-directed work teams to make up for the paucity of trained supervisors (many of whom had been inducted into military service). The result, to everyone's surprise, was increased productivity and performance. Self-directed teams performed better than groups of managed individuals. Yet, despite this showing, after the war ended, and engineers and supervisors returned to the workforce, GM disbanded the self-directed teams and went back to the prewar hierarchical management structures. Indeed, most U.S. managers and unions resisted self-directed work teams until TQM came along in the 1980's.

Self-directed work teams were used extensively in England and Sweden in the 1950's. Japanese industry has been using them since the 1970's.

Proctor and Gamble has been employing them since the 1960's, with good results. Today, self-directed work teams can be seen in such companies as Boeing, Caterpillar, Ford, Digital Equipment, General Electric, General Motors, LTV Steel, Nucor Steel, and Metropolitan Life Insurance.

CEO Pay and Its Effect on the Corporate Team[17]

A component of employee willingness to join with management in partnership arrangements is management's willingness to be more modest in its own demands for high pay and fringe benefits. The average pay for CEO's of big U.S. companies in 1992 (including bonuses) was $3,842,247, 56% more than the 1991 level. The highest total pay for an American CEO was $127 million. Ten CEO's earned more than $22.8 million; twenty were paid more than $11.2 million.

As CEO remuneration has increased, the gap between executive pay and worker pay is also widening. Back in 1980, the average CEO pay was a mere $624,996, 42 times the pay of the average factory worker. The comparable 1992 ratio was 157:1.

In Japan, by contrast, average CEO pay in 1991 (later data are not available at this writing) was $872, 646, or 32 times the pay of the average Japanese factory worker. Part of the reason for the relatively modest Japanese CEO pay level is that Japanese executives rarely job-hop. This prevents the bidding wars that are a factor in raising our own executive compensation to such high levels.

U.S. public sector pay ratios are even lower than those in the Japanese private sector. Top federal pay in 1994 was about $135,000 for senior career executives, only about five to six times the pay of the average public sector nonprofessional worker.

Much of the total remuneration for U.S. private sector senior executives comes from bonuses linked to near-term performance of the company's stock. For several reasons, such bonuses, unheard of in Japan, may not even be a good idea. First, salaries on the order of many hundreds of thousands of dollars are almost certainly enough to motivate hard work and to provide an incentive to do well. Second, near-term stock price performance is as often the result of bull markets as it is of corporate performance. Third, in most cases, such plans do not penalize executive pay for any downward movement in stock prices, and therefore the executive (unlike public stock holders) has nothing tangible at risk. Fourth, as noted in an earlier chapter, when near-term equity increase is used as a basis for bonus determination, there is an unhealthy incentive to improve the short-term bottom line, possibly at the expense of sustained long-term results.

There is no hard link between high executive pay and "excessive" demands by union members for wages, benefits, or restrictive job rules. But it would seem to be self-evident that grossly excessive executive pay and benefits must cause some resentment among the work force. Disparities of 157:1 between the pay of executives and workers are hardly consistent with a clear call for corporate partnership, especially when awarded in the face of declining corporate performance.

U.S. CEO pay should not necessarily follow the pattern of Japanese practice, or of our own public sector practice. Nor should outstanding executives be deprived of rewards consistent with their contributions. But, companies determined to achieve high performance through corporate partnership between workers and managers must give some thought to setting executive pay scales at levels not grossly disproportionate to the corporate value of any one individual. This can't help facilitating the creation of a partnership.

Corporate boards are attending to this issue as never before. *Business Week* published a survey (April 26, 1993) relating executive pay to corporate performance. It showed that, over the last three years, some of the highest-paid CEO's turned in corporate losses, while some of the lowest-paid achieved the best corporate results. Since high CEO pay does not guarantee good performance, and "low" CEO pay does not bar it, it would seem that other factors are at least equally relevant to corporate success. Among the most important of them is improved performance of the work force achieved through corporate partnerships.

6

TQM Reward Systems

How Do TQM Reward Systems Differ from Traditional Ones?

Dr. Deming, it will be recalled from chapter 2, has professed some strong views on the subject of reward systems. He urges the elimination of numerical goals, including Management by Objectives, and abolishment of annual performance appraisals. Though controversial among TQM practitioners, these Deming admonitions are worth considering as a point of departure for discussion.

Numerical Goals and Management by Objectives

Management by Objectives is indeed flawed on several counts. First, worker input is only one of a number of factors that govern performance. Other factors include things over which the worker in traditional organizations may have little or no control, such as the quality of the process, tools, environment, team mates, and suppliers. Second, basing reward on output compared to an objective or quota ignores the random variability inherent in all processes. And, third, objectives are empty statements unless supported by a strategy.

When evaluating performance, we cannot know whether performance outcome, good or bad, was the result of something within the worker's control, whether it resulted from random variation, or whether it stemmed from some factor in the system other than the employee's effort. It follows that meeting or not meeting an objective should not be the sole or even the primary determinant of reward.

Perhaps the strongest argument against the use of objectives or quotas as a basis for performance measurement is that they are, by themselves, empty of real meaning unless the objective is supported by a strategy. To say, for example, that it is our objective to "increase production by 10%" or "reduce defects by 25%" is the equivalent of a bumper sticker statement unless the objective is supported with a strategy developed and agreed to jointly by the performer and the supervisor.

The strategy is important not only because it forces the parties to think about and agree upon a means for accomplishing the objective, but also because it provides a reality check on the objective itself. If a strategy to achieve the objective cannot be found or agreed to, it may mean that the objective is flawed and needs to be modified to "fit" the strategy that seems to make sense.

Once the strategy is agreed on, management by objective gives way to "Management by Strategy" (MBS). Performance, then, can be judged and rewarded based on how well the strategy is adhered to, the imaginativeness and creativity demonstrated by the performer in finding and effecting solutions to unexpected problems, and the ability of the performer to modify the strategy as necessary to take advantage of opportunities and to deal with changes to the business environment. MBS is a big-picture way of managing; it leads to a more global perspective than MBO which, by definition, focuses on the relatively narrow issue of whether or not the objective has been met.

TQM provides the framework for assigning "global" responsibility to performers at the working level. Empowerment gives people a degree of influence, if not control, over their processes, tools, environment, team dynamics, and suppliers. Decentralization gives performers unprecedented control over support functions. Information and involvement give people at all levels of the organization a base of knowledge adequate for strategic management responsibilities. Links to customers and suppliers put workers in touch with the wider business environment.

A study conducted by General Electric showed that Best Practice companies tend to have four defining characteristics in common: short product development times, treatment of suppliers as partners, very low inventory costs, and *an emphasis on the management of processes, not functions*. From its study, GE concluded that it had been managing the wrong things: it was setting goals, and measuring against the goals, but not paying enough attention to how the goals were being achieved. Accordingly, the company changed its management focus from *what* things got done to *how* things got done. One result was that the corporate audit staff, which used to concern itself with such relative trivia as the $5,000 petty cash box, turned its attention instead to a $5 million inventory, looking for ways to reduce it through process improvement.

Performance Appraisal

Performance appraisal can, for any one of several reasons, be counterproductive. Perhaps the most important reason is that, by rewarding individual achievement, appraisal fosters competition between people and is a disincentive to cooperation. Second, appraisal fosters an environment where looking good becomes more important than doing well. And, third, people who get low performance ratings can become victims of a self-fulfilling prophesy through the inevitable loss of confidence. Low performance ratings can result from factors outside the person's control, such as poorly designed processes, a biased or "tough" supervisor, short-term stress or illness, or ineffective support.

Despite these widely accepted objections to periodic performance appraisal, appraisal remains a centerpiece of the manager-employee relationship in most U.S. organizations, especially for white collar workers. It is a convenient basis for performance feedback, the primary determinant of promotability and pay, and at least a secondary determinant (seniority is often primary) of retention standing during periods of downsizing.

Though there are other ways to provide performance feedback and to determine promotability, pay, and retention, performance appraisal is so deeply rooted in our business culture that few organizations are likely to abandon the practice.

Fortunately, there are ways in which periodic appraisal can be made consistent with TQM principles. First, we can provide an incentive for cooperation by balancing rewards for individual performance with rewards for team performance. Thus, any selfish emphasis on individual performance achieved at the expense of support for the team results in an overall lowered performance score. By linking everyone's individual reward to team performance, the individual is motivated to support team mates while remaining motivated to individual performance as it contributes to the team.

Second, to overcome the appraisal-fostered propensity to place immediate appearance ahead of longer-term substance, a shift from supervisor-driven appraisal to a more widely-based appraisal input should be considered.[1] Some organizations have adopted an appraisal format known as 360-degree feedback, in which the supervisor's primary involvement in the appraisal process is not to provide appraisal, but rather to orchestrate appraisal input from peers, customers, and subordinates. With appraisal information from this wide group, the supervisor is in a far better position to rate and guide employees than he or she would be using only personal observations.

Wyatt Company, a consulting firm, has found in a survey of 897 U.S. companies that 26% are now incorporating some form of customer input into their appraisal of employees, 15% include evaluation by peers, and 12% obtain subordinate evaluation (anonymous) of supervisors.

Third, the adverse effect on the morale of those who receive low performance ratings for reasons beyond their control can be minimized by creating what has been called a 5-90-5 appraisal system. Under such a system, 5% of the employees would receive ratings of "outstanding", 90% "good", and 5% "need improvement." The 5-90-5 distribution would not be applied as a quota, but rather as a general guideline.

By awarding a performance rating of "good" to some 90% of the employees, Deming's Point Number 12, which seeks abolishment of performance appraisal, is virtually met since awarding almost all employees a rating of "good" is tantamount to no rating at all. Yet, the 5-90-5 formulation retains the option to identify a small number of employees as "outstanding" or "in need of improvement."

The small "outstanding" group are those who consistently demonstrate extraordinary ability and diligence. By keeping the size of this group as small as about 5%, we seek to avoid identifying as "outstanding" those who may have done well in a given performance period as a result of random variation or as a result of circumstances not of their doing. The equally small group identified as "needing improvement" can be dealt with as special cases in need of training, reassignment, or, possibly, termination.

General Motors Powertrain Division has adopted the 5-90-5 formula, stating in its rating guidelines: "Exceptional, given its most elementary definition, is rare. To identify more than a few individuals as such negates the 'exceptional' label [which should] require consensus by acclamation, not debate." GM Powertrain seeks to align itself closely with Japanese practices in which compensation for the broad middle rank (90%) of employees will be based largely on rank, expertise, and years of experience, rather than on "merit."

Other U.S. organizations that have adopted variations of the 5-90-5 system include Xerox, Motorola, American Cyanamid, Ford, and General

Motors. Most had five-tier appraisal systems, with a constant concern about borderline ratings between 4 and 3 and between 3 and 2. Most have gone to a three-tier system. Recognizing that there is a stigma associated with being on the bottom tier, the systems are treated virtually as pass-fail, with the distribution formulas ranging from 20-70-10 to 10-80-10 to 5-90-5.

Appraisal As A Feedback Mechanism

Reliance upon formal annual appraisal as the primary mechanism for employee performance feedback and counseling is a standard feature of appraisal sessions. While pro-forma feedback is generally provided at the time of the annual review, only rarely does that review session contain surprises. People should be (and generally are) made aware on a continuing basis both of praiseworthy performance and of any need for improvement. The annual review session serves most often to confirm the obvious.

Performance review sessions do, however, provide a good opportunity for meaningful dialogue of a broader kind. In a TQM organization, the dialogue between employee and supervisor might be started with some thoughts from the supervisor on TQM values: empowerment (What does it mean? How is it working? What should we be doing differently?); process improvement (comment on process improvement efforts earlier undertaken, identify processes that are candidates for improvement, suggest some process benchmarks); customer obsession (provide information on who the most important customers are, discuss recent customer survey results, solicit ideas on how customer delight might be increased); strategic planning (describe company values, vision, strategies, and seek comments). The Baldrige criteria make another good topic for the annual performance appraisal dialogue (How are we doing with respect to the Baldrige categories? How might we improve?).

To enhance the dialogue, the employee might be asked to come to the appraisal discussion prepared to comment on his or her plans for the coming performance period, career goals, what further contributions the employee could make if given wider opportunity, and the biggest question of all: "If you were CEO (or department head), what would you do to strengthen the company (or department)?".

TQM Appraisal Factors

Traditional organizations generally reward people on the basis of four factors: job knowledge, performance, effort, and attitude. TQM organizations value these same four factors, but also base reward on the additional factors that are at the heart of TQM values: teamwork (both local and corporate), empowerment, process improvement, customer focus, and strategic planning. People in TQM organizations must be motivated to practice these TQM values. By including them in the list of appraisal factors, both management and work force are reminded to incorporate them into their professional value system.

Evaluation of Supervisors by Employees

Evaluation of supervisors by employees is increasingly practiced. Its purpose is to provide feedback to supervisors, to empower employees to have a voice in the way (and by whom) they are supervised, and to provide higher level supervisors with a ground-floor perspective about the practices and abilities of subordinate supervisors.

Generally, the means used for employees to rate their supervisors is known as "skip review." Employee ratings of their supervisors are given to the supervisor's supervisor, rather than directly to the first-level supervisor. Thereby, confrontation and the possibility of retribution are avoided, and the next-level supervisor obtains information to be used in rating and guiding lower-level supervisors.

Gain Sharing [2]

The belief that productivity rises when employees are given a stake in company profits is widely accepted conventional wisdom, and it is an intuitively logical concept.[3] Yet, actual hard evidence about the relationship of rewards to motivation is thin. Peter Drucker has reported (*Adventures of A Bystander*) on this matter from his early study (1943) of General Motors employees. Drucker concluded that while pay and promotion (termed "extrinsic" rewards) were not important motivators, dissatisfaction with them was a powerful demotivator. Thus, while people with comfortable pay and organizational status were not strongly motivated by additional pay or promotion, those who deemed their pay and status to be unsatisfactory performed at less than their capacity.

Drucker found, in the same study, that "intrinsic" rewards (achievement, contribution, responsibility) were strong motivators. Thus, for people at satisfactory levels of pay and status, additional motivation comes primarily from non-monetary intrinsic rewards such as recognition, empowerment, and job enrichment.

Initial results of a more contemporary study by Rutgers economist Douglas Kruse were recently reported in *Fortune*.[4] Based on 20 years worth of data, Kruse found productivity increases of from 3.5% to 5%, on average, after companies adopted profit-sharing programs. Cash plans were found to have more than twice the impact of deferred-payment plans. Profit-sharing was found to raise productivity more in small companies (less than 775 employees). Some 16% of employees in medium-size and large companies share in profits; 25% of small firms offer profit sharing.

Queried in the *Fortune* article as to whether cash alone makes the big difference, or whether the reported positive results stem from the implied combination of monetary incentives with employee involvement and information-sharing, Kruse had no answer. Though he suspects that money is the key, the link with empowerment and involvement could explain why smaller companies, more likely to empower and share information, get better results.

While hard data about the effectiveness of gain sharing remain less than wholly compelling, we must fall back on the obvious. TQM seeks to involve employees as partners, and partnership implies sharing. Some form of gain sharing or profit sharing is the working-level equivalent of executive bonus plans keyed to profits or equity value. Indeed, when companies link some part of executive compensation to corporate gain, and do not offer the same link to working-level employees, the dissatisfaction with extrinsic rewards identified by Drucker may result in demotivation at the working level.

Organizations across the spectrum of the U.S. economy share gains with employees in one way or another. The U.S. Navy Aviation Depot in Cherry Point, North Carolina, monitors gains resulting from TQM implementation, and shares them on a 50-50 basis with civil-service employees. Beth Israel Hospital in Boston does the same. Merck, DuPont, Tandem Computers, and Syntex Corporation all offer stock-option plans. At Springfield ReManufacturing, workers own 30% of the company's stock. Microsoft's stock sharing program has boosted an estimated one in five of its employees to millionaire status.

If you should decide to plan your own gain sharing program, be sure to take into account these six parameters:

1) How gain is to be measured.

2) Size of the sharing work unit.

3) The baseline: setting it and whether it should be moving or fixed.

4) Gain distribution ratio: employees to organization.

5) Whether payout should be relative to salary or equal for all.

6) The payout period.

The following guidelines, keyed to each of these parameters respectively, will help you design a successful gainsharing program.[2]

1) The measurement of gain must encompass the cost of labor per unit of output, materials, and quality. It might also include the Customer Satisfaction Index and overhead rate as bases for determination of gain.

2) The size of the sharing work unit must be small enough to allow the worker to see the performance/reward connection, yet large enough to ensure cooperation between cross-functional work units. Most organizations opt for using the largest possible work units; sometimes the entire organization shares equally.

3) Setting the baseline requires agreement on an historical standard. Workers will prefer a fixed baseline, since a moving baseline gradually raises the performance standard. A frequent compromise is to agree that, after two payout periods, the standard will be raised. In any case, the standard must be raised, as needed, to reflect technology improvements.

4) Distribution ratios can and do vary all across the board, from 70-30 to 30-70. Many organizations settle on a 50-50 distribution: half to the company for improvement, and half to the employees. Companies often allocate at least some of their 50% to improvement of quality of worklife, including such things as child care, safety, cafeteria, decor, and recreation facilities.

5) Payout is generally an equal percentage of salary. Some organizations, however, distribute an equal dollar amount to all, which makes the percentage high for lower paid workers, and low for those at the top of the salary scale. Since those at the lower income levels are generally in greatest need of the added motivation that comes from gain sharing, this seems to be the best choice.

6) Payouts need to be frequent enough to provide a constant incentive to employees, but the payout period needs to be long enough to smooth out seasonal and other earning cycles. Payout periods should never be less frequent than once a year. Some organizations pay out quarterly.

Two-Track Promotion

A consequence of the TQM-inspired flattening of the organizational hierarchy is the reduction in the number of management positions, and a consequent reduction in opportunities for promotion.[5] To further complicate the problem, the TQM-motivated shifting of control and support functions to self-directed work teams reduces the number of staff positions to which people can aspire. Two problems result: first, there must be new mechanisms devised to reward deserving people with increased status if not outright promotion, and, second, decisions must be made with respect to what will be done with displaced supervisory and management people.

The creation of two-track promotion is a good answer to the first dilemma. The first promotion track is through the traditional managerial hierarchy, albeit with fewer levels and with fewer positions at each managerial level. The second promotion track is a "professional" hierarchy, with a professional level corresponding to every managerial level, equal (or at least approximately equal) in status, perquisites, and pay.

To take the engineering function as an example, ascending managerial ranks are often something like: division supervisor, department manager, group director, and chief engineer. Corresponding professional ranks might be: senior engineer, department engineer, group engineer, and engineering scientist.

Or take a law firm, where progression through the "ranks" is entirely based on increasing professional stature: Associate, Partner, Senior Partner. Management status is generally conferred on only one Managing Partner. Despite the fact that most of the attorneys in a large firm have no managerial position, there is no doubt about relative status conferred by the three different professional levels. Status in the firm comes from increased responsibility and the ability to take on increasingly complex work. This same idea can readily be applied to organizations of any kind; we need only transform our cultures to accept the new paradigm: stature comes from professional capability, not managerial rank.

The second problem brought on by TQM-inspired flattening of the organizational hierarchy is, as we said, that of how to deal with the issue of displaced supervisors and managers. This issue is one of TQM's more difficult challenges. Because these people generally rose to supervisory and management positions because of their strong performance, the organization needs to do everything possible to retain their skills for the organization, and to preserve their dignity, self-confidence, and loyalty to the company.

Establishment of a two-track promotion system is an important step in this direction. Displaced supervisors or managers can be moved laterally from management status to the corresponding professional status. Ideally, there should be little or no loss in pay attendant to the lateral transfer, and responsibilities assigned for the newly established professional position should be at the level of importance attributed to the vacated management position.

Skill-Based Pay[6]

Since the mid-1970's, increasing numbers of blue-collar employees have been paid on the basis of the breadth of their skills. Especially for team-based organizations, it made sense to pay more to people with a wide variety of skills because of the greater flexibility thus provided to job-balancing and work-flow management.

Skill-based pay is now making its way into the white collar departments of organizations. Because TQM-driven downsizing has left offices with fewer workers, the remaining ones must be capable of performing a wider variety of jobs than before, and white-collar skill-based pay is designed to motivate that outcome.

Most companies, recognizing the efficiencies that result with fewer people who possess an array of skills, are willing to provide training, both in the blue-collar and white-collar areas, to achieve the goal of wider skill sets for their workers.

Ralph Stayer, CEO of Johnsville Foods, has eliminated annual across-the-board raises and substituted a pay-for-responsibility system.[7] Under the new system, whenever people take on new responsibilities (budgeting, for instance) or training, they are given an commensurate increase in pay. Stayer comments that, "Where the old system rewarded people for hanging around, regardless of what they contributed, the new one encouraged people to seek responsibility."

Another leading practitioner of skill-based pay is the Polaroid Corporation which initiated it company-wide in 1990. Along with skill-based pay, Polaroid's employees have been formed into work teams and empowered to redesign their work processes for greater efficiency. Although the Polaroid system encompasses everyone in the organization (including the senior executives), the company candidly admits that it has been more effective in the manufacturing part of the business.

Polaroid points to cost savings that result from employees having developed a wide array of skills. "They don't have to wait on somebody else to do something . . . they're able to keep the line going, to move the material," according to Mr. Richard Terry, Polaroid's compensation manager. "The work teams have picked up some of the responsibilities of the supervisors, as well, like scheduling assignments and overtime," he said.

The focus for Polaroid's white collar employees has been on learning new technologies. But here the process has so far worked less well, according to Mr. Terry: "We have not seen the same dramatic change in the white-collar jobs."

Part of the problem is that skills and competencies are more difficult to measure in managerial jobs. Professor Edward Lawler of the University of California, a strong advocate of skill-based pay for white-collar workers, says that these early difficulties will be overcome:

> Slowly, but surely, we're becoming a skill-based society where your market value is tied to what you can do and what your skill set is . . . . In this new world where skills and knowledge are what really counts, it doesn't make sense to treat people as jobholders. It makes sense to treat them as people with specific skills and to pay them for those skills.

Non-Monetary Rewards [8, 9, 10]

Ben & Jerry's Homemade Ice Cream, a $50 million corporation located in Waterbury, Vermont, has designated a Joy Committee to lift the spirits of its 325 employees. Steelcase Furniture and Marriot empower employees to design their own benefits package, realizing that young unmarried people might want their benefit allowance allocated differently from employees with large families. Gardner's Supply Company empowers single employees to obtain health coverage for their unmarried partners. Johnson's Wax, Lands' End, and Tandem Computers provide swimming pools at the workplace. FelPro gives chocolates on Valentine's Day and an extra day's pay for birthdays.

Tom's of Maine, a producer of personal-care products, lets workers donate 5% of their paid time as volunteers in charitable efforts outside the company; people can choose whether to allocate their 5% on a weekly (two-hours a week) or monthly (one day per month) basis. Tom's even offers a service that matches employees with a charitable effort. Currently, 33% of employees, often working as teams, use the opportunity by working in schools, hospitals, shelters, or churches. In assessing the worth of the program, now in its fourth year, Tom's asserts that the community outreach effort allows workers in different parts of the company to get to know one another, feel proud to be with Tom's, and to be happier with their own lives. Doubtless, it also strengthens Tom's standing in the community.

Day-care has become one of the most prized non-monetary offerings. Numbers of organizations are offering day-care on the premises at modest cost for the children of employees. Others make arrangements with local day-care facilities to take their employee's children on the basis of a discounted and sometimes subsidized group rate. Many young, two-parent families find it necessary or desirable for both parents to work. For single parent families, the income that comes from work is generally essential. The difficulties faced by these young people in finding responsible care for their preschool children are legion. Employers who meet this need create loyalty well worth the cost.

Quality of Work Life

Quality of Work Life encompasses such things as safety, comfort, parking arrangements, lunch facilities, lighting, work space environment, and cleanliness. While there are no data to support this, common sense suggests that TQM goals such as quality, high performance, partnership, and corporate loyalty are greatly enhanced when quality of work life is high. Conversely, and perhaps even more intuitively compelling, when the attributes defined as quality of work life are less than adequate, TQM goals would be more difficult to realize.

7

Training and Education

Purpose

The link between training and performance is obvious. People are generally more effective and productive as their technical skills are honed, and as they learn more about their products and processes. Effectiveness and productivity also increase as people learn more about customers and competitors, and about the vision and strategies of their organization.

Beyond skill enhancement, company-sponsored training provides yet another link to performance, which, though less apparent and less measurable is, no less real. It creates a covenant between the organization and the person by conveying a bonding message: "The company is investing in your professional growth because your future is with us, as a partner; the organization's well-being depends on the collective ability and effort of its people."

For traditional organizations, company investment in training is useful. For TQM organizations, where employee involvement in decision-making, work-team self-direction, customer focus, partnership, and continuous improvement rise from clichés to core realities, training is more than useful – it is essential.

Training requires investment of capital resources, and investment capital is always in short supply. Training investment thus needs to compete with an endless list of alternative investment possibilities: plants, equipment, product redesign, process improvement, corporate acquisitions, advertising, and so forth.

The case needs to be made, therefore, that training is not only a good investment, but that it is often a better investment than many of the alternative investment possibilities. Obviously, this is not to argue categorically against investment in such things as new facilities, new products, or new marketing strategies. It is intended as a reminder that the ultimate success of these investment alternatives depends on the ability and dedication of the organization's people, and that their ability and dedication are in part a function of training.

Intellectual capital is no less vital to corporate success than financial capital. *Los Angeles Times* columnist Michael Schrage has observed that "While you can buy innovators, you can't buy innovation – you have to build it into your company [through investment in training]."[1]

To argue his point, Schrage quotes Alcoa President C. Fred Fetterolf to the effect that (financial) capital is no longer king:

> What we are really interested in now is an engineering community that can solve problems without capital . . . . We're working hard to recognize the heroes that solved a problem and didn't spend a dime.

Fetterolf's kind of thinking represents a dramatic break with the past where the surest route to success was management of large capital projects. There is a clear link between the new emphasis on low-cost problem solving and the TQM emphasis on process improvement, using both kaizen and reengineering. See chapters 10 through 12.

The ingenuity needed to solve problems without capital, the ability to innovate, and the will to seek new and better ways to do things are enhanced with training.

General Motors and IBM are only two of the many organizations that have had to undertake radical downsizing and transformation. These and other companies had failed to keep up with their competitors' pace and quality of innovation, despite the investment of huge sums in capital equipment and plant facilities. It is at least possible that, had some of that investment in capital equipment and plant facilities been diverted to more and better training, innovations in product and quality innovations might have been stimulated to keep them at the forefront of their respective industries.

How Much is Enough?[2]

Anthony Carnavale, chairman of the National Commission for Employment Policy, says that American industry will have to devote a greater share of investment resources to workplace education and training if our programs are to be consistent with world-class standards. "The basic logic of competition is taking us there . . . France and Australia already require employers to spend 1.5% of their annual payroll on worker education, and German companies spend an average of 4% a year." American companies, Carnavale says, spend an average of 1.02% of their payroll on training (a total of about $30 billion), and that is concentrated in an elite 10% of our most progressive companies.

Carnavale adds that the great bulk of the $30 billion spent by our companies on education and training goes for things like executive semi-nars in Palm Beach, or courses for engineers, managers, or sales people. Only about $270 million is spent on training workers in basic skills.

Though the training investment by U.S. organizations is on average far too low, a number of well-managed U.S. companies provide a benchmark for the rest.[3] Xerox, for example, spends about 4% of its payroll on training. Motorola spends 3.6% and its employees are given an average of 36 hours per year of training. Corning expects each of its employees to devote 5% of working hours to training and invests 3% of payroll to make it happen; ordinary workers, not professional educators, do most of the training. At Federal Express, each employee is expected to spend two hours at least once a year with an interactive PC-based program that tests job knowledge and identifies training needs; 4.5% of payroll supports an average of 27 hours of training per employee. Andersen Consulting spends 6.8% of payroll to provide an average of 109 hours of training per year for each employee. Most supplement classroom training with com-puter and interactive video programs.

When giving TQM seminars to working-level people, more than once I have heard the observation that companies would be well served with a greater investment in training. The comments are not in any way casual; instead, they have been supported with such statements as "even when our company buys new equipment, we are often not adequately trained in its use." To people on the company front lines, the need for training is not abstract; for them, training can make the difference between good and mediocre performance. Under-utilization of costly equipment, low quali-ty, and low productivity can be clear and telling consequences of insuffi-cient or ineffective training.

While any generalization about how much training is enough is proba-bly dangerous, I think a good benchmark is 4-5% of payroll. Assuming that one-fourth of the investment is used to pay for the course (instructor, course materials, classroom), and that three-fourths is used to pay for the time of the people being trained, a 4% (of payroll) training budget would result in people spending an average of 3% of their time being trained (some 60 hours per year, or about 7-8 days training per year).

What Kind of Training Should Be Provided?

Job-related technical or proficiency training bears the most self-evident correlation to quality, productivity, and effectiveness. Yet training in the "soft" skills may be at least as important. Among them would be business literacy, information about customers and competitors, the vision and strategy of the organization, and the concepts, practices, and implementation of TQM.

• Work-related training and education are an essential basis for empowerment. Empowerment can not be successfully conferred upon a worker who lacks sufficient job knowledge to be capable of independent performance.

• Business literacy should be provided for people at every level of the organization. Contrary to the view of some management sophisticates, basic business literacy is easily within the grasp of every intelligent worker. I have personally provided such training to people at the level of maintenance and loading dock workers, and can testify not only to their full and ready comprehension, but also to their ability and eagerness to offer company-specific ideas for improvement.

People understand intuitively much of what comes under the general heading of business literacy, but it is useful to remind them in terms of company-specifics that higher quality and productivity lead to better products at lower prices, and that this in turn leads to higher sales, greater market share, and, hence, to greater job security and higher wages. Education in business literacy might begin with generic considerations, but to be useful to the people and the company it should include company-specifics (How are we doing against competition? How is product A doing relative to product B? How are we doing in region A as opposed to region B? For each of these and related questions, why?).

• Information about customers and competitors is important. Most people other than customer-contact personnel have little or no opportunity to see or even to know about external customers. Yet, people will develop both greater interest in and insight into the company's products and services when given information about who the company's customers are, what their needs and expectations are, how they use the product or service provided by the company, what problems they might have with the product or service, and what they think of the company's products and services compared to those provided by competitors.

Just as most people have little or no knowledge of their company's customers, they generally have no information about its competitors. The more people can learn first hand about competitors' products and services, and customers' reaction to them, the stronger will be their ability and incentive to improve the company's products and services in ways that will beat the competitors' offerings.

• Training in the plans and strategies of the organization is essential if people are to view (and comport) themselves as partners in the corporate enterprise, and if managers are to gain value from a dialogue with the workforce on corporate issues. When people are given training and information about the company's customers and competitors, coupled with insight into the company's plans and strategies, the call to partnership will be both strong and well-founded. The response of these newly won partners will be to contribute their energies and their ideas as partners, not merely as employees. There is a big difference.

• Training in TQM is essential. Implementation cannot succeed unless everyone, *all levels and every department in the organization,* understands TQM concepts, practices, and implementation methods. The training must aim for comprehensive understanding of each of the four elements of TOM: empowerment, process improvement, customer obsession, and strategic planning.

• Literacy and numeracy education, when needed, can be the basis for corporate turnaround. Not only does training in basic skills improve the ability of people to deal with increasingly complex work requirements, but it provides them with enhanced self-confidence, a better understanding of their business, and motivation for continued self-improvement.

Training Payoff: Some Case Studies

The Will-Burt Company, a 280-employee machine-parts factory in Ohio, provides a compelling case-study in the benefits of corporate investment in training. The company was near liquidation eight years ago because of high defect rates and chronic absenteeism. Today, its products are selling at double last year's levels and defects have been sharply reduced.[4]

The company's training program, which initially included courses in mathematics and a few other subjects, was developed by professors enlisted from the nearby University of Akron. All employees were required to participate. The program has been expanded over the years to include such topics as quality control and blueprint drawing, and is capped by a comprehensive two-year course in manufacturing that leads to a "mini-MBA," so far awarded to two dozen staffers.

Will-Burt believes that its recent giant strides, both in winning new business and in improved plant performance, are in large measure due to its innovative employee training program. Its business successes include winning back a multimillion dollar contract for publishing machinery that it had lost to a Mexican manufacturer. Plant performance improvement is evident on several fronts: employee tardiness has dropped from 70 a day to two in seven months; per capita costs for disability benefits has dropped from $525 to $3 a year, and product defect rates have declined markedly. Company President Dennis Donahue states that, "Once employees start learning about how the business runs, they become more aware of costs and they become more careful. They become interested in helping us save." The total cost of Will-Burt's training program is a relatively modest 0.8% of payroll.

Administering a program like Will-Burt's is not without difficulty. Courses meet once a week and require homework. Initially, a number of workers declined to participate – some because courses repeated things they had learned earlier, others because they simply wanted to be left alone. One person resigned because of the program; it was later learned that he felt threatened about exposing his inability to read and write. More than two dozen who volunteered for the mini-MBA program have dropped out. To spur interest in the program, Will-Burt offers incentives. Employees who complete the mini-MBA receive bonuses, improved eligibility for promotion, and this year one graduate is to be selected for the plant's board of directors.

The Will-Burt program has become a model for others. The Chevron Corporation and Japan's Matsushita Company have asked to visit Will-Burt to study its techniques. The Ohio plant of Volvo, the Swedish car company, wanting to start a training program of its own, hired away Will-Burt's best trainer. The National Association of Manufacturers is adopting the Will-Burt program (together with Motorola's and others) to create a training package for its 13,000 members.

Hampden Papers, a century-old paper mill in Holyoke, Massachusetts, has in recent years made the transition from low-tech paper manufacturing to high-tech computer-operated machinery that can turn out as much paper in a minute as the old equipment produced in a day. Becau: for literacy and a breadth of understanding in this new, f high-tech environment, Hampden pays for any worker to classes to earn a high school equivalency degree.[5]

The mill hired a private teaching organization to administer tests to the workers. To avoid embarrassment, results were not to be shared with the company. The in-plant classroom is set off from the factory and equipped with three personal computers. Enrolled workers can drop by any time in the afternoon for individual instruction from two teachers. They must put in a regular work day, but the company pays for time spent in the classroom.

Hampden Papers also pays all the costs for any worker or executive to attend college or graduate school, including business and law school. The cost of the two programs is 1.97 % of overall payroll. While the mill concedes that it is "tricky to measure the benefits," it notes that workers who take part in the classes have lower rates of absenteeism and job turnover. They also tend to get higher performance ratings from their supervisors. Robert Fowler, the company's president, has enrolled in law school under the company's college reimbursement program: "To practice what I preach!"

In a similar effort to expand course offerings beyond the usual, employees at Griffeth Rubber Mills in Oregon are offered business administration and math. At Plumley Companies, Inc. in Tennessee, the curriculum includes courses in Japanese and German.

The Granite Rock Company, a 1992 Baldrige winner, provides reimbursement for all requested outside education and training, whether work-related or not. In addition, Granite Rock sponsors numerous in-house seminars on diverse topics including law, teamwork, leadership, quality, safety, products , sales, service, and technology. Any employee may attend on company time; attendance is voluntary. The in-house seminars are taught by a mix of outside speakers, customers, suppliers, and company executives.[6]

The Honda plant in Marysville, Ohio, when faced with a recent need to reduce output during a sales slump, rejected layoffs or shortened hours. Honda decided to use the time to double the amount of training, reasoning that it would constitute an investment in future productivity. Training is provided in such diverse topics as corrosion theory, hydraulics, electronics, pneumatics, and process analysis, all presented in the context of real-world problems. The course listing offers 600 subjects, including nontechnical ones such as Japanese, export marketing, and the methodology of the J.D. Powers & Associates quality survey. Honda workers must also study such humdrum topics as inspection, cleanliness, safety, low-level maintenance, and the jobs held by co-workers to provide multiple skills.[7]

The Ritz-Carlton Hotel chain, another 1992 Baldrige winner, conducts a two-day orientation for new employees that serves as a model for organizations of every kind. Given to new employees at all levels, from chambermaid to concierge to managers, the training session begins with a salute to the new employees, aimed at building the dignity of service: "You weren't hired, you were selected. You are ladies and gentlemen serving ladies and gentlemen."[8]

The traditions, values, and vision of Ritz-Carlton are presented and discussed. People are instructed in the basics of courtesy and helpfulness; they are hosts and hostesses, members of an elite team always searching for ways to improve. To emphasize the importance of quality service, the chain's president and chief operating officer conducts the orientation at each new hotel.

Ritz-Carlton's orientation training and quality emphasis pays off in business results. The hotel chain's employee turnover averages 30%, versus an average of 45% at other luxury hotels. Occupancy rates average 70.2% versus the 61.7% industry average. The lower operating costs that result from training and quality emphasis enable Ritz-Carlton to charge rates less than those charged by comparable hotels.

Motorola calculates that every $1 invested in training yields $30 worth of productivity gains within three years. Though most courses at Motorola University (the company's name for its training center) are technical, process improvement, and team building training are also provided. Motorola assembled a team of procurement specialists and assigned them to study their processes for the purpose of shortening procurement cycle time. Before starting their work, team members were given two days at Motorola University to take a course called "High Commitment, High Performance Team Training," subtitled "collaborative-problem solving" by a Motorola executive. The team, which won a gold medal at the company's annual quality competition, felt that the training had given them the tools necessary to achieve their award-winning improvements.[9]

When TQM was introduced at Corning's ceramics plant, 21 job classifications were replaced with one (Celcor Specialist), people were formed into teams, and teams were given full authority over their work. The initial result was unimpressive: confusion reigned and quality and productivity declined. Teams had been formed, and empowerment had been granted without adequate preparation. Corning retreated to the beginning, and required that people be trained in the 21 sub-specialties, pass competency tests, and only then be certified as a Celcor Specialist with a 20% increase in pay. Training required the equivalent of one day per week, some on the job and some in classrooms, over a period that sometimes extended to two years before competency tests were passed. The training has resulted in increased productivity, reduction in waste, and a sharp improvement in quality. A Corning foreman states, "There's a heavy up-front cost in training, but the payback is quite impressive."

There is no question that training received before the employee enters the work force yields good results.[10] An extra year of high school has been found to add $96,000 to a male worker's lifetime income, and $51,000 to a female's. A 1992 study by two Princeton economists found that an additional year of schooling for one twin raised his or her wages by 16%. Though the relative value of pre-work training to post-work training is speculative, post-work training may be even more relevant to work performance both because the student is more mature and because employer-sponsored training is generally more applicable to job needs.

The *Journal of Labor Economics* reported on a 1989 study of employee training sponsored by large employers in the south and midwest. The study found that a 10% increase in spending on training produced a 3% boost in productivity over two years, which was twice as large as the pay hikes caused by the training.[11]

Orientation Training for New Employees

People rarely join a company with a bad attitude. Most come in happy to have gained employment, eager to do well, and determined to succeed. Often, this cheerfulness, optimism, and determination are met by impersonal mass processing and a bunch of routine forms to be filled out. Rarely is the new employee told anything of real interest about the company; company literature may be handed out, but it almost certainly will not contain "insider" information.

The new employee is now an insider, a prospective partner. The company's purpose in these first hours and days on the job should be to win the employee's interest and to begin to win loyalty. The importance of new employee orientation can hardly be overstated: these are the moments when the employee really wants to know and is open to positive first impressions.

The right agenda for a new-employee orientation program must fit the particular needs of the company. But the generic agenda which follows should provide a good checklist.

Session 1, Company Level:

(a) Who we are; how we do business; our values; what societal needs we fill; who our competitors are; who our customers are; who our suppliers are; a profile of our workforce and our management.

(b) Corporate vision (the next 3-5 years); the strategy we expect to employ to achieve that vision.

(c) Overview of the organization; who does what; meet senior people; a few words of welcome from each; question and answer session.

(d) Tour of the facilities.

Session 2, Department Level:

(a) Orientation to the employee's particular function; how decisions are made; how problems are solved; composition of the employee's team; the need for teamwork.

(b) How the team fits into the corporate whole; who are the teams customers and suppliers, both external and internal.

(c) TQM training.

Session 3, Local Level:

(a) Meet mentor; mentor begins to impart experience; mentor introduces employee to the mentor's network; employee is introduced to other mentors and employees.

(b) Initial job instruction is provided; provision is made for follow-up as required.

TQM Training

Training in TQM concepts and practices must be extended to everyone in the organization: every department and every level. Limiting TQM training to managers or to professional levels is a mistake for two reasons: first, it fosters the we-they relationships that TQM seeks to overcome, and second, it fails to enlist the full involvement of sub-professional people in customer-focused improvement of processes and products.

TQM training should be done in "family" groups, of which there are generally several in every organization, such as the top management family, department-level management families, and work-unit families. Often, people are members of more than one corporate family. For example, a department manager might simultaneously be part of the top-management family, the department-level management family, and the work-unit family.

Managers are well advised to undertake TQM training twice: once with their peers and once with the group they manage. The peer interaction that takes place during management-level TQM training is a profoundly good team-building experience. The heart of TQM training is the very set of topics that managers should discuss among themselves, but rarely do: empowerment (both of the workforce and the managers), involvement, open book information flow, customer focus, kansei, product improvement, process improvement, corporate vision, corporate strategy, and competitive and other benchmarks. TQM training that stimulates discussion of these and related topics and uses workshops to move from discussion to improvement planning and commitment are a good experience for the management team, both for bonding and for development of programs and strategies.

When managers repeat TQM training the second time with the groups they manage, the departmental or work-unit team undergoes the same team-building experience. Group discussion leads to bonding between team members and between the members and their manager. When managers participate in TQM training sessions with their people, the managers must go out of their way to create a non-threatening atmosphere, where people are encouraged, even provoked, to "tell it like it is" from their perspective. This opportunity to bring about an honest dialogue on matters of corporate consequence is one of the richest results of TQM training.

An added virtue of double training for managers is that it leads to their greater understanding of TQM concepts and practices. That, in turn, leads to enhanced ability of managers to lead the organization into this new way of doing business.

TQM training, indeed all training, should be done on a "just-in-time" basis. That is, training should be followed immediately by implementation. To provide training, and then do nothing about implementation for many months, is more than a mere waste of training resources. People become disillusioned and cynical about TQM, and its ultimate implementation will have been made more difficult.

TQM training sessions should be full-day sessions, three to five days long, and at an off-site location. Sessions should include no less than 10 and no more than 30 people (20-25 is optimum). Class-size of less than 10 limits the range of discussion; classes larger than 30 limits individual participation to the more aggressive members.

Initial TQM training of management and senior staff is generally best done by an outside trainer-consultant. Following that initial training, large organizations generally choose to develop a cadre of in-house trainers to train the remainder of the staff. Training materials can be developed in-house, or training packages can be bought from any of a number of reputable trainer-consultants. The Naval Air Systems Command, the 1989 winner of the "Presidential Award for Quality and Productivity Improvement" (the federal sector equivalent of the Baldrige Award) followed that approach, using an outside trainer to train some 200 top people, including a cadre of 12 very senior professional-level employees to serve as in-house trainers for the rest of the staff. The in-house trainers continued to perform their regular jobs, and were double-hatted to spend about 15% of their time providing TQM training. The Navair TQM training assignment was billed as career-enhancing, and it attracted excellent people.

Xerox Corporation has taken a different path for the development of in-house trainers. Xerox managers, upon having received their TQM training, are expected to then provide the same training to their subordinates. This "cascade" training approach at Xerox is known by the acronym LUTI: Learn, Use, Train, Inspect. Managers are expected to "learn" TQM, "use" it, "train" their subordinates, and then "inspect" their subordinates' usage of TQM to assure correct implementation.[11]

The Xerox approach has some advantages: it forces supervisors to learn TQM well-enough to be able to teach it, it obliges managers to participate in discussion of TQM issues with their people, and, when properly carried out, it creates a bond between managers and employees.

Training in Small Companies[12]

Smaller organizations may choose to use their initial TQM outside trainer to train everyone in the organization. The cost-effectiveness cross-over point would seem to be a company size of about 400-600 people. When the company has fewer people, it is generally not cost effective to develop your own in-house TQM training capability.

We may think of training as the province of large organizations, the kind of thing that small organizations don't bother with because it requires resources and staff support often beyond their perceived means. Not so. Martha Mangelsdorf reports in *Inc.* magazine that the most successful small companies do train, and small companies that become large and successful trace their growth and high performance, in part, to excellence that resulted from early and aggressive investment in training. Companies that fit this mold include the printer, Quad Graphics, the retailer, Crate and Barrel, and the restaurateur, Lettuce Entertain You Enterprises.[13]

Indeed, TQM, with its emphasis on employee involvement in decision-making and independent action, requires people who know what they are doing and who have the confidence in themselves that comes with knowledge.

Books have been described as the poor man's consultants. Mangelsdorf points to one small (then 30 employees) company, Pro Fasteners, that launched its TQM strategy by giving to each employee, as "required reading," a copy of Phil Crosby's *Quality Without Tears*.[14] Weekly discussion groups were convened to review sections of the book. Though it became evident that some had not done the assigned reading, use of the book as a catalyst for discussion was sufficient to convey Crosby's quality philosophy to each and every employee.

The Print and Copy Factory has established a lending library of books, tapes, and videos on self-improvement topics for its employees. The Granite Rock Company, as was noted earlier, provides frequent on-site seminars, taught sometimes by customers and suppliers, but often by managers and by working-level people. When people learn enough to teach, and are faced with having to organize their thoughts and prepare materials sufficient to lead a seminar, profound learning takes place, confidence is built, and company role models are created.

To reduce per person costs, several small companies can team together to hire expensive outside experts. To the same purpose, several small companies can share specialized knowledge among themselves. For example, at periodic get-togethers, one company might, in its turn, speak on shipping, another on inventory control, and a third on sales methods. Perhaps small companies can link with large ones in the trading of expertise.

I strongly encourage clients to involve employees in deciding on the methods and content of training programs. Management must serve as the spark plug to get people interested in the idea of learning for improvement, should facilitate staff discussions aimed at designing the program, and should guide implementation arrangements. The training program will best serve the needs of the people and the organization when it is developed jointly by management and the people with both individual and corporate objectives in mind, and when the people have some meaningful role in its implementation.

TQM in Academia [15, 16]

Lester Thurow, then Dean of the MIT Sloan School of Management, announced in December of 1992 that the school was adopting TQM as its internal operating philosophy:

> [We are undertaking] a major effort to bring TQM into the management of the Sloan School. While we may have received relatively good marks on our teaching of TQM, there was – and is – a lot to be desired in our internal practices . . . . Wherever possible, we are trying to take better advantage of our students. They are now running the orientation program, have established a student government, and have been empowered to make some of the maintenance decisions that are most central to their well-being.

PACE, the Philadelphia Area Council for Excellence, undertook a successful campaign to bring TQM instruction into local business schools. PACE representatives served on advisory boards at the University of Pennsylvania and Drexel University that were instrumental in integrating TQM into business and engineering curricula.

PACE sponsored an education survey of 125 Philadelphia area businesses in 1990 (35% responded). 82% of respondents said that, when hiring, they would give special preference to college graduates who had been trained in TQM. 78% believe that quality-related courses were important to the success of their businesses.

Apprentice Programs [17]

Non-college-bound students of the last several decades could expect easy entry into well-paying blue-collar jobs. But with today's demand for greater technical skills, high school diplomas are no longer sufficient to assure meaningful employment. Many of our nation's young people are drifting into dead-end jobs, at great loss both to themselves and the nation.

There is growing interest in devising a national apprentice system, modeled after Germany's, which integrates the last years of high school with the early years of work. The Clinton Administration's Labor and Education Departments are putting such a system together and hope to have a program of national proportions in place by the year 2000. Even prior to the Clinton efforts, a dozen states and nonprofit foundations had initiated similar efforts. However, according to Jobs for the Future, a Boston-based clearinghouse for apprentice programs, these local efforts remain small, involving just 2,000 students at some 250 companies as of mid-1993.

Anthony Carnavale estimates that a full-blown program to accommodate the annual crop of 6 million U.S. teens who do not go to college will cost about $12 billion a year. While the initial investment will be seen as substantial in this era of deficit cutting, the payoff in greater-than-offsetting economic and societal gains would seem to make this an investment that the nation can hardly afford not to make.

There is also some concern that the German approach perpetuates a class system. To meet that concern, the apprentice program could be linked (at even greater cost) with education at community colleges to make possible a later transition to four-year colleges for trainees who prove to have the academic aptitude and interest.

Apprentice programs must be linked to certification by employers of successful graduates. Just as the certification of plumbers and carpenters is recognized by employers across the nation, other job skills will need to be documented and standardized to make possible a system of testing and certification. Motorola, for example, is developing a set of skill standards for the American Electronics Association, which received a grant from the Bush administration for that purpose.

Disposing of a Red Herring

When I have advocated increased corporate investment in training, managers sometimes respond that the mobility of U.S. workers argues against it. "As soon as their skills improve, we'll lose them to another organization." This is perhaps true, but unless companies expand and improve training, the company itself could be lost to more progressive and farseeing competitors. The "Catch 22" reality is that, when companies strengthen the bond between themselves and their people through training and empowerment, turnover will lessen even though the training has increased the employees' attractiveness to other organizations.

8

Leadership in a TQM Organization

Leadership Characteristics

Max DePree wrote in his book, *Leadership is an Art*, that signs of outstanding leadership appear primarily among the followers.[1] When people are performing with excellence, when they have been transformed from employees to partners, and when they seek to widen their roles and their contribution, we can be sure that leadership is of the highest caliber.

Charisma is not a necessary quality of leadership, nor is appearance or size or charm or public speaking ability. There surely are some about whom people say "that person has natural qualities of leadership," or "was born to be a leader." But there are many with great charm, good appearance, and a commanding platform presence who would be ineffective as leaders. There are others, though less than attractive and devoid of charm, for whom people would give their all.

What, then, are the characteristics of great leadership? And can these characteristics be learned, or must one be born with them?

Knowledge: To lead an organization, large or small, the leader must be seen by the people as one who has vast knowledge about the work, or about some important aspect of it. The leader should be seen as one who can make creative contributions by virtue of superior knowledge or insight, someone with whom people can discuss problems or ideas and expect informed consideration in return. This is not to assert categorically that leaders must emerge from the discipline that they lead. John Sculley, former CEO and Chairman of Apple Computer, came from PepsiCo, but

Sculley, through innate brilliance and hard work, became a widely recognized authority and a leading visionary, not only for Apple, but for much of our science-based industry. Knowledge, while crucial to first-class leadership, can be gained on the job, particularly in the more senior leadership positions.

Corporate status: People want to know that their leader is highly regarded in the rest of the organization and preferably in the business community generally. People want their organization not only to be internally well led, but they want it to be externally well-represented. People know that their leaders need to have corporate status to compete effectively for corporate resources, for "plum" assignments, and for customers. People bask in the reflected status of their leader. Those who work for leaders deemed to be high in the corporate and industry "pecking order" gain status in their peer group.

Participative: Leaders must be people-oriented. They must instinctively want to ask that all important question to which David Kearns directed our attention in chapter 3: "What do you think?" Jack Welch, CEO of General Electric, commented about the obsolescence of autocratic managers in the 1991 GE Annual Report:

> In our view, leaders, whether on the shop floor or at the tops of our businesses, can be characterized in at least four ways.
>
> The first is one who delivers on commitments – financial or otherwise – and shares the values of our company. His or her future is an easy call, onward and upward.
>
> The second type of leader is one who does not meet commitments and does not share our values. Not as pleasant a call, but equally easy. The third is one who misses commitments, but shares the values. He or she gets a second chance, preferably in a different environment.
>
> Then there's the fourth type – the most difficult for many of us to deal with. That leader delivers on commitments, makes all the numbers, but doesn't share the values we must have. This is the individual who typically forces performance out of people rather than inspires it: the autocrat, the big shot, the tyrant. Too often, all of us have looked the other way – tolerated these "type 4" managers because they "always deliver" – at least in the short term.

And perhaps this type was more acceptable in easier times, but in an environment where we must have every good idea from every man and woman in the organization, we cannot afford management styles that suppress and intimidate.[2]

Network: In empowered organizations, the leader ceases close monitoring of his people, but must be available to resolve roadblocks that are beyond the ability of people to overcome. When the leader is part of an effective network, when the leader is "well-connected" in the industry or business, roadblock removal is often a simple matter of a call to the right person.

Someone once wrote that the function of senior Japanese executives is to "sit and sip," which meant that they stayed out of day-to-day operations, devoting their efforts instead to sitting and sipping (tea, I assume) with colleagues to maintain relationships horizontal to their level outside their organization, thereby maintaining a readiness to employ the network on behalf of the company whenever required. Networking provides leaders with ready access to benchmarking, and with knowledge of "world-class" practices and standards.

Listeners and scholars: Leaders must want to learn. We've discussed the importance of asking people, "What do you think?" This admonition to listen to others applies not only to people in the organization, but equally to suppliers, customers, competitors, professional society affiliations, spouses, neighbors, and tennis and golf partners. Sources of information and of ideas that improve our ability to perform and to lead are endless. These sources should not be limited to people in your particular business or technology. I have always found biographies of interesting (not always "important") people to be a great source of stimulation and insights into the way the world works. Writing and teaching have been, for me, among the most important sources of creative energy. The leader is responsible for giving vision and strategic direction to the organization. Listening and scholarship are essential to imaginative and innovative vision and strategy.

Integrity: People cannot respect unprincipled leaders. Integrity, as it applies to leadership, includes not only the usual adherence to the law of the land and to the ten commandments. It includes, as well, insistence on quality; placing customer long-term satisfaction ahead of company short-term profitability; fairness to people in the organization; courtesy; and total professionalism.

Confidence: Leaders should be confident of their knowledge, their corporate status, and their "right" to be leaders. Leaders lacking a strong sense of inner security are cautious about delegating responsibility and authority, concerned that their stature will be correspondingly diminished. Insecure leaders cling to and cherish their authority because it fortifies low self-esteem. Without a strong sense of self, leaders cannot effectively lead, and will not empower their people in any meaningful way.

Teachers: Good leaders are often good teachers. They are committed to conveying as much as possible of what they know to their people, not only because unit effectiveness is thereby raised, but because continuous learning is essential to raise people to their potential and to raise them to the full partnership that TQM seeks to bring about.

Egalitarianism: Successful leaders of empowered organizations must understand that everyone in the organization is a person. Everyone is entitled to pride, dignity, and a strong sense of self-worth. Stuffed shirts, pomposity, and arrogance are an anathema to empowerment and partnership. As suggested in an earlier chapter, executive dining rooms and preferred parking contradict the TQM call to partnership.

Some years ago, before the implementation of TQM in our auto companies, an industry analyst stated that U.S. auto senior executives think of their workers as beings from a different gene pool.

The executives sit in handsome offices, are well-dressed, earn high salaries, are university-educated, and possess the self-confidence and optimism that comes from being able to aspire to ever-higher positions and increasing income. The workers, by contrast, spend their working hours in dirty and noisy environments, are dressed in grease-spattered working clothes, earn relatively modest incomes, are always subject to downsizing. Without much formal education they haven't a hope in the world of being promoted much higher than first-level foreman.

Given the vast gulf that separates senior executives from ordinary workers, the gradual assumption of superiority by the occupants of mahogany row is easy to understand. But it is wrong, not only because it interferes with the TQM call to partnership, but quite simply because the assumption of superiority by any one group over another is stupid on its face.

Leaders need to recognize the possibility that a cult of superiority may have crept into the management ranks. Look for it, and stamp it out if you expect to lead successfully, and if you expect to achieve successful implementation of TQM.

Recall from chapter 4, Max DePree's account of the millwright who was at once a poet. Such a man, surely the intellectual equal of any executive, is representative of many workers at every level of the organization. With that truth in mind, egalitarianism, full partnership, is the only policy that makes sense in defining the relationship between the different levels in the corporate hierarchy.

The Role of Leaders

Much has been said and written about leadership, and definitions of what constitutes leadership abound. The fact that there are so many views on the matter suggests that leadership may elude rigorous definition. Supreme Court Justice Potter Stewart's comment on pornography provides a parallel: "I can't define it, but I know it when I see it!" But, just as the Court went on to describe the elements of pornography, it is important for us to describe the elements of leadership in an empowered organization, even if we cannot define it with rigor.

Most would agree that the primary role of the leader is to stimulate excellence from people. (I will use the term "people" in lieu of the term "subordinates;" in a truly empowered and egalitarian organization, there still exists a hierarchy, and discipline remains, but everyone is a person. No one is a superior, and no one is subordinate.)

To create an environment in which people are stimulated to excellence, the leader is responsible, with the active support and involvement of his people, for a number of things:

• The leader defines what needs to be done, assigning *initial* roles to teams and/or individuals, and coordinating and integrating output to bring about the required result. As the work matures, empowered people are themselves responsible for refining or changing roles, and for coordinating and integrating output to achieve excellence.

• The leader defines and promulgates a vision and strategy for the future, telling people not only what must be done here and now to deal with the task at hand, but giving people a sense of what the future holds.

• The leader defines and provides the resources needed to do the job, including processes, tools, suppliers, expert assistance, and internal support.

• The leader tests people's abilities and provides any necessary training for their initial assignments. As the work matures, people's jobs need to be enriched through cross-task training and through training in support tasks that can be assumed by work teams.

• The leader provides information to people about the company's products and services, its financial situation and prospects, its plans for the future, its customers and suppliers, the geopolitical environment, and anything else that will enable people to manage their piece of the company effectively, and encourages them to think of themselves realistically as partners with management.

• The leader blazes trails and removes roadblocks when the team needs help. Empowered teams will sometimes come to barriers that are beyond their ability. Management or professional assistance must be readily available.

• The leader recognizes and rewards accomplishments that go beyond the expected. There is little more important and satisfying to most people in the workplace than an occasional word or gesture of praise for a job well-done or for a good and timely idea.

• The leader offers encouragement of continuous improvement and of risk-taking to bring it about; continuous improvement, one of the center-pieces of TQM, requires change. Change, in turn, implies risk. Management must encourage risk-taking and forgive (even reward) failure in the honest and effective pursuit of continuous improvement.

• The leader displays professionalism, to include freedom from harass-ment of any kind, good manners and courtesy within the organization and outward to customers and suppliers, intolerance of corporate infighting, and a high level of corporate and personal ethics and integrity.

• The leader provides the freedom to work without monitoring or supervision; only by providing that freedom on a continuing basis will people mature to full empowerment.

Though the leader is responsible for each of the steps just listed, it bears repeating that the *empowered people must be involved* in every one of them. Their active involvement and help in defining and implementing each of the steps is essential because, during the formative stages, it assures support during the implementing stages, and it prepares people for their increasing assumption of responsibility for these and other steps as the work matures. In addition, the involvement in management actions of a diverse cross-section of people assures the best possible outcome.

Micro-Management is Not Leadership

One of the most difficult transformations in TQM is the elimination of micro-management Because managers generally come from the ranks of excellent performers, it is doubly hard for them, especially those new to management, to let go and cease close involvement with the work. If managers fail to step away, empowerment, which is a centerpiece of TQM, is doomed.

People so often complain, "My supervisor tells me I'm empowered, but he/she keeps hovering and checking and watching. I'm not really free to do much of anything without approval." The general response of the supervisor is one of surprise: "I can't believe it. People are not coming close to exercising the empowerment they've been granted; they continue to insist on coming to me for everything."

What's needed here, as in every dysfunctional unit, is communication. The supervisor and the people need to talk about their concerns and their differences, and come to agreement on how to deal with the situation. Such a dialogue is greatly enhanced by the presence of an informed third party to guide and possibly to mediate the discussion.

Leadership Requires Trust

Another leadership concern that needs to be dealt with is the matter of trusting people. Sometimes the "best" managers, the most conscientious ones, are the very ones that find this most difficult. Their deep sense of responsibility for the output of "their" work unit leads to the belief that the only way to assure excellence is for the manager to stay personally involved, to direct and to check everything.

Max DePree has written on the need for managers to *abandon* themselves to the strengths of others, not just to others who are experts, not just to those with a university degree, but to the strengths of all members of the workforce.[3]

Only when leaders are ready to trust the workforce can true empowerment become a reality. When particular individuals prove themselves to be untrustworthy, it is the leader's job to provide the necessary additional support, usually in the form of motivation or additional training; sometimes process improvements are necessary. When none of this works, people need to be transferred to work for which they can be trusted, or they must be removed from the workforce.

Trust is a *Catch 22* phenomenon. It isn't extended until people prove themselves trustworthy, yet they don't become fully trustworthy until they are trusted! When leaders let go, extend trust and abandon themselves to their people, most people will respond by performing to the level of excellence expected of partners. Those few that fail to respond can be given added support or removed.

Sam Walton's Leadership Rules[4]

Just before he died in 1992, Sam Walton, founder and CEO of Wal-Mart, wrote *Made In America: My Story*, in which he told the Wal-Mart story and described his management methods. His ten rules of leadership, summarized below, warrant recounting; they are what TQM leadership is all about:

Rule 1 – Commit to your business. Give it your all.

Rule 2 – Share your profits with your associates. Treat them as partners.

Rule 3 – Motivate your partners . . .

Rule 4 – Communicate everything to your partners . . . . Information is power . . .

Rule 5 – Appreciate everything your associates do . . .

Rule 6 – Celebrate your successes . . .

Rule 7 – Listen to everyone in your company . . . figure out ways to get them talking.

Rule 8 – Exceed your customers' expectations.

Rule 9 – Control your expenses.

Rule 10 – Swim upstream. Ignore the conventional wisdom.

More advice from Walton:

• Be a fanatic about getting managers off their chairs.

• Push responsibility and authority down.

• A lot of people think its crazy for me to fly coach. But its not fair for me to ride one way and ask everybody else to ride another. (This from a man who was worth some seven billion dollars!)

The Deming Prize Leadership Audit [5]

Florida Power and Light received the Japanese Deming Prize in 1989. John Hudiberg, then president of FP&L, has recounted the leadership questions posed by the Japanese counselors preparing him and other FP&L executives for the Deming Prize examiners:

• What is your job? Not your title, but your job.

• What are the eight most important things you do, in order of importance?

• How do you measure your performance?

• Based on these measurements, how are you doing?

• Where do you want the company to be next year? In five years?

• How do you propose to get there?

• What would you do if one or more of your objectives were not being achieved?

• If all were being achieved, what would be your next objective?

I cite Hudiberg's recollection because of the power inherent in the set of questions posed by the JUSE (Japanese Union of Scientists and Engineers) counselors. These are questions that all leaders should be asking of themselves. Where there is no good answer, or where the answer is thin, leaders are well advised to work on the question and to develop substance that will fully satisfy the thrust of the question.

Akio Morita, co-founder, chairman, and CEO of Sony Corporation, and former recipient of the Deming Prize, has said that management has only two responsibilities: to establish an atmosphere that excites and challenges employees, and to set out well-defined goals to set off the "creative spark" which is in everybody. He commented further that management sets the atmosphere by encouraging exploration of the "un-obvious," by rewarding "craziness that is the very common guise of genius," but most fundamentally "by letting people know they can count on management's support."[6]

Leadership from Desert Storm [7]

Lt. General William Pagonis, in charge of logistics for the Desert Storm operation and a highly regarded leader, wrote an article for the *Harvard Business Review* in which he stated his leadership principles. They serve to confirm those detailed in this chapter and include:

• Successful leadership requires two traits: expertise and empathy. Leaders must take active roles in shaping the environment, both organizational and external. The leader's personal "presence" is important, but it results from expertise and empathy, not charisma.

• Leaders must know the strengths and weaknesses of their organization. They must learn how and what to communicate, must know the mission, and must give and get feedback. Leaders must practice Tom Peters' MBWA: Management By Wandering Around.

• On the subject of organizational development, Pagonis notes that leadership almost always involves cooperation and collaboration, which occur only in a conducive context. That context results from combining centralized control with decentralized execution.

• On vision and strategy: the leader must shape the vision; simple is better. Subordinates must shape the strategy by which the vision is to be realized. The strategy must be specific and quantifiable.

• Leaders are responsible for educating their people.

9

TQM Management Infrastructure

You Already Have It!

Though TQM requires a managing infrastructure, that infrastructure is the business management infrastructure that every organization already has in place. The business managers are the TQM managers. No dedicated TQM bureaucracy is required.

Every company has a top management group, often known as the Executive Committee, that gives direction to the business from the corporate level. This same group of people can be "double-hatted" as the Quality Council (or whatever name you choose to give it) and chartered to give *corporate* direction to TQM.

Similarly, every department and division of the company has a management group that directs the work of the unit. These same people can be "double-hatted" as the Quality Management Board for that unit, and chartered to give *unit* direction to TQM implementation.

The Quality Council

As was noted in the opening chapter, TQM has a single purpose: to improve business performance. It is a means to that end, not an end in itself. Integration of the Quality Council with the Executive Committee is a way of assuring that this principle continues to dominate our view of TQM. The same people that manage the business manage TQM, and the sole purpose of TQM is to manage the business more effectively than before.

Because TQM provides a coherent and integrated set of management methods, the interleaving of business issues with TQM issues, and the "double-hatting" of operational management with TQM management, obliges line executives and managers to invest some of their time in business fundamentals in the context of dealing with operational issues. Executives and managers are thereby encouraged, while dealing with everyday operational issues, to take actions designed to improve business fundamentals (people, processes, customers, and planning) rather than merely solving the immediate operational problem at hand.

The transformation of "quality" into a topic meriting top executive attention stems in large part from the transformation of the term itself. Whereas quality once dealt exclusively with such measurable things as dimensions, voltages, and defect rates, it now includes not only product excellence, but also the means by which product excellence is achieved: empowerment, process improvement, customer focus, and strategic planning. Thus, broadly defined, TQM is what general management is all about. It is indeed Total Quality Management.

Despite the fact that TQM is equivalent to general management, numbers of organizations implementing TQM nonetheless continue to delegate TQM implementation responsibility to second or third tier managers. Human Resource Departments are often assigned responsibility for TQM; Quality Assurance Departments run a close second.

The CEO or a highly credible first-level operating executive should assume the TQM "czarship" in close partnership with other members of the Quality Council, as just described. When it is deemed necessary for some lower-ranking manager, such as the Human Resources or Quality Assurance manager, to assume TQM implementation responsibility, that person should be designated as a member of the Quality Council. The obvious shortcoming of this otherwise feasible arrangement is that the HR or QA managers, assuming that they are not first-tier executives, will not be members of the corporate Executive Committee. The link between TQM management and general business management will thus have been broken. TQM will have become a program with its own goals, not a business management strategy.

One or two members of the Quality Council should come from the workforce, having been elected by their work mates. When the organization is unionized, these work force representatives to the Quality Council should be union officials. While these people will not (generally) be members of the Executive Committee, they can make important contributions to the Council by conveying the views of their working-level colleagues, by bringing the workforce perspective to Quality Council deliberations, and by reporting back to their colleagues on Quality Council deliberations and actions. It is a means for bringing about the corporate partnership so important to TQM vitality and success.

The role of the Quality Council, in addition to cross-coupling business management with TQM principles, is to see to it that TQM is being successfully implemented across the organization. Quality Council members should be the best-informed people in the organization about TQM concepts and methods. They should be sure that TQM is happening in every corner of the organization.

Since the Quality Council is chaired by the CEO, and its members are heads of departments and divisions, the Council is the natural body to set corporate TQM policy, provide resources for implementation, encourage actions consistent with TQM principles, benchmark the TQM strategies of other organizations, publicize corporate TQM aspirations and accomplishments, and measure TQM success by its relationship to improvement in corporate business fundamentals.

Quality Management Boards

Every department, division, or other work unit with more than 30-50 people should have its own Quality Management Board. Thus, there can be several tiers of QMB's, depending on the size of the organization. The chairperson of each QMB will be the senior person in that work unit (i.e. the department head), and QMB members will be the direct reports or other senior members of the unit.

Because the QMB chairpersons are members of upper-tier QMB's, or of the Quality Council, they will receive TQM policy guidance from that higher-level affiliation and will be responsible for conveying information about TQM status in their work unit upward to the next level and laterally to peers.

QMB's, like the Quality Council itself, are made up of the very people who manage the work unit. By "double-hatting" work unit managers as members of the QMB's, and interleaving the unit's business issues with its TQM issues, the organization gains in two ways. First, TQM at the work unit level does not become a program with its own purposes; it remains a way of managing the organization and its activities. Second, by requiring unit managers to focus on TQM methods *as they manage the business of the unit*, we assure that these managers invest some of their time on business fundamentals rather than spending all of their time putting out fires.

QMB's are responsible for successful implementation of TQM in their respective work units. In addition, they have another special responsibility. It is the role of the QMB to identify processes in need of review and improvement, and to charter Process Improvement Teams to undertake the improvement effort.

Before we proceed to a description of the composition and role of Process Improvement Teams, let it be noted that thinking about process improvement is an organization-wide responsibility. TQM challenges and empowers everyone to think about how to do things better. Senior executives will have ideas, as will unit managers, teams, and individual performers throughout the organization. But responsibility for collecting process improvement ideas and transforming them into action generally belongs to the QMB for the work unit with primary responsibility for the process needing improvement.

Many, perhaps most, processes are cross-functional; that is, more than one work unit is involved. When several QMB's have a stake in the process under consideration, they must negotiate among themselves to determine which QMB will assume primary responsibility for the improvement action. When there is disagreement, the next-higher QMB or the Quality Council must adjudicate. The responsible QMB then establishes a Process Improvement Team.

Process Improvement Teams

Process Improvement Team members are selected by the QMB from among those who work with the process, who know its strengths and weaknesses, and who are known to possess the kinds of analytical strengths and motivation needed to assure success. PIT members are sometimes selected from outside the process to assure objectivity or to provide expertise not available from within the process.

The number of people needed to constitute a successful Process Improvement Team is generally five to nine. Synergistic interaction is more difficult with fewer than four or five members, and more than nine or ten members complicate teamwork and communication.

Process Improvement Teams need to meet at least once weekly, and should meet for no less than two hours each time. There are cases where, for an urgent process improvement effort, the PIT meets for several hours every day until the improvement effort has been completed. Hammer and Champy advocate that process reengineering teams meet full-time until the job is done. The problem here is that too much time devoted to the PIT effort causes people to have insufficient time to do their regular job. Hammer and Champy get around that problem by advocating that PIT members be entirely separated from their regular job, and reassigned to the new process following completion of the PIT effort. Another approach used in some organizations I have worked with is known as the "15% rule." The rule says that work (especially white collar work) is generally elastic, and that most people can afford up to 15% of their time away from their regular work doing PIT (or other TQM) work and still get their regular job done to full satisfaction.

10

Kaizen and Reengineering

Process is King

Everything we do employs a process. Whether we do our work efficiently, achieve a quality outcome, and complete it on a timely basis depends in large part on the process we employ.

Virtually every worker wants to do a good job. Everyone wants to succeed, be esteemed by bosses and peers, and achieve self-satisfaction. When managers blame low quality or inefficiency on worker attitude, unions, or lack of a work ethic, the real culprit, more often than not, is a badly designed process.

Processes that yield unsatisfactory outcomes need to be redesigned. When defect rates are unacceptably high, it is necessary to determine the root cause and to change the process so that defects are prevented by process restructuring. When the process is too slow, the process needs to be examined for such things as needless steps, ways to improve flow, and possible automation.

The worker, too, is part of the process. Thus, when the worker flounders, one of three things is needed: (1) the worker needs to be better trained; (2) a new and more capable worker needs to take the place of the weak one, with the unsuccessful worker either dismissed or transferred to work within his or her capability; or (3) the process needs to be changed to compensate or adjust for the worker's weakness.

When faced with a floundering worker, managers often limit their options to the first two. But the third option, changing the process to accommodate the worker's limitations, is often the least disruptive and most cost-effective. For example, should good eyesight or great strength be required, one could add magnifying lenses and levers. One manufacturer had a process that required the worker to select from among several tool-size options for different steps in the process. The tools were all stenciled with size information, but hurried workers often chose the wrong tool. The answer, it turned out, was simple: color-code the tools. Red was big, green was medium, and white was small.

Perhaps the biggest payoff of all in improving processes comes from examining every step of every process to be certain that we need to be doing it at all. Much of what we do can be eliminated with no adverse consequence to the product being built or the service being offered. More on this later in our discussion of reengineering.

Process improvement is fundamental to greater corporate strength. We cannot produce quality products and services without processes that yield excellence. We cannot shorten product development cycles without improving the product development process. We cannot bring better people into the organization unless we improve our recruitment process. We cannot improve our understanding of customer requirements unless we improve our market research process. And so on. In short, the process is king!

The Red Bead Experiment

Dr. Deming, during his seminars, employed a simple game to illustrate the importance of processes, and the futility of reliance on inspection. Known as the "Red Bead Experiment," the game made use of a small transparent plastic box containing some 2,000 small beads, 80% white and 20% red, randomly mixed.

Deming introduced the box, together with a small scoop, to his students and stated that he, as founder of The Universal White Bead Company, needed five "willing workers." Five student volunteers came forward and Deming next called for two additional volunteers to serve as inspectors and one additional volunteer to be chief inspector. He commented with a wry smile that the ratio of five workers to three inspectors seemed about right for an American manufacturer. He also noted that the ratio of two inspectors to one chief inspector seemed to conform roughly to industry averages.

Deming informed his newly assembled "staff" that each worker was expected to produce 50 beads per day, and that only white beads were acceptable; red beads were defects. He then illustrated the process that the workers were to use to produce their daily quota: the small scoop, which held exactly 50 beads, was to be dipped into the box, and 50 beads were to be withdrawn. He admonished his workers once again to remember that only white beads were acceptable; red beads were defects.

The first worker stepped up to the task, dipped the scoop into the box full of beads, and tried hard to bring up only white ones. The worker was asked to submit the scoop full of 50 beads for inspection, and the inspectors, checked by the chief inspector, counted them, looking for defects (red beads). Let's assume that for worker number one, 9 red beads were counted. This number was duly recorded on a big board. Deming strongly declared 9 defects to be an unacceptably high level, and admonished the second worker to be more careful. Worker number two tried even harder, but withdrew – let's say – 12 red beads, as counted and recorded by the inspectors. Deming pretended to be irate, saying that he would not tolerate this level of incompetence. Worker number three, we'll assume, was lucky: only 6 defects. Deming promised that worker a vice-presidency if performance continued at that level. And so it went for five "days" of production for each of the five workers. They all tried hard to move their scoop around to avoid extracting red beads – but, of course, to no avail.

Because the red beads were randomly mixed among the white ones, and because the process mandated by management (Deming) precluded the use of fingers or other devices to selectively extract white beads, continued "manufacture" of some number of red beads was inevitable. In Deming's experiment, the results of 25 total withdrawals were recorded (five workers working for five "days"), and the total number of defects (red beads) was divided by the total number of withdrawals. To no one's surprise, the average number of red beads was invariably very close to 10 (20% of 50).

With the Red Bead Experiment, Deming was communicating three important lessons. The first thing learned is that when workers produce low quality, it is generally because of a poorly designed process; only rarely is it attributable to the worker's attitude or skill level (most workers want to succeed). The second lesson is that process output varies randomly around some average result. The third is that, while inspection will generally (though not always) identify defects, defects will continue to occur at some predictable average rate and a predictable range of variation, unless the process is changed in ways that will reduce or eliminate defects altogether.

Deming's lesson was to *prevent* defects through process improvement rather than to *detect* them by inspection.

Deming used the results of the Red Bead Experiment to introduce his students to the rudiments of Statistical Process Control. Using the simple formulas of SPC, he calculated the Lower and Upper Control Levels to be approximately 6 and 14, respectively. Thus, in the 50-bead extraction process, "workers" could expect that in 99.7% of withdrawals, from now until doomsday (as long as the process remains unchanged), the number of red beads would continue to vary randomly between 6 and 14, averaging at 10.

Another important purpose of SPC, perhaps its most important application, is its use for developing insights into process weaknesses, and, concurrently, as a basis for the development of ideas leading to process improvement. See chapter 12 for a further discussion of Statistical Process Control.

Kaizen [1]

Kaizen is a Japanese word that means improvement. In the TQM context, it has come to mean a continuing accumulation of small increments of improvement to existing processes. Japanese quality strategy employs the Kaizen idea as the basis for process improvement and is different from innovation, which is seen by Japanese as the American penchant for major change and capital investment.

Japanese like to invoke the fable of the tortoise and the hare to illustrate their point. The tortoise (Kaizen) creeps steadily along while the hare (innovation) takes an occasional leap. In the end, it is the tortoise, with its steady forward movement, that wins the race.

An interesting Kaizen example comes from one of the large Japanese companies which presents an annual award to one (or a team) of its employees for outstanding contributions to the corporation's quality strategy. Some years ago, the award was presented to the ladies who serve tea in the company cafeteria. Their contribution had been to analyze and improve their tea-serving process to provide better distribution and reduce waste. While their effort clearly did little to advance corporate fortunes, it was deemed to be important because it was representative of the Kaizen ideal of small increments of improvement to an existing process. By giving the annual award to the tea-ladies, this giant corporation was endorsing the Kaizen principle.

Contrasting the 1980's experience of Ford and General Motors provides additional support for the Kaizen idea. Ford's quality strategy was centered on the notion of improving its existing processes. For example, in one study jointly sponsored by Ford and the UAW, it was determined that Ford "could shave more off the price of a car by improving the way it shipped parts between plants [rather] than by putting in expensive new robots." General Motors, on the other hand, pursued innovation, spending huge sums on robotics and automation (a staggering $67 billion in the decade of the 80's).[2]

Ford's steadfast efforts at reducing overhead and improving its manufacturing processes caused it to win hands-down the quality-productivity race of the 1980's.[3] By 1990, labor hours required to assemble a mid-sized car was 40 for GM and 27 for Ford. A 1990 study by Harbour and Associates concluded that if GM could learn to produce cars as efficiently as Ford, it could trim 60,000 workers from its payroll and boost annual pre-tax profits by $4 billion.

Reengineering

Reengineering is not the same as Kaizen. A reengineered process is not merely an improved process, it is a wholly new process. Reengineering got its initial impetus from the increasing recognition that many of our processes, in part or in whole, particularly administrative and service-oriented ones, are obese. Many of the things that our inflated processes do are not at all necessary; many others add little value. These unnecessary or low-value activities needlessly clutter our agendas and divert resources and attention from things that are necessary. To become competitive, we needed to redesign these bloated processes wholly to rid them of needless steps, red tape, and superfluous reviews.

Added to the 1980's cumulative recognition of process obesity was the realization during this same period that there were altogether too many administrative, support, and mid-management personnel. It became apparent to those undertaking TQM process improvement that large numbers of people performed non-jobs, caused overhead rates to be needlessly high, and got in the way of those who were doing "real" work to support real customers. Some relevant observations follow:

AT&T has stated that: "AT&T is learning that running leaner and meaner means deciding what doesn't need doing, rather than trying to do everything done before with fewer people."[4]

Hillary Clinton, in Senate testimony on the White House health care proposal put the case for reform in health care administration this way: "A Mozart quartet being played in the 18th century and being played in the 20th century still requires four people. The problem with the American health care system is, if you can imagine, that quartet has added people to hold the chairs, to hand the violins in, and has required the musicians to stop at the third or fourth page of music to call somebody to make sure they can go on to the next bar."[5]

Peter Drucker has been quoted as having said: "To start cost-cutting, managements usually ask: 'How can we make this operation more efficient?' It is the wrong question. The question should be: 'Would the roof cave in if we stopped doing this work altogether?' And if the answer is, 'Probably not,' one eliminates the operation."[6]

General Electric : As was noted earlier, GE has coined the term "administrivia" to define the multitude of unnecessary paperwork, meetings, reviews, and support activities.

Recognition of the now all-too-apparent fact that we have burdened ourselves with numbers of nonessential and nonproductive functionaries has led to a nationwide rash of "downsizing." Virtually every U.S. organization is finding it possible to get more work done with fewer people, in large part by improving processes to reduce or eliminate altogether those activities that added little or no value, and by eliminating the many support jobs and mid-management jobs that empowered organizations no longer need. Quality has risen, and rework is less, making it possible to downsize even farther.

The federal government is following the example set by the private sector. Budgets and staff sizes are being reduced across the government. Vice President Al Gore, assigned responsibility for "reinventing" the government, has held town-meetings at many government agencies seeking "reinvention" ideas and support from civil servants. One of the vice-president's favorite rhetorical devices is to ask, "Do we have too many mid-level managers?" His question is always answered with applause and shouts of approval.

Organizations across the country have taken note that there is a cadre of mid-level (and even senior) managers that neither lead nor decide, whose sole function is to collect information from performers, analyze it, provide it to decision makers, and convey decisions back to performers. These are generally good people with titles like coordinator, liaison, facilitator, planner, or assistant.

In TQM organizations, these non-managing managers have become redundant and excessive. Workers are now empowered to collect data about their jobs and to make job-related decisions; they also deal directly with corporate decision-makers, and even with suppliers and customers as necessary. There is no longer a need for many of the mid-management people formerly "required." They can be, and are being, assigned to more productive work.

Though radical redesign of processes is hardly a new idea, the term "reengineering" found its way into the popular vernacular only recently through the work of Hammer and Champy. Their 1993 book, *Reengineering the Corporation*, defines reengineering as "the fundamental rethinking and radical redesign of business processes to achieve dramatic improvements in critical, contemporary measures of performance, such as cost, quality, service and speed."[7, 8, 9, 10, 11, 12]

One excellent example of a dramatically reengineered process has been reported in the business press. Blockbuster (the video cassette distributor) has teamed with IBM to reengineer the marketing and distribution of compact discs. The current process, which requires record stores to stock multiple copies of every title, requires costly inventory and even more costly shelf space. The reengineered method will be to stock all titles in the memory of a remotely-located central computer. The customer will select a title, can listen to it in the store's listening booth, and can order a copy to be made on the spot. No CD's are kept in the store. They are called up from the distant central computer either for listening or for instant copying on the store's CD-maker. For billing purposes, information is automatically posted of the numbers of each title copied at each retail outlet. Many stores will be linked to each central computer.

Another important influence on the concept of reengineering has come from some studies of process queuing. George Salk and Tom Hout, in their book, *Competing Against Time*, found that, on average, work-in-process receives value for only 0.05-5% of the time that it is in the value-added system of the company.[13] For example, an insurance company takes 22 days to process an application, but in that period of time, only 17 minutes of actual work is required to do the processing. For the remaining time, the application is in transit between workers or sitting in somebody's in-box. (Note: this works out to 0.22%, assuming that 22 calendar days equals 16 working days, and that there are 480 working minutes in each day.)

The Hammer-Champy book reports on a queuing reduction example taken from IBM Credit. To finance sales made to IBM customers, IBM Credit employed a five-step process: log the request, perform a credit check, make any necessary amendments to the standard loan agreement, determine the appropriate rate of interest, and prepare a quote letter. The five step process took 6-10 days (during which the customer could change his mind), and involved four different "experts." The actual work took 90 minutes. Doubling productivity would have reduced this to 45 minutes, but elapsed time would still have been 6-10 days. Solution? Simply have one person do all five steps. No hand-offs. The old process had been over-designed to handle the most difficult (but very rare) applications. Most were simple and could be handled by plugging numbers into standard models. The 6-10 day turnaround is now four hours.

For years, I have wondered about the need for invoices. When my small consulting practice does an item of work for a client, generally in response to an oral agreement or a purchase order, it is always clear to both parties when the work has been completed. Yet, to get payment, it is always necessary to submit an invoice. Why? Ford asked itself that same question, and has done away with invoices from all of its suppliers. That simple and obvious action made it possible for Ford to reduce the size of its accounts-payable department by 75%, from 500 people to 125. Now, Ford pays upon receipt of goods by matching incoming shipments to outstanding purchase orders at the receiving dock.

DuPont, like Ford, no longer expects invoices from its vendors, nor with a growing number of suppliers does it bother with purchase orders. Outside vendors are linked electronically with DuPont's internal inventory control system and respond with delivery when inventory runs low.

Another example of reengineering which involves the sales function comes from Phoenix Design (a Herman Miller Furniture subsidiary). Phoenix sold office furniture in the traditional manner, by sending sales representatives to customer's offices to gather requirements, from which a designer would later develop a draft design. After a back-and-forth iteration, usually about six weeks long, the sales rep would show the customer a proposal. Now, thanks to some PC's and appropriate software, sales people have become their own designers and are generating proposals in 4-5 days. One dealer has made a sale in each of the 70 times it has used the new system. Phoenix is now moving toward the next step, the use of laptop systems that will enable the salesperson to work on designs in the customer's office.

Aetna Life and Casualty has completely reengineered the way in which it issues policies. The company originally had 22 business centers with a total staff of 3,000, and took 15 days to get a basic policy done, in part because 60 different employees had to handle each application. Now the operation has been pared down to 700 employees in four centers, and customers get their policies within five days. How? Because a single sales rep tied to a PC network can perform all steps necessary such as calling in to an actuarial base, for example, to process an application. The reengineered operation has given sales people greater autonomy, too, by linking each salesperson to a team of 16 inside people.

ITT Sheraton required 40 managers and 200 employees to operate a 300-room hotel. Their reengineered hotels have 250 suites, 14 managers and 140 employees, with higher customer satisfaction. "We redesigned the processes of the company and eliminated everything we didn't need to do. Most of the managers had been filling out forms for the bosses." One other noteworthy feature of the Sheraton reengineering effort: it began by taking into account the customers preference for suites over rooms.

Some automobile insurers are reengineering their process by moving toward decentralization of the vital estimating function. The traditional claims process requires the insured to come to the insurance company's estimating station to obtain an estimate of damage and authorization for repair. For badly damaged and undriveable cars, arrangements are made for the insurance company estimator to go to the car to make the estimate. These costly actions are in some cases being replaced by arrangements between the insurance company and trusted repair shops authorizing the repair shops to do the work and simply bill the insurance company. The obvious risk of overcharge is monitored by spot checks and by statistical comparisons of average charges. A repair shop so favored would, in most cases, go out of its way to maintain the relationship, and cheating would probably be rare. The reduction in costs for the insurance company and the added convenience to customers are factors that justify any small element of risk.

By now, a pattern common to reengineering efforts should have begun to form. The following rules will help to focus your reengineering effort.

Rule 1: Consolidate. Through extension of the Frederick Taylor and Adam Smith philosophies (narrow jobs, economies of scale) we have become captives of specialization. Most workplaces consist of many people, each doing a narrow and highly specialized piece of the whole, and requiring platoons of support personnel and supervisors to plan, coordinate and integrate the fragmented output into a cohesive whole.

We have lost sight of the merits of consolidating the entire job (or the largest possible pieces of it) in the hands of a single individual or small team. One important goal of process reengineering is to eliminate the need to pass work from one specialist to another, eliminate repeated waits in successive in-boxes, eliminate the need to balance the workload of serial specialists, and restore the pride that comes with full responsibility for a deliverable end-item. Workers responsible for the entire job will make their own decisions about the sequence in which the work is best done, they will be responsible for and will be judges of quality, and they will in many cases deal directly with customers and suppliers.

Our further goal is to eliminate the need for the numerous planners, coordinators, and integrators no longer needed when responsibility for the complete job (or very large pieces of it) is consolidated in the hands of a single person or small team. The performer will become the most important point of contact about the work because no one knows more about it than he or she.

Consolidation needs to include assignment of support tasks such as procurement to the performing individual or team. When operations people need new pencils or software or computers, they are often better qualified to select and buy the right items than some central procurement office. The economies of scale hoped for through central purchasing ignore the costs inherent in maintaining a procurement office; they also ignore the costs of delay inherent in central procurement when compared to empowerment of performers to buy as the need arises from the local discount office supply store.

Rule 2: Be flexible. For any given task, there can be variations in complexity. Dentists, for example, have a standard process for drilling and filling teeth. Most times, the dentist's standard process is perfectly adequate, but occasionally there are complications that require extraordinary steps. For those rare occasions, the dentist needs a process that is both different and more complex. To provide another example, road crews filling in potholes also have a standard process that suits most needs, but here, too, there can be complications requiring extraordinary measures.

Neither the dentist nor the road crew would employ their extraordinary process to deal with the ordinary problem. Yet, most businesses do just that. We have developed extraordinary processes to deal with worst-case situations, and we apply the extraordinary process to all cases, including the simplest and most ordinary, just to be sure that *no* case falls outside the capabilities of the process.

When we apply for a credit card or initiate an insurance claim, we know that the actual time needed to work on our application or claim might be measured in minutes, certainly no more than an hour or so. Yet we also know that it will almost certainly be a matter of many days or (more likely) many weeks before the processing is complete. Part of the reason is the involvement of many people, which we dealt with by establishing our Rule 1: Consolidation of Work. But there is another reason why simple tasks take a long time to complete, and that is the frequent use of extraordinary processes for even the simplest and most ordinary cases. For this, we need Rule 2: Processes Need to Be Flexible.

To illustrate, most credit card applications and insurance claims are straightforward and can be dealt with using simple and standard processes and "boilerplate" paperwork. Only a small percentage of applications and claims are difficult or complicated. For these few, we may need more extended consideration, paperwork that is nonstandard, and the involvement of specialists. Thus, we need several processes, one for the easy, standard, and most usual cases; another for the unusual and somewhat more complex cases; and perhaps a third for those very rare cases that give all the headaches. Above all, we must avoid using the third process for all cases just because it is designed to deal with every possible level of difficulty. A filter of some sort is needed at the front end of the activity to sort out the various levels of difficulty, and to then shunt the work into the appropriate process.

Rule 3: Employ technology. Computers have made it possible to speed work in so many ways. We have pointed to the Phoenix Design example, where the PC and the laptop computer can compress a many week iterative design process into just a few days (and potentially just a few hours). The use of computers by DuPont to eliminate purchase orders and to make suppliers responsible for inventory management is representative of similar buyer-seller innovations undertaken across the country. The Aetna and IBM Credit examples could make use of a computer-stored library of standard form modules, easily assembled or modified through word processing to fit special needs, and of computer-conducted rapid search into credit or other history to determine rates or acceptability.

The computer can be programmed to provide instant analysis, instant information, instant advice, and an instant link to established patterns and standards. It can be used to transform generalists into specialists, and unskilled clerks into highly capable case managers.

The automobile insurer could be computer-linked to the repair shop for instant analysis of the customer's claims history, the repair shop's work history, and a comparison of the estimate with those for comparable damages; the repair shop could even send pictures to the insurance company of the damage via fax or computer modem. Adjustments or discussion between the parties could take place as necessary.

The IBM/Blockbuster example may be the most fascinating application of technology, if only for its scope and the complete transformation of a traditional business form into something wholly new.

Rule 4: Begin with the customer. No amount of reengineering will yield good results if, in the end, customers are not pleased with the outcome. Every one of the examples listed above leads to increased customer satisfaction.

One computer company, believing that its customers needed greater technical support from its sales force, poured millions of dollars into

reengineering its selling operations by providing extensive technical training and electronic backup to its sales force. At the end, it turned out that
customers made no use of the new capability. They were interested only in
the price which, ironically, was pressed upward by the misguided reengineering effort.

The lesson is clear. Before undertaking an investment in reengineering,
be sure that your customers will value the outcome.

Rule 5: Lead from the top. Reengineering requires a considerable and
sustained investment in resources, and will almost certainly lead to vast
organizational and procedural change. Cross-functional involvement and
cooperation of numbers of people and corporate activities will be required
to accomplish it. When the reengineered process has finally been defined,
some, and possibly many, existing corporate or departmental structures
and traditions will need to change as a consequence. None of this can
happen without a certain amount of resistance from the established order.
To overcome the resistance, and to assure cooperation at every level and
in every part of the company, reengineering needs to be led by a strong
and very senior person, and must have the full and visible support of the
CEO.

Rule 6: Simplify. Recently, the *Washington Post* published "Slips and
the Lisp: What Do School Administrators Do All Day?" by Elizabeth
Austin, a writer living in suburban Chicago. The article makes such a
compelling case for our urgent need to return to simplicity from foolish
and self-inflicted complexity that I cite relevant parts of it below.[14]

> My 7-year old daughter is disabled. Her disability is so
> severe that it has required the attention of a psychologist, a
> nurse, a learning disabilities specialist/team facilitator, a lan-
> guage arts specialist, two speech therapists, several Board of
> Education workers and the principal of a school she doesn't
> even attend.
>
> What sort of disability is so severe that it requires such a
> phalanx of experts? She has trouble saying the sounds *sh*, *ch*,
> *j* and *th* . . . .
>
> The district's traveling speech lady screened the second
> grade for speech problems. After listening to my daughter
> talk, she sent home a completely incomprehensible report.
> For example, my daughter's *th* was found to be "stimulable in
> the final position."

The author goes on to present a lengthy litany of bureaucratic detail. Multiple forms, numerous meetings, even a redrawn lease on the family's apartment to include the daughter's name as a renter. The article continues:

> In a final meeting, the therapist explained the (remedial) plan to me, then walked me through a six-page "Explanation of Procedural Safeguards Available to Parents of Children with Disabilities," a statement of parental rights required by the state . . . . The statement let me know that the district was required to give me 10 days of advance notice of its intentions, "in language understandable to the general public and provided in the native language or other mode of communication used by the parent," later adding: "If the native language or other mode of communication of the parent is not a written language, the State or local educational agency shall take steps to insure that the notice is translated orally or by other means to the parent in his or her native language or other mode of communication . . . ."
>
> I signed the three-page Individual Education Plan, the Notification of Multi-Disciplinary Conference/Individual Education Plan Recommendations, the Consent for Initial Special Education Placement and the form signifying that I understood my rights in these difficult cases. That covered it for me – although the speech therapist still had to fill out a 14-page form detailing my daughter's case, a task that takes an hour or two . . . ."

The most interesting (and painful) part of Ms. Austin's article is its ring of familiarity. Not only do all of us encounter such needless complexities in our dealings with bureaucracies and the law, but we encounter them in our own business organizations. Perhaps not quite as blatant, but the CYA principle, the red tape, and the hierarchy of approvals needed for the simplest things in most of our organizations would sound just as silly in the hands of a satirist of Ms. Austin's caliber.

Balance

I would urge TQM implementers to consider all important processes as candidates for reengineering. Application of the rules listed above, study of the examples, and hard thinking about wholly new ways to do things are likely to yield strikingly good results.

I also want to urge you, for two reasons, not to drop the TQM classic principle of Kaizen. First, small increments of improvement, though they yield less dramatic results, are far easier to come by; remember the Tortoise and the Hare. Second, many processes do not warrant investment in reengineering, either because they are already "world-class" or because they are of only minor importance to your business. To summarize the point, every process can benefit from the continuous small steps of improvement embodied in the Kaizen principle; only some processes merit the time and resources needed to do reengineering. Both Kaizen and reengineering should be included as elements of your TQM strategy.

11

Process Improvement Methods

Benchmarking

The search for ways to improve processes, whether by small steps through *kaizen*, or by breakthrough using *reengineering*, is all too often limited to a search through the minds of those seeking the better way. While discussion among process participants often leads to good ideas, benchmarking can lead to great ones.

Benchmarking, in the TQM context, has come to mean looking outside the immediate organization to find out how those who are best-in-class do the same thing, and then adopting the best-in-class standard as a bench-mark of excellence to be met or, better yet, exceeded. The value of benchmarking comes only in part from the insights gained directly from seeing how others do things. Its main strength comes from using the information gained from benchmarking as a stimulus to entirely new realms of thinking.

Even though I have been involved with TQM for almost a decade, every time I read another article or a new book about some aspect of TQM, or talk to others in the field (all of which is benchmarking), I learn something. Only rarely is the new insight taken directly from what I see or hear. In most cases, the new insight results from new thinking on my part that was stimulated by the different perspective gained from my encounter with the views of other people.

Benchmarking is often the most important part of the "research" that leads to process improvement or process breakthrough. Again, not neces-sarily because we learn directly "copyable" ideas, but rather because we combine our own experience and perspective with those learned through the benchmark undertaking to find a wholly new way of thinking about the process or product at hand.

Benchmarking may strike some as odious – the equivalent of business spying. To others, who see their organizations as business leaders, it may appear unseemly: leaders innovate, they don't look to see what others are doing. The opposite view is worth looking at. All businesses, particularly those that aspire to leadership or world-class status, need to be fully aware of what goes on in the world around them. Good ideas and best-in-class practices are not the sole province of any "leading" organization or of any one business category. We all need to be benchmarking all of the time to maintain excellence, because the standards of excellence rise continuously.

Benchmarking can be done in any of three different categories: functional, product, or strategic.

Functional benchmarking can often be done with organizations in fields of business entirely different from your own, because many functions are generic. To cite just a few, virtually every company has a human resources function, a strategic planning function, and an accounts payable function. No matter what business you are in, these and other generic functions will be similar to those in any other business.

For example, the human resource, strategic planning, and accounts payable departments of a company in the business of software development could benefit from benchmarking the same departments of a company in the business of making lawn mowers or selling insurance policies. Though the functions may be generic, the way they are accomplished will differ from one organization to the next. Again, directly usable ideas may or may not result from the benchmark comparisons between three such disparate companies, but software, lawn mower, and insurance companies are almost certain to have developed their human resource, strategic planning, and accounts payable functions along very different lines. Each company is likely to find its way to new thinking about these functions as a result of benchmarking interaction with the others.

Xerox Corporation has been a pioneer in the application of benchmarking to process improvement, and often proclaims its success with functional benchmarking.[1] Consider four examples:

• Xerox benchmarked cataloguing, warehousing, and warehouse picking with L. L. Bean, the Maine-based catalogue-distributor of equipment for campers and sports people.

• Xerox benchmarked inventory control with American Hospital Supply Company.

• Xerox benchmarked shipping with Caterpillar Tractor Company.

• Xerox benchmarked 24-hour telephone service response with American Express Company.

None of these benchmarked organizations had anything at all to do with making copiers, which is the primary business of Xerox. Yet the four functions that Xerox chose to benchmark are generic to many companies, and both Xerox and the benchmarked organizations benefited from the benchmark experience.

As was noted earlier, the Granite Rock Company provides what may be the most unusual example of reaching outside for benchmarking purposes. Granite Rock is in the business of providing crushed rock and cement, generally to contractors. Given the substantial cost of cement delivery trucks, delivery routing and turnaround time are two of the company's key metrics. The company sought to benchmark its delivery process with another cement company, but could find no other that measured delivery time and maintained a delivery time data base. In its search for a benchmarking partner, Granite Rock turned to Domino's Pizza, a worldwide leader in on-time delivery of a rapidly perishable product. Domino's vast data base and extensive analysis provided the basis for a continuing (and expanding) benchmark relationship (since 1990) between these two very different companies, each of whom had in common one very similar and very central operating challenge.

The most appropriate benchmark "partners" are obviously those with applicable functions that have a reputation for excellence. Both Xerox and Granite Rock made a thorough search of professional journals, professional society proceedings, and professional networks to select best-in-class partners for their benchmark undertakings.

Product benchmarking, in contrast to functional benchmarking, must be done with organizations in the same or similar businesses. Its purpose is to examine competitive or alternative products and/or services to identify best-in-class features. Again, such features only represent ways in which performance standards have been met by someone else. They aren't necessarily directly applicable to your products and services, but they should stimulate your own product-improvement ideas.

Ford undertook a product benchmarking effort in developing its Thunderbird. The effort began with identification of 357 features, ranging from power door locks to engine performance. Ford then surveyed competitive cars – generally more expensive than the Thunderbird – to identify best-in-class for each of the 357 features. With the benchmark standard in mind, the company then undertook its own design for each of the 357 features, seeking to equal or exceed the best-in-class standard, but with characteristics unique to Thunderbird. Ford met or exceeded 270 of the targeted standards. The remaining 87 were left to be worked on for incorporation into a later model.

Strategic benchmarking is a third benchmarking category. Here, one would look at strategic performance standards either for an industry or for a best-in-class practitioner.

A major airline selected key areas of its maintenance and engineering operations for comparison with four leading international competitors. The airline's managers toured the competitors' facilities, studied their organizational structures, examined their information systems, and analyzed their cost structures. After comparing their own performance to that of the international competition, the managers set new cost and productivity standards and made far-reaching strategic changes.

The State of Montana has undertaken to benchmark the state's manifold processes. One of those selected for benchmarking was the process by which Montana puts on its annual state fair. Research indicated that the best-in-class process for fair-giving was that used for the Canadian National Exposition, an annual fair in Toronto. Montana officials traveled to Toronto for the benchmark exchange, and altered their own processes accordingly.

Getting Started with Benchmarking

To start a benchmarking program, begin by drawing up a plan. Look deeply into your own organization and identify its most important functions, processes, products, and strategic considerations. Select a limited number that would be most likely to benefit from benchmarking. Then, determine specifically what it is you wish to compare: what, exactly, are you trying to find out?

The next step is to identify the organizations with which benchmarking is likely to be most beneficial. Though you may have ideas from the outset as to who the best-in-class organizations are, expand your horizons with additional research. You might begin with a search of available literature (technical/professional journals and annual reports are good sources). Supplement these findings with further research based on your involvement with trade and professional organizations and societies.

The last step in your benchmarking start-up effort is to approach the prospective benchmarking partner(s). Your proposal needs to address two things:

First, the case must be made that the prospective partner will benefit from the benchmarking interaction. Several possibilities suggest themselves:

• Offer to open your doors to them in exchange for their cooperation.

• Offer to share your analysis of their operation (everyone benefits from a well-done outside audit).

• Offer mutually beneficial business interactions as a *quid pro quo* for the benchmark exchange.

Second, you must convince the prospective benchmarking partner that you will respect the privacy and confidentiality of any exchange that might be agreed to between the partners. This will, in general, be less of a problem with companies in different lines of business. When the benchmarking partners are current or prospective competitors, there may be some important privacy and confidentiality conditions attached to the interaction. Both sides need to be sure that the arrangement protects information that either deems proprietary.

Recall that Baldrige documentation specifies "Award recipients are expected to share information about their successful quality strategies with other U.S. organizations." Much useful information about processes, products, and strategies can be exchanged without proprietary infringement. Moreover, world-class companies are almost without exception willing, and often even enthusiastic, to share information that will better the competitive position of colleagues in the business world.

The Plan-Do-Check-Act Process Improvement Cycle

Albert Einstein once remarked that his best work was 90% inspiration and only 10% perspiration! Even for lesser mortals, analysis generally benefits when the door remains open to an element of spontaneity and intuition. Granting that important point, experience nonetheless shows that Process Improvement Teams are more likely to succeed when their efforts are guided by a pattern.

The Plan-Do-Check-Act process improvement cycle, which provides such a pattern, is so well known in the TQM world that it is widely referred to as PDCA. The importance of the PDCA cycle is not its specific structure or content, but the fact that it provides a path that begins with a requirement to plan before doing, and to check before acting. The tendency for improvement teams, when left unguided, is to leap immediately into doing (inventing the improvement) and then directly into acting (implementation of the improvement), thereby ignoring altogether the planning and checking functions, without which the chance for error is high.

Consider each of the four PDCA steps.

The **plan** step should include:

Identification of the process output and establishment of baseline metrics. That is, what is the process meant to accomplish? How are results measured? What are the data results for the process as it now stands (before improvement)?

Identification of customers for the output. Who wants the output from the process? What are the customers' requirements and expectations?

Comparison of the output of the current process with customer requirements and expectations. Look for unneeded output, as well as for unmet expectations. Both yield ideas for changes that should be made to the process.

The **do** step should include:

Detailed identification of the current process. Prepare a process flow chart.

Identification of a "zero-base" process to yield the desired output. (A zero-base process is an idealized process that ignores real-world limitations, such as constraints on resources.) Prepare a process flow chart describing the zero-base process.

Compare the current process with the zero-base process. Take into account the unneeded output and unmet expectations identified during plan step one. These comparisons should provide clues on how the current process might be changed to conform to the zero-base process ideal.

Pull together benchmark information and the results of statistical process control analysis; brainstorm, and use process improvement tools to generate process improvement ideas.

The **check** step should include:

Perform a pilot run of the new process, preferably on a small and controlled basis. Monitor performance data. Compare these data with the baseline data accumulated in plan step one.

Discuss the proposed process changes with those who manage adjacent processes, with customers, and with suppliers to be sure there are no adverse impacts.

Adjust the proposed new process as required.

The **act** step should include:

Obtain formal support as necessary for the proposed change.

Formalize and implement the change.

Recycle for continuous improvement. Think about possible next steps to improve the process even farther. Bring these ideas to the attention of the Quality Management Board for future action.

The specific content of the four step PDCA cycle is less important than the fact that there is a process of some kind that includes planning and evaluation. Xerox uses a nine-step process improvement cycle which in content is almost identical to the PDCA cycle.

Kearns and Nadler, in their book about Xerox's TQM strategy, make special reference to the importance of identifying the customer and the customer's requirements. Kearns, as CEO of Xerox, attended a workshop intended to provide instruction in process improvement methods. The class was divided into teams, and each team was assigned a process to study and improve. Kearns' team picked operations reviews, a process used by Xerox top management to review periodically (as often as monthly) the performance of Xerox units. The process was deemed ineffective; neither top management nor unit managers were satisfied with the results.

In reviewing the process, Kearns' team addressed the question of who was the customer for the reviews. They came to the breakthrough realization that the process' customer was not top management (which had always been the assumption) but rather unit management. Top management was the supplier, responsible for supplying guidance to unit managers. Thus, top management needed to ask their unit management customers how the operations reviews needed to be changed to satisfy the needs of the unit managers. This undertaking provided the basis for changes to the process and improvements in its effectiveness.

GE Work-Out

"Work-Out" is the name given to a process improvement strategy originated by General Electric in 1989.[2] By 1991, it had become so widely used that more than an eighth of its total workforce had been involved in at least one Work-Out session. Work-Out is a three-day give-and-take forum with two primary objectives: to solve problems and to take unnecessary work out of jobs. The second goal is achieved either by removing "administrivia" and other non-value-added work, or by process restructuring.

Work-Out sessions are generally chartered by management (though they can be proposed by anyone in the organization). Management selects the 40 to 100 participants for each session (sometimes including suppliers and customers). On the morning of the first day, the manager initiates the session by outlining its agenda. Following this, however, management withdraws from the process until the group's recommendations are ready for management review.

Work-Out participants, guided by an outside facilitator, break up into five or six teams to deal with various parts of the agenda. The teams work for 1½ days to develop recommendations, and an additional half day to prepare a presentation. The manager then returns on the afternoon of day three to hear recommendations from each team. For each recommendation made, the boss must give one of three responses on the spot: acceptance, rejection, or a request for additional study or information. Should the manager call for additional study or information of any of the recommendations made by the Work-Out group, he is obligated by the Work-Out rules to assign responsibility then and there for the additional work, and to designate a date-certain for its completion.

Responsibility for Process Improvement

The best assurance of success for process improvement efforts is to assign responsibility and accountability to the Process Improvement Teams. Only when the teams undertaking the improvement effort think of the process as theirs can they be expected to take the aggressive and responsible actions that lead to best outcome.

Identification of PITs as owners of their process not only results in a more serious-minded process improvement effort, but it is also one of the most important components of work force empowerment. When management reserves for itself the right to review and judge PIT recommendations, and to challenge the bases for PIT conclusions, the stage is set for loss of interest, lack of rigor, and third-rate results.

This is not to say that management is out of the process improvement loop. Chapter 9, which addressed the TQM management infrastructure, described the role of Quality Management Boards in process improvement. QMB members, who are mid-level and lower-level managers, decide which processes are to be reviewed and improved, designate PIT members, and write the PIT charter, specifying the objectives of the process improvement effort. But having taken these steps, the QMBs then need to back away and give the PIT freedom to do its job without second-guessing from the QMB. The QMB is entirely free to call for periodic briefings from the PIT, to attend PIT meetings (as members, not bosses), and to provide inputs and guidance to the PIT as work proceeds. But responsibility for outcome needs to remain assigned to the PIT.

When management says to the PIT, "We will accept whatever you come up with," the PIT is obliged to take the effort seriously; its pride and reputation are on the line. These are the conditions that lead to determined effort and good outcome.

12

SPC, Six-Sigma, and All That

Statistical Process Control [1,2]

Statistical Process Control, known widely as SPC, is useful for analysis of repetitive processes. Manufacturing processes that produce continuing streams of like products are good candidates for the application of SPC, as are repetitive administrative operations such as processing bills, purchase orders, and payroll actions, and white collar "production" activities such as processing insurance claims.

Though SPC is applicable only to repetitive processes, it should be emphasized that the frequency of repetition can be low. Process cycle time might be very short (fractions of a second) for some manufacturing operations, but it can be long (days or weeks) for some administrative processes (or even for certain manufacturing processes). Whether cycle time is long or short, the same SPC principles apply. However, SPC has little if any value in analysis of processes that are used only once, and then changed for the next application.

Though SPC can get complex in certain special situations, most applications are simple, and the concepts are straightforward. There are numerous texts available describing SPC, and I don't propose here to get into the details; readers who need them will want to consult the available technical literature. For our current discussion, however, it is useful to say a few words on what SPC is, and how it serves to help us in our analysis of processes. In all my reading of SPC texts, this big picture story is often not told at all, and I have not seen it told concisely in a way both useful and comprehensible to the executive-level implementer. The following should serve to fill in what other texts leave out.

SPC begins with something known as a *control chart* (figure 12-1), where the output from a process is posted. Let's say we're making car doors, and the specified height of the door is 44.40". We measure the first door that comes from the manufacturing process, and it measures 44.44". The second door measures 44.46". The third measures 44.36". And so on. These measurements are posted on the control chart.

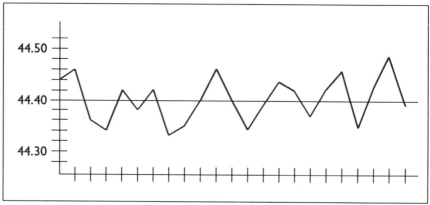

Figure 12-1: Control Chart

We can say two things about this or any other control chart. First, since processes are rarely perfect, the measurements of process output will always vary somewhat from the desired or specified level. Our purpose in process improvement must be to reduce variation, for it is the enemy of quality.

Second, the variation in process output will be random: that is, we cannot tell from the first three or three hundred measurements what the fourth or 301st measurement will be. Random variation is an important concept, and it applies to any repetitive operation, whether we are manufacturing a product or processing salary actions or insurance claims.

Once 20 data points are posted on the control chart, we can use the information from them to compute a value known to statisticians as the three-sigma value, but known in SPC parlance as the upper control level and the lower control level, or more simply as UCL and LCL. (Statisticians require a minimum of 20 data points as the basis for calculating UCL and LCL. Fewer than 20 gives unreliable results.)

There are several formulas to compute UCL and LCL. While each is simple, requiring no more than 8th grade math, the choice of which formula to use and the added complication of sampling constants require a complexity of understanding disruptive to our discussion of concepts and application. Readers requiring such an understanding will want to consult one of the many available SPC texts – though it might be noted that SPC implementers rarely do their own UCL/LCL calculations. Most make use of one of the many easy-to-use and inexpensive software packages available for that purpose.

Having computed UCL and LCL, we can post them on our control chart (figure 12-2), and thereby create a powerful tool for process analysis. The potency of this display chart as an analytical tool comes from a statistical fact: 99.7% of all data points reflecting the output of any process will fall between the UCL and LCL as long as the process remains unchanged and undisturbed – or, as statisticians put it, stable and in control. Random variation within the confines of the UCL/LCL boundaries is known as common cause variation.

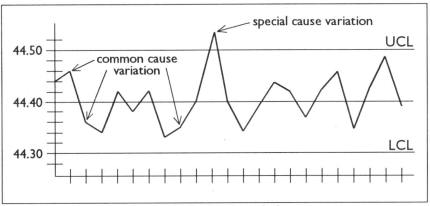

Figure 12-2: SPC Control Chart

Since, for a process stable and in control, only 3 data points out of every 1,000 will fall outside the UCL or LCL, it is likely that whenever a data point does fall outside these boundaries, it will indicate that the process has gone out of control. We call such data points *special cause variation*.

Process analysts regard special cause events as messages from God, since they provide an opportunity to improve the process. The analyst must examine the process to see what the process conditions were at the time the special cause event occurred, and change the process in a way that will inhibit that adverse condition from happening again.

In the case of the car door example, consider that the stamping operation involves a number of process conditions (technical parameters), such as pressures, angles, voltages, and speed. For the "standard" process to produce doors with dimensions within the UCL/LCL boundaries, the pressures, angles, voltages, and speeds need to be within certain specified levels. We would suspect that when the process yields a "special cause" outcome (outside the UCL/LCL boundaries), one or more of the process conditions might have gone out of standard. If our examination of process conditions shows one of the conditions to have been out of standard at the time the special cause event occurred, we have identified where we need to improve the process to avoid a repetition of that outcome. If a pressure anomaly caused the special cause event, for example, we need to work on the process to stabilize pressure to keep these anomalies from happening again.

If every time we have a special cause event we examine the process conditions that prevailed at the time, we gradually tighten down on the process, making it more and more stable and less and less likely to produce an anomalous or special cause outcome.

Every time the process is improved, after new process outcome data points are measured and posted, random variation is reduced, and the earlier values of UCL and LCL are no longer applicable. Process output values, though they will still vary randomly from the desired value, will converge increasingly to the desired value with each successive improvement (tightening) of the process. After 20 new process outcome data points are posted, new values of UCL and LCL can be computed. (Remember that statisticians require at least 20 data points to have the necessary confidence in UCL/LCL values.) Every time the process is improved, UCL and LCL will move closer to the desired output value.

One additional concept needs to be advanced. Processes have not only process parameters (UCL and LCL), but also what might be termed *product* parameters, upper and lower specification levels (USL and LSL). Thus, for the car door, calculated values of UCL and LCL were 44.50" and 44.30". Assume that, for the specification value of 44.40", the specified tolerance is plus or minus 0.10". Thus, for this particular case, the values of UCL and LCL correspond exactly to the values of USL and LSL.

Process Capability

For every process, a value known as Process Capability, or Cp, can be computed. Cp = (specification limits) divided by (process limits), or (USL − LSL) /(UCL − LCL). For the car door case just described, where the values of UCL and LCL are the same as USL and LSL, respectively, where both are symmetrical about the specified value, and where the average process output value is the same as the specified product value (39.40"), the value of Cp is 1. Since we know that 99.7% of all data points will fall between the UCL and LCL boundaries, and since in this case the USL and LSL boundaries are coincident with UCL and LCL, we can see that for a process with a process capability (Cp) of 1, only about 3 data points out of a thousand will fall outside USL and LSL.

Six-Sigma Quality

Consider a process capability of 2, also known as a six-sigma process. Six-sigma processes (Cp = 2) have an error rate of about 3 parts per million (3.4, to be exact), about 1,000 times better than the three-sigma processes (Cp = 1) we considered in the car door example. The three-sigma processes, you'll recall, have an error rate of about 3 parts per thousand (2.7, to be exact).

Six-sigma quality levels are important today because they have become a kind of world standard. Motorola led the way to six-sigma by committing itself several years ago to that high standard. Increasing numbers of American organizations have made or are making six-sigma the goal for their process improvement efforts.

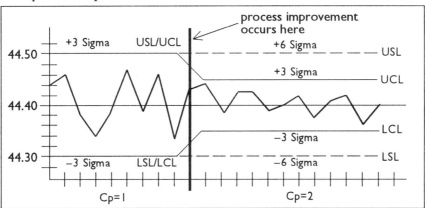

Figure 12-3: Understanding Six-Sigma.
$Cp=(USL-LSL) \div (UCL-LCL)$. *Cp=width of car door÷width of car.*

Figure 12-3 depicts a six-sigma process. Notice that the quantity USL-LSL is twice as large as the quantity UCL-LCL. Consequently, Cp = 2. To understand the six-sigma concept, ignore for the moment the USL and LSL lines. We are left with a three-sigma process, where, as always, about 3 data points out of 1,000 will fall outside the UCL/LCL boundaries. Most of those special cause data points will fall inside the USL/LSL boundaries, and therefore will be within spec (within acceptable tolerance levels) even though they fall outside process bounds. For the depicted process, only 3.4 data points out of a million will fall outside the USL/ LSL boundaries.

Motorola describes the six-sigma process in another, even simpler, way. Consider the USL/LSL boundaries as a garage door (spec width), and the UCL/LCL boundaries as a car (process width). When the car (process) is about the same width as the door (spec), we can barely get through, and the chances of scraping the sides are high. When the door (spec) is twice the width of the car (process), only very rarely would we scrape the side. That, says Motorola, is the advantage of a six-sigma process, where the process yields only half the variation allowed by the specification.

The importance of a six-sigma process is evident when we consider the real-world situation of a product composed of many parts. Take the example of a product containing 500 parts, each coming from a process with a capability of 1 (Cp = 1). Each part would have 2.7 defects per thousand. Thus, the 500 part product would have a defect rate of 1.35 defects per unit (500 x 0.0027) on an average. A defect rate of that high level would be unacceptable for virtually any product. If, on the other hand, the 500 part product consisted entirely of parts built to six-sigma quality standards (3.4 defects per million), the 500 part product would have 0.0017 defects per unit (500 x 0.0000034). Such a defect level would be acceptable for most products.

Taguchi Loss Function

Genichi Taguchi, a Japanese quality "guru," and winner of the Deming prize in 1960, was dissatisfied with the simplistic emphasis on meeting

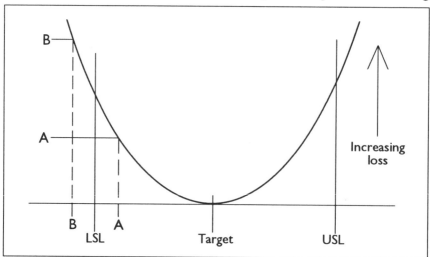

Figure 12-4: Taguchi Loss Function

specifications. Taguchi expressed his concern by constructing the parabolic curve shown in figure 12-4, with which he was able to make an interesting point. Suppose that a part is manufactured and it measures at the low end of the spec tolerance (value A). Now we make the same part again, and it measures just a bit less (value B). Value A is just inside the spec tolerance, while value B is just outside. By definition, value A is acceptable and value B is unacceptable even though the two values are virtually identical.

Taguchi expressed his concern about this simplistic outcome by projecting values A and B onto the parabolic curve that he identified as the Loss Function. Viewed in this way, the only process-output value that would have zero loss would be the target value. Value A, as projected onto the loss curve, results in a certain loss. Value B, also projected onto the loss curve, results in a slightly higher loss than value A. Viewed in the context of their compliance with spec tolerance limits, A was acceptable and B was unacceptable. Viewed in the context of their respective "loss" value, neither A nor B is acceptable; only the target value or something very close to it is acceptable. Taguchi has said that his loss function expresses "loss to society."

The Ford Motor Company once made a movie that lent important credibility to the Loss Function concept. The movie documented the manufacture of Ford transmissions in a plant in Batavia, Ohio. The same transmissions were also being made for Ford in a Mazda plant in Japan. Over time, it became apparent that unacceptably high numbers of the Batavia-built transmissions were breaking down after a time in customer cars, while those built in Japan remained reliable. Yet, the transmissions from Ohio and Japan were exactly the same – the same drawings, same specs, same materials.

The Batavia operation was, of course, deeply concerned. Japanese built transmissions were brought to Batavia for analysis. Units were disassembled and parts were measured with great precision. It soon became apparent that parts from the Japanese-built units uniformly measured at or very close to the target value. On the other hand, while parts from the Batavia-built units measured within spec, many measured at the outer edges of spec tolerance. The Japanese had worked on their manufacturing processes, and had reduced variation to very low levels.

Analysis showed that operational difficulties from the Batavia-built units resulted from *tolerance-stack-up*. When shafts, for example, were at the outer edge of the allowed spec limit, and the holes they fit into were at the inner edge, tight fit and binding would result and, over time, wear would cause breakdown. Some who viewed the Ford movie argued that the problem could have been resolved by adjusting the spec tolerances. Possibly, but Taguchi's point remains nonetheless valid: as you approach the outer edges of spec tolerance, "loss to society" inevitably increases.

The outcome at Ford was that the Batavia plant worked on its processes, reduced variation, and began delivering transmissions with the same lifetime reliability that had been achieved at the Japanese Mazda plant.

13

Customer Obsession

CARE: Customers Are Really Everything

Use of the term *obsession* in the title of this chapter is intended to convey the depths of my conviction on the subject. Customers are more than important, they really are everything.

Without customers, there is no business. From that simple truth, it follows that the very purpose of business must be to gain a profound understanding of customer requirements and expectations, and do everything necessary to meet and, if possible, exceed them.

A simple device for learning customer requirements and expectations is to put yourself in the customer's shoes. Barbara Sobel did that.[1] As Director of the Human Resources Administration for New York City, Sobel wanted to see how her "customers," those who apply for assistance, were being treated. Dressed in worn-out clothes, and posing as a poor and needy person, Sobel went to an HRA office to apply for assistance. The long lines, disinterested and inattentive personnel, and endless forms to which she was subjected became grist for her reformist mill.

Tom Peters reports a story about Milliken, a 1989 Baldrige Award winner.[2] The marketing manager, wanting to know more about customer requirements for Milliken floor coverings, went to a local hospital that used Milliken's products and asked to work for a time with the custodians responsible for floor-cleaning. After two weeks of mopping, sweeping, vacuuming, and washing Milliken's floor coverings, his understanding of customer requirements and expectations was raised to new levels. Having for the first time seen Milliken products from the point of view of the users, the manager was able both to adjust his marketing strategy and to suggest technical changes to the products. Through real-world involvement with his product, the manager learned things that simply aren't available to desk-bound executives.

The Doctors, a movie starring William Hurt, is similarly instructive. Hurt plays the part of a successful physician, always splendidly dressed, totally confident, ever in control, with a beautiful house, luxury car, and lovely wife. His patients, sick, bristling with tubes and needles, fearful, bedridden, with little understanding of either their illness or the treatment being administered, wearing hospital gowns that expose their backsides, are a weak and sorry lot compared to the strong and handsome physician. The story then takes a dramatic turn as the doctor is himself struck with severe illness. As a patient in his own hospital, he finds himself subject to the same indignities and uncertainties visited upon the other patients. The result? Having gained a firsthand understanding of patients' requirements and expectations, the doctor is transformed. Following his recovery, he becomes a gentle and caring physician, doing everything possible for his patient's peace of mind and dignity. As a senior physician, he establishes a policy requiring all interns to undergo a period as patients so that they, too, learn firsthand the same lessons.

By awarding 300 points out of a total of 1,000 to Category 7, "Customer Focus and Satisfaction," Baldrige documentation pays implicit tribute to the overriding importance of customers relative to other business considerations. The other six Baldrige categories, each extremely important in its own way, collectively add up to only 700 points in the Baldrige scoring system.

The criteria listed in Baldrige Category 7 provide a good framework for development of a comprehensive strategy aimed at determining, understanding, and fully satisfying customer requirements and expectations:

- Customer expectations: current and future

- Customer relationship management

- Commitment to customers

- Customer satisfaction determination

- Customer satisfaction comparison

Customer Expectations: Current and Future

Determination and understanding of customer requirements and expectations begins with identification of customer groups , and acknowledgment that each group might have unique requirements and expectations. Not all customers are the same. Your products and services need to be tailored accordingly.

How a business categorizes its various customer groups can have an important impact on the resulting estimate of their needs and expectations. Tregoe, Zimmerman, Smith, and Tobia, in their book *Vision in Action*,[3] describe a tractor company that had been segmenting its customers by geography. Though there were some differences between the needs of tractor customers from different geographic areas, the overall outcome of geographic segmentation was predictably unimaginative. When the tractor company changed to segmentation by customer user groups, such as grassland, wheat farmers, and dairy farmers, its understanding of customer needs deepened. Further segmentation of each category led to a still more profound understanding of needs. Segmentation of the grassland category, for instance, led to identification of markets not previously identified: golf courses, schoolyards, parks, cemeteries, and grass along highways.

Another example of the power of segmentation of customers into different categories described in *Vision in Action* is a bank that initially categorized its customers simply into consumer, commercial, and government. Additional segmentation of the consumer category into recently married, married with children, married with grown children, and single, led to better understanding of customer needs. When the bank took segmentation still farther, grouping each customer category by age, income, and education, understanding of customer needs and expectations deepened even more.

In addition to profiling groups of its own customers, every business should seek to profile the customers of competitors. What is there about the needs and expectations of this group that causes them to be drawn to your competitor? What is it about your offerings that has failed to attract them? What might you do to your products and services, or to your marketing methods, to win the business of this important group?

Identifying and profiling customer groups is only the first step. The next and more difficult step is to identify the needs and expectations of each group. Ways to do this include questionnaires, telephone surveys, personal visits, and focus groups. Each of these, particularly personal visits and focus groups, can be effective.

tant requirement is to develop some format that will bring
tain a continuing and easy dialogue with customers. Com-
just with customers with whom you have a successful
relationship, but also those with whom your relationship is uneasy or even
hostile. Messages from this latter group may be among the more important ones for you to get.

To gain insights into customer needs and expectations, Boride Products, a ceramics division of Dow Chemical, has created an annual Customer Appreciation Day. Customers are invited to one day of discussion
of the company's plans and ways in which products and services can be
improved. A second day is spent "bonding" with customers on sailboats
and on the golf course. Discussions during the first day, and even to some
extent on the second day, result in deepened understanding both of
customer requirements and in how those requirements can be better
satisfied.

Lexus U.S., the luxury car distributor, requires every executive to call
one randomly-selected customer each day to gain insights into requirements and expectations. The continuing dialogue has proven to be an
effective mechanism for increased understanding of customer needs and
expectations.

Motorola has established "Customer Champions" whose operating
philosophy is that, in order for Motorola to understand the customer's
requirements, it must understand the requirements of the customer's
customer. The Customer Champions serve as Motorola's ambassadors to
important customers. When the customer's have questions, comments, or
complaints, their designated Customer Champion is responsible for re-
solving any problems and for bringing the customer's comments and
concerns to the attention of those in the organization who can use the
information to improve Motorola's operations, products, or services.

Focus groups are an effective means for gaining deeper understanding
of customer requirements. I have by pure happenstance taken part in two
focus groups, both managed by a local marketing organization. The first,
sponsored by an unidentified motel chain, was a two-part activity. It
began with an unsolicited call from the marketing organization asking if I
traveled on business. My affirmative answer led to an invitation to join a
focus group which was to take only one evening, and for which I was to
receive a small honorarium and dinner. The offer seemed interesting, so I
agreed.

On the appointed evening, members of the focus group (there were
about 10 of us) began with a tour of several model motel rooms set up
side-by-side in a large open area. Each of us was separately asked to

comment on various features in each room, and at the end to give an overall appraisal. We were then placed around a conference table, and spent the next hour or so in intense discussion about the things that were important to us about motels.

I was later asked by the same marketing organization to join another focus group to discuss banking from the customer's point of view. My conclusion about the focus group format is that it was, in each case, powerfully effective. People in the group interacted in synergistic and imaginative ways with one another, guided by a skilled facilitator. In both cases, the proceedings were videotaped for later analysis.

Still another technique for gaining insight into customers needs and expectations comes from a matrix method used by a large paper company, among others. The process begins with a questionnaire (figure 13-1) in which customers are asked to score the paper company on a number of attributes (eight, in this case): on-time delivery, product quality, price, and so forth. The questionnaire then asks customers for a rating of the paper company's competitors against the same attributes. Finally, the questionnaire asks the customer to rate each attribute as to its relative importance.

Attribute	Cust. Rtg. of Company	Cust. Rtg. of Competition	Competitive Advantage	Importance
1. On-time delivery	8	7	+1	10
2. Product quality	10	8	+2	10
3. Price	10	8	+2	7
4. Lead-time	7	8	-1	7
5. Attitude	8	10	-2	8
6. Sales Representation	8	7	+1	9
7. Technical Support	8	9	-1	9
8. Billing Accuracy	7	9	-2	10

Figure 13-1: Measurement of Customer Satisfaction

When the paper company receives the filled-out questionnaires, it completes each one by noting the difference between the score that it received for each of the attributes and the score its competitor(s) received. That difference is posted on the form in the column labeled "Competitive Advantage."

The completed sets of questionnaires are aggregated, the quantities are averaged, and a matrix (figure 13-2) is assembled to portray the results in a way that invites action. The bottom right quadrant of the matrix, you may guess, is the area of special interest for our paper company. The attributes posted in that quadrant are the ones that score high in impor-tance and low in competitive advantage. Action is needed on these attributes (technical support and billing accuracy, in this case) to raise them from competitive disadvantage to competitive advantage.

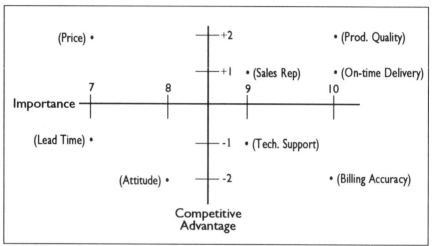

Figure 13-2: Matrix Ranking of Customer Satisfaction Parameters

A special effort needs to be made to be sure that customers' future needs are identified, as distinct from their current needs. Changes are constantly taking place. Technological, cultural, economic, and demo-graphic factors are ever changing. Though it is generally difficult to forecast the future with precision, every producer of goods and services needs to peer as far into the future as possible to determine the potential effect of these changes on customer needs and expectations, and upon the producer's need to satisfy them. Action is needed as early as possible to conform the producer's products and services to the expected evolution of customer requirements.

Customer Relationship Management

Customer's don't just buy a product or service. They also buy a host of less tangible things that can be summed as "relationship." They buy prompt delivery; courtesy; accurate billing; attractive packaging; environ-mental responsibility; integrity and ethics; prompt, accurate, and cheerful response to future inquiries; understandable descriptive literature and user manuals; reliable supply of parts; and ready source of maintenance and repair at reasonable cost. The customer is buying, not just a product, but a relationship to support effective use of the product.

Customer relationship management is sometimes thought of as the "warm and fuzzy" aspect of customer interaction. The listing in the preceding paragraph should dispel that "PR" impression. Customer relations is about substance, not about fuzz. It is as important a part of customer satisfaction as the product itself. Perhaps even more so, because its impact is sustained over a longer period of time, and involves more personal interaction.

Management of customer relations begins with the identification of key components such as those just listed. For each component, standards must be set, responsibilities assigned, and a strategy devised for implementation.

The company must provide easy-to-use mechanisms for the customer to obtain information, deliver comments, and complain. Customer comments should be seen for what they truly are: a goldmine of suggestions and ideas for improvement of products, services, and relationships. No one likes criticism, and, when we hear it, the tendency is to respond in ways designed to pacify the critic rather than to elicit further details that might lead to new thinking and breakthrough improvement.

The requirement here is for the company to consolidate comments and criticism, analyze them for important and actionable ideas, follow-up to get further information if needed, and provide the aggregated and actionable information to those in the company in a position to use it as a basis for improvement. Special effort should be made to respond to customers who took the time and trouble to tell you what was on their minds, including your expression of gratitude for their input.

Because not everyone is endowed with an equal ability to succeed in customer-contact positions, special effort needs to be made to hire appropriate people into those positions. They need to possess an interest in others, empathy for the (often contrary) views of others, and readiness to accept (even to welcome) criticism of the company and its products, knowing that such criticism is the necessary basis for improvement. The career path for such people needs to be designed to demonstrate that customer-contact positions are important and can lead to important management or other desirable positions in the company.

Customer contact personnel need to be given special training in the areas of company products and plans to make them effective representatives of the company in their customer interactions. They need to be schooled in the techniques of listening, of soliciting information, and of "mollifying" and pacifying irate customers in ways designed to retain their business. They need to understand that doing these things, and doing them effectively and cheerfully, is among the most important work in the company.

Customer contact personnel need to be fully empowered to take whatever action they deem necessary to perform their job to the fullest. That is, without on-the-job guidance or permission, they need to be empowered to get information, resolve problems, and draw upon and coordinate company units to help with the problem or to bring about needed improvements.

Commitment to Customers

When people buy something, whether for themselves, personally, or on behalf of their companies, they seek to minimize risk. Knowing this, there is hardly a business today that fails to offer some kind of guarantee or warranty arrangement. "Your money back if not fully satisfied" is pledged by virtually every magazine subscription, department store, and catalog retailer. Though most producers of industrial goods and services are somewhat less generous, full replacement of defective products or, at a minimum, repair of defects for an extended period has become the norm for American business.

Generous guarantees are a relatively recent phenomenon. Only recently, major consumer items were guaranteed for relatively short periods of time, if at all. Today, our car manufacturers, for example, routinely offer two-year and often three- or four-year full guarantees, something unheard of a few years ago. Overseas competition forced our automobile and other manufacturers to this new and highly desirable state of affairs. But it is the advent of TQM-inspired quality strategies that have made such extended guarantees technically and financially possible. Things last longer now and are far more reliable during their usage cycle than before.

TQM implementers need to look across the full line of their product and service offerings to determine the adequacy of guarantees and warranties. Customers need to think of their purchase from you as a risk-free arrangement. You will want to be sure that appropriate guarantees and warranties are in place.

Customer Satisfaction Determination

Methods used to determine customer satisfaction are much the same as those used for determination of customer requirements and expectations, earlier described. Questionnaires, telephone surveys, personal visits, and focus groups are all useful. Again, personal visits and focus groups are often the best ways.

The customer satisfaction questionnaire or discussion needs to be designed with two goals in mind. The first is that it should be consistent from one time to the next, and should lead to quantifiable results so that data can be aggregated and trends monitored. Second, it should ask not only about the customer's level of satisfaction, but must also ask why. Knowing that a customer is satisfied or dissatisfied without knowing the reason is an exercise in frustration and futility.

Inquiries about customer satisfaction need to be tailored to the particular customer and the particular product or service. Though you will want inquiry formats to be as similar as possible for easy aggregation and cross-comparison, it is possible, even likely, that the formats will differ somewhat for the various customer categories (segments and groups) and various products.

To design the inquiry format in ways that will elicit a maximum amount of reliable information, you will want to be as knowledgeable as possible about how the customer uses your product, and your inquiry needs to parallel that usage. At good approach, therefore, is to convene a focus group of typical customers and ask them to help you design the format.

Notes appended to Baldrige criterion 7.4 state that:

> An effective (actionable) customer satisfaction measurement system is one that provides the company with reliable information about customer ratings of specific product and service features and the relationship between these ratings and the customer's likely market behavior.

Directly or indirectly, you will want to gain not only a rating for your product, but some insight into the reasons for the rating and what purchase actions the customer is likely to take based on his rating.

Another word of advice: make it easy, even inviting and interesting for the customer(s) to respond. Everyone has received long and often dreary questionnaires seeking our ratings and comments on products or services we have bought. Often, telephone calls come just as dinner or the evening news begins. Intrusive and untimely inquiries stiffen resistance, and the resulting answers are reluctant, hurried, and probably of little value. A few cooperative sessions are more useful than many reluctant ones.

Some companies have found that a persuasive letter accompanying the questionnaire can improve both the rate and the quality of responses. The letter needs to explain why responding is ultimately in the customer's best interests: "When we know your needs, we can serve you better." Another good device is to promise a donation to charity for every response received.

When employees leave a company, most personnel departments conduct exit interviews to see what can be learned about the reasons for voluntary termination. You might think about doing the same for customers that voluntarily terminate their relationship with your company. Why are they going to the competitor's product or service? What might you have done to hold them? After some time has passed, a follow-up discussion asking how they like the competitor's product or service, and telling of the adjustments you have made to your offering that warrants their return to your fold, might be of value.

Dissatisfaction indicators are often the richest sources of actionable information about customer attitudes. Among such indicators are complaints, claims, refunds, recalls, litigation, repairs, and misshipments. Each dissatisfaction indicator is an invitation to a "please don't leave us" interview, or an exit interview if that unhappy outcome has already occurred.

On the other hand, when *new* customers are won, an "entrance interview" might be a good idea. What caused them to turn to your company's offering? Now that they have begun to use your offering, what do they think of it? What must you do to keep them as customers?

When products or services are sold through intermediaries, there is often a difference between the satisfaction ratings (as well as the requirements and expectations) of the intermediary and end user. Needless to say, in that event, the requirements and the ratings of both are important and need to be learned and accommodated.

I can't leave the subject of customer satisfaction determination without recalling a wry comment on the subject from Dr. Deming. As a guest in a hotel, Deming found the usual questionnaire. There were, he said, 48 questions, to which he added a 49th. Q. What do you think of our coat hangars? A. Not much. Whereupon Deming received a letter from the manager saying that he didn't like them either, and promised to change them. He did, at a cost of $20 each for 500 rooms.

Customer Satisfaction Comparison

Benchmarking your customer satisfaction findings with those of competitors and alternative suppliers is important. To be fully useful, comparisons should be made by customer group, product line, and product features. Trends are important indicators; if you are gaining on your competitor, you're probably on the right track. If the reverse applies, questions need to be asked and actions need to be taken to counter adverse trends.

Kansei

The Japanese word *kansei* means "to take to perfection," or "to complete." Guided by the kansei philosophy, Japanese producers strive to move beyond mere customer satisfaction to customer delight and excitement. The idea is that with TQM, high quality will routinely lead to customer satisfaction. To leapfrog competitors, producers will need to provide products and services that go beyond satisfaction to the higher realm of customer delight and excitement.

Happily, examples from American producers are all around. Dodge/Plymouth vans introduced an optional built-in infant's safety seat that helped to set their vans apart from competitor's vans. Reebok developed pump-up sport shoes to distinguish its product and to delight and excite its customers; Reebok followed the pump-up feature with a recent announcement that its Telos shoe will be made of 70% recycled materials. A local jewelry store provides no-cost annual cleaning of customer's jewelry. A dentist offers patients high-fidelity earphones and a choice of music while the work is going on. The Oldsmobile Bravado, a four-wheel drive vehicle, provides a compass built into the rear view mirror. Biojector has developed a needle-less hypodermic injector. Great Plains Software, upon routing customer calls to customer service representatives, simultaneously provides its representatives with a computer screen display listing hardware and software owned by the customer, along with a history of previous calls. Similar information is displayed when calls are received from the company's "partners:" resellers, installers, and software developers associated with the company. American Express offers air mileage redeemable through a number of cooperating airlines to its credit card customers (one mile for every dollar charged) as a way to distinguish its card from competitors. Smith-Kline-Beecham Pharmaceuticals modified its delivery crates to make them useful for other purposes by customers. A Saturn automobile dealer in Louisiana offers a free customer maintenance clinic one Saturday a month. While the clinic is being conducted, the customers are treated to barbecued hot dogs and soft drinks.

A couple of German innovations are interesting. On some BMWs, when you shift into reverse, the passenger side mirror tilts down so the driver can see the curb. On the S-class Mercedes, standard side mirrors fold in so the car can fit into tight parking spaces, and the rear headrests can automatically fold down to give the driver an unobstructed view.

The list of kansei examples could go on, but these few examples serve to illustrate the idea. Every producer of goods and services needs to ask what added feature (or entirely new product) might lift its offerings from "satisfyers" to "exciters and delighters."

The search for kansei ideas needs to be endless and it needs to be systematic. Today's kansei offering, if the customer likes it, will be tomorrow's standard feature as competitors swiftly find a way to meet and exceed your feature.

Finding and Filling a Niche

Customer's are always sending messages, and we're often too busy "running the business" to listen. One small company began a boating equipment mail-order business. In the back of the catalog, as a kind of afterthought, a modest amount of camping equipment, rain gear, moccasins and other outdoor items was included. To everyone's surprise, the apparel items attracted more orders than the boating equipment. The company, known from the start as Lands' End, listened to its customers, and now sells in excess of $650 million each year of what began as an afterthought!

Southern Audio Services began as a producer of home audio speakers; the first year gross was a modest $11,000. A local retailer forecast an uphill battle in this already crowded market, and suggested that Southern Audio enter a niche market. During the ensuing discussion, the idea of speakers especially designed for pickup trucks came up. Within a few weeks, Southern Audio had built and tested a prototype. The product became a best seller. In the eight years since, sales have doubled each year, reaching $6 million in 1992.

Fletcher Music Centers, a Florida retailer of pianos and organs, was doing business primarily with retirees. Fletcher began to realize that its business was more than simply selling pianos and organs. To serve its unique clientele fully, it needed to meet its customer's physical and social needs as well as their musical ones. Fletcher began selling organs with oversized print and controls. No-cost music lessons are offered as a social event. Fletcher's sales have doubled despite a general decline in the organ market.

Gary Hamel and C.K. Prahalad, in an article in the *Harvard Business Review*, put it this way:

> There are three kinds of companies: those that simply ask customers what they want, and end up as perpetual followers; those that succeed, for a time, in pushing customers where

they do not want to go; and those that lead customers where they want to go before they know it themselves.[4]

Dedication to the principles set forth in this chapter, including kansei, are the means by which companies can join the elite group of those that "lead customers to where they want to go before they know it themselves."

Internal Customers

Our discussion (and the Baldrige criteria) has focused entirely on the relationship of companies with external customers. TQM, however, prescribes a focus on internal customers, as well. Most members of the work force rarely, if ever, encounter an external customer. Yet every member of the organization is continuously interacting with internal customers.

Internal customer/supplier relationships are always in flux. The people in manufacturing are customers of the people in engineering in the sense that engineering provides drawings and specifications that manufacturing uses to do its work. At the same time, the people in engineering are customers of manufacturing when they await prototypes and change requests. Similarly, the manager is a supplier of work and resources to the secretary, and the secretary supplies the manager with typing, filing, and other services.

This notion of internal customers emphasizes the obvious need for cooperation and mutual support within the organization. Everyone working in an organization of more than one person has internal customers and is, in turn, an internal customer. Our job, as a supplier of services and support to people at the next desk or in the next department, is to gain the best possible understanding of their requirements and to do everything possible to satisfy them. Sound familiar? Of course. These are the same admonitions that apply to the company's relationship to its external customers.

One of the complaints I hear most often from traditional (pre-TQM) companies is that the various departments do not work in harmony. Each thinks the others are bloated with resources and inadequate in support. Don Petersen, former CEO of Ford, commented on this in his book, and suggested that internal customer/supplier relationships be fortified by bringing departments together to work it out.[5] His advice is to assemble, in one large room, representatives from each department, placing those from each department at a separate round table. Each table is given some time to assemble its concerns about the other departments and to put together a list of recommendations to improve upon those concerns. Each group is then asked to make a presentation of its concerns and recommendations. Finally, a full-group discussion takes place, facilitated by the CEO. Action items are generated and recorded for follow-up.

14

The Public Sector Challenge

Contrast

As documented in this book and elsewhere, the quality movement is strong in the United States private sector. Companies all over America are developing TQM strategies, and large numbers of them have become first-rate practitioners. World-class implementation, which once took 5-10 years, is now being done far more rapidly because of the many benchmarks and the vast amount of sharing and expert instruction available to new entrants. AT&T Universal Card became a 1992 Baldrige winner only three years after start-up.

Private sector productivity is rising in every part of our economy. For many of our companies, quality has risen to world-class levels. Market share lost during the 1980's to overseas competitors is being reclaimed. Much of this success is directly attributable to the widespread and effective implementation of TQM.

By contrast, our public sector TQM movement has been less successful. The President's Award (which, as noted earlier, is the federal public sector equivalent of the Baldrige Award) has been around since 1989, and, in 1990 and 1993, the examiners could not find a single federal agency worthy of the award.

TQM efforts are underway at many federal agencies, perhaps even most of them. But with some notable exceptions, TQM in the public sector is often little more than a *buzz word*. For some reason, it has been deemed by many in the federal sector to be more trouble than it is worth: "just one more thing to do," "one more set of reports to prepare," "useless," "nothing new," "the fad of the moment," "it interferes with my real work."

Why the difference? The reason most often proclaimed by public sector managers is that public sector agencies are sheltered from the threat of competition. Private sector companies must succeed or die. Individuals at every level in the company understand the link between competitiveness and job security. They are energized by that link to seek improvement.

While public sector organizations also feel a sense of urgency and crisis, it is of a very different kind. Job security for individuals in public sector agencies is often linked more to the whims of public budgets and to political forces than to individual or corporate productivity. Individual workers and operating-level managers have only limited influence over their agency's budget, and generally none at all over political forces.

The absence of competitive incentives in many (not all) of our public sector agencies is doubtless part of the reason. To provide a different kind of incentive to their agencies, our most effective public sector leaders have sought to invoke the challenge of excellence, pride in work, and service to the nation. Their success has been limited because they have not dealt with the root cause, which is out of their reach.

The root cause of public sector "malaise," to borrow President Carter's term, is the low opinion the public has of government and federal workers, and the consequent low value that public sector employees often place on their own work. The performance of public sector workers is less than it would be if they felt themselves to have important and esteemed roles in our social fabric. Our political leaders have failed to counter either the negative (even hostile) public impression or the malaise of the federal workforce. Indeed, they have fueled it by running against government, even while heading it themselves.

Until recently, top-level public sector leaders have made no serious and sustained effort to lead the federal public sector into TQM implementation. Advent of the Clinton/Gore quality management strategy, popularly known as "Reinventing Government," gives reason to hope that things will turn around.

Reinventing Government

The Clinton administration strongly supports implementation of TQM in the federal government.[1] The administration's effort to bring about the "reinvention of government" is more formally known as the National Performance Review. Under the active, informed, and enthusiastic personal direction of Vice President Gore, the drive to reinvent government has, for a number of reasons, become a model of excellence.

The first of those reasons is that Gore began the effort with an extended series of "town meetings," held at virtually every agency of the federal government. His personal appearances and strong advocacy have sent a message government-wide: "We mean it." In each of his town meetings, the Vice President has had the agency head at his side, which has the dual effect of committing the agency head to the TQM transformation and letting the staff know that the agency head is so-committed.

A second reason is that the Vice President resisted what must have been a strong temptation to simply proclaim a quality strategy and insist on compliance. Instead, his town meetings were designed to get people at all levels of the agencies to tell the Vice President what they thought needed improving. The result has been the gradual building of a list of problems common to virtually every agency. Among them are such things as unwieldy personnel practices that form a barrier to recruitment of the best people, travel policies that encourage and even force wasteful expenditure, rigid budgeting and financial control systems that encourage waste and discourage savings, a surplus of mid-level managers, and procurement regulations that force over-specification and thereby assure excessive cost. Each one of these items would have been predictable by any experienced government operative, but by getting the people to tell him in very public and widely publicized forums, these same people now have a vested interest in helping to devise the solutions.

Third, the Vice President has formed a task force of some 200 federal workers from a variety of agencies, on detail from their respective jobs. Designed to assure continued interest and input from the agencies, the task force will also be both a source and a sounding board for ideas, and a liaison back to the agencies of action items designed to correct the prevailing wastefulness and inefficiencies.

Fourth, Gore has engaged the assistance of a strong team of TQM professionals, including David Osborne and Ted Gaebler, authors of *Reinventing Government*, the book that helped shape the objectives of the performance review.[2] He is avoiding start-up and implementation mistakes by relying on the advice of people who know the pitfalls and traps through experience.

Fifth, the Vice President has himself become an expert in TQM concepts and practices. His leadership of the transformation needed to bring about the "reinvention of government" has credibility that it simply would not have achieved if he had limited his role to signing the reports and cheerleading the effort.

The Vice President's most frequently used symbol of foolishness in government has become the ashtray, better known in government procurement channels (Gore says with a smile) as "ash receiver, tobacco, desk type," described in 10 pages of specifications and regulations.[3] The ashtray testing specification is Gore's special favorite:

> You put the ashtray on a plank, a maple plank. It has to be maple, 44.5 millimeters thick. And you hit it with a steel punch, point ground to a 60-degree included angle, and a hammer. The specimen should break into a small number of irregularly shaped pieces, not greater in number than 35. But wait, now we get to the specification of the pieces: each must be 6.4 millimeters or more on any three of its adjacent edges.

And so on. To drive home the absurdity of it all, Gore poses a rhetorical question: "Would western civilization be threatened if the ashtray broke into 36 pieces?"

Gore displays a photograph of a pile of books, 1,008 pounds of them, which are the federal regulations for hiring and firing of employees, and compares this enormous stack of government regulations with the enlightened private-sector equivalent, a skinny 20- page personnel manual used by the Saturn plant in his home state of Tennessee.[4, 5, 6] His town meetings have produced a rich lode of stories about wasted money: $1,500 laptop computers routinely purchased for $3,500 (in one case after approval of the purchase by 23 officials!), $3 notebooks purchased for $6, and the barriers that discourage returning leftover funds at the end of a fiscal year. And so on, with hundreds of additional examples, all provided by government workers at Gore's town meetings. None of these examples is an isolated case; they are representative of how the system works. We need only recall the overpriced hammers and toilet seats of an earlier era.

The Importance of a Vision

In arguing that the government needs to get on with reinvention, Gore points to the success of the American private sector. Ten years ago, he asserts, it would have seemed impossible to hope that in less than a decade American car companies would again become "world models of economical quality." But competition and the threat of profits and jobs drove our car companies and the unions to change their way of operating. And now government, battling rampant public disillusionment with their services, must show they can do the same thing.

All of this is true, and the earlier-listed strengths of the Vice President's effort suggest that he has a good shot at bringing it off. But once the implementation strategy is agreed upon at the top level of the administration and once required legislative changes win congressional support, the TQM cultural transformation will need to take place out in the agencies. Bureaucracies will need to be won over, individual bureaucrats will need to be unleashed from the straitjackets of rules designed to inhibit creativity and the application of common sense, and workers at all levels will need to assume the responsibilities for action that come with empowerment.

And, finally, something will need to done to counter the public's negative impression of government. While public admiration for government may be too much to hope for in the foreseeable future, simple tolerance or acceptance would be a step up from the disdain or outright hostility that now so widely prevails.

My own experience with almost a decade of attempts to bring TQM to the federal public sector persuades me that none of this will be easy. Bureaucracies are notoriously difficult to turn around, whether public sector or private. Bureaucrats are accustomed to seeking low profiles and the safety of rules, and many federal workers have ducked responsibility for so long that embracing it or even accepting it may at first seem disconcerting. And public negativism about government is rooted deeply.

But there is a more optimistic side to this. The Vice President, in the midst of his round of town meetings, said this about federal workers: "They've been waiting for a situation where somebody will take their ideas seriously, where they don't feel like if they stick their necks out with a creative suggestion, they're going to get there heads chopped off. And now is the time for that change to take place." The enthusiasm seen at Gore's town meetings suggest that he may be right. Government workers really do seem ready for a change; ready to take pride in their work, ready to be responsible, ready to be creative.

The development of a vision of public service designed to *turn on* public sector managers and people is one of the actions that each agency head should be charged with undertaking at the start. Visions such as those provided in chapter 16 can serve as benchmarks.

The vision or mission statement for a public sector agency should be descriptive of the agency's support to society. What socially important function is the agency providing? What do American taxpayers get for tax dollars allotted to that agency? A vision/mission statement that speaks to these questions serves two important purposes, First, by proudly proclaiming the purpose and social value of the agency, its staff members are given a sense of purpose, pride, and dignity. Second, the same proclamation tells the public that this agency is important to the quality of life of American citizens; the nation simply cannot sustain its position as a desirable place to live without education, social services, safety, interstate highways, census, air travel, and the host of other services either provided or enhanced by government agencies.

Public disdain for the federal government and its employees (excluding the military) is widespread. It is conventional wisdom to hold that government can do nothing well, and that government employees are people who couldn't survive private sector competition. A great Mike Luckovitch cartoon, which appeared in the *Atlanta Constitution*, captures the public mood perfectly. It pictures the corridor of a federal office building. Two office doors appear side by side, one labeled "Federal Bureau of Looking Busy," and the other labeled "Agency for the Killing of Time." Behind the door of the latter agency is a bureaucrat, who proclaims to his assembled staff, "People, under Al Gore's plan, we'll merge with the department next door. Prepare to assume dual responsibilities."

Having spent about an equal number of years in the private and public sectors, I have come to the conclusion that this widely-held view of government is a bum rap. The ratio of strong to weak performers is about the same in large private sector organizations as in government.

Inefficiencies and indifference to the purposes of the organization are more a matter of the organization's size than of public versus private sector. Very large and highly centralized organizations, whether called General Motors or the Department of Defense, tend to become slow, unresponsive, and remote from their customers. And just as TQM has made a profound difference in our private sector, it can make an equal difference in the public sector.

But, let me say it again, it begins with a vision. Only when people understand and believe in their organization's purposes will they be ready for empowerment, improvement, and customer focus.

If we want high performance from the public sector, public sector people need to be given a reason to hold their heads up high. A vision/mission statement that portrays the purposes of the organization in ways that demonstrate the agency's importance to the nation is a first step in that direction. (See chapter 16 for the Census Bureau's vision, which is a good one.) Agency top leaders, cabinet officers, and their immediate sub-cabinet staff must proclaim their agency's vision/mission statement from the rooftops both to the agency's people and to the public. Our top political leaders need to remind the public that government is not there for its own sake, but to serve and support the essential needs of the public. Without the services that only government can provide, our society would quickly deteriorate to third-world status.

The importance of public support for government's contribution cannot be overstated. The public is the government's customer. Unless that customer is satisfied, or better yet excited and delighted with government's performance, genuine and sustained pride in work will continue to elude the federal workforce. And as long as pride in work is denied to the federal worker, performance will never reach world-class levels.

Nonessential or low-value government services must, of course, be as aggressively curtailed as political realities permit. The TQM focus on empowerment, process reengineering, customers, and planning should help our political leaders bring that about.

Vice President Gore addressed the National Conference of Governor's in August, 1993, describing the administration's Reinventing Government strategy. During the subsequent discussion, Governor Lawton Chiles of Florida made a telling point, stating that persuasion of the public needed to be an important part of the administration's strategy. Florida, the Governor said, had made numerous quality-inspired improvements; yet people in the state continue to criticize the very things on which improvements had been made. They were simply unaware that things had changed for the better. People are so accustomed to criticizing government, said Governor Chiles, that unless great efforts are made to inform the public and to win their active and enthusiastic support, government will continue to be held in low esteem even after it has been reinvented.

The Governor's advice reemphasizes the importance of the vision/ mission statement. The public needs to be made aware of the value it receives from government. Citizens need to be told about it by top elected officials, and they need to see it in terms of visible improvements in public sector performance. Only then will federal workers see their work and themselves as important players in our national endeavor, and only then will they fully deliver on the promises of reinvented government.

15

ISO: The Link with International Trade

What is ISO?

In today's climate of intensely competitive international trade, companies must identify and put into place mechanisms that will facilitate success in world markets. Foremost among such mechanisms is ISO certification.

ISO is the International Organization for Standardization. With membership from more than 90 countries including the United States, ISO has agreed on a set of quality assurance and quality management standards, and will *certify* companies that meet those standards. Because certification standards are the same worldwide, international trade is facilitated when buyers can be confident that certified companies in another part of the world meet these worldwide quality standards.

While ISO has no formal link to TQM, ISO documentation recognizes that companies embracing mature and successful TQM strategies are likely to be eminently certifiable by ISO. John Rabbitt and Peter Bergh, authors of *The ISO 9000 Book*, state that "ISO 9000 certification was merely a milestone marker in [the Foxboro Company's] TQM journey."[1] Greg Hutchins, in his book *ISO 9000*, states that "ISO is a useful first step on the journey to the Malcolm Baldrige National Quality Award."[2]

Rabbitt and Bergh assert that "ISO 9000 . . . ensures a structured working environment that captures improvements and integrates them into a stable and structured operation, thereby keeping those good ideas [from TQM continuous improvement] from eroding." Thus, ISO is not only a *useful first step* to TQM, it can help to put in place a working environment that facilitates TQM success.

Overview of ISO Content

While it is not within the scope of this book to go farther into the details of ISO, the 20 aspects of a company's quality program prescribed by ISO standards, each of which is subject to a rigorous audit during the certification process, are listed below.

1. Management responsibility
2. Quality system
3. Contract review
4. Design control
5. Document control
6 Purchasing
7. Purchaser supplied product
8. Product identification and traceability
9. Process control
10. Inspection and testing
11. Inspection, measuring, and test equipment
12. Inspection and test status
13. Control of nonconforming product
14. Corrective action
15. Handling storage, packaging, and delivery
16. Quality records
17. Internal quality audits
18. Training
19. Servicing
20. Statistical techniques

16

The Hoshin Planning Process

Hoshin Kanri Planning: Features [1]

The term *Hoshin Kanri* and the planning process it prescribes come from Japan. The term translates into English literally as "Policy Management" or "Direction Control," and has in usage come to define a particular planning process, often known in the United States simply as Hoshin Planning. TQM implementers may wish to consider the Hoshin Planning process, or some adaptation of it, for use in preparation of their corporate strategic plan, the outline for which is set forth in chapter 17, Strategic Planning.

The Hoshin Planning process, which has been adopted by Hewlett-Packard and other American organizations, is characterized by a number of features, all of which are of interest to TQM implementers:

Vision - The Hoshin Planning process begins with the creation of a vision for the organization. Its purpose is to instill creativity in planning the company's future, and to provide a sense of purpose and even inspiration to employees.

Long-term emphasis - Hoshin requires development of plans that project no less than 3-5 years into the future, and which are consistent with the company's vision statement. The long-range plans, in turn, form the basis for development of the company's short-term (one year) strategy.

Targets are always linked to means - Short-term plans must be actionable. This all-important feature of the Hoshin planning process insists that strategic objectives be supplemented with specific plans (or means) for their accomplishment. Necessary resources must be identified, people need to be assigned, realistic and achievable timetables are called for, and, to avoid ambiguity, metrics are required for evaluation.

Consensus among corporate players - Plans developed by planners remote from operations are often disputed or even ignored by those responsible for operations. The Hoshin process requires that planning be done by, or at least with, the people responsible for performance, and that each work unit involved with execution confirms the plan's achieveability and accepts responsibility for tasks assigned to it.

Cascade - Hoshin planning begins at the top of the organization. Top-level plans are deployed to the next level down, and become the basis for plans at that level. The cascade continues until work unit plans become the basis for individual performance plans.

Catchball - There is an emphasis in Japanese organizations on relentless communication among its members. The term *catchball* is used to convey the idea of tossing information around from one department to another, from one person to another, upward in the hierarchy, downward, and laterally. Everyone should be informed of what is being considered during the planning process and of what emerges as the plan.

Deployment - The plan, once completed, must be made widely available in the organization. Everyone should know what is in it. Everyone should use it as a basis for departmental and personal actions. The plan must not be filed and forgotten until the next planning cycle. It should be a living and relevant document.

Contingencies - Every plan contains elements that could go wrong. The Hoshin process seeks to anticipate possible problems, and to plan for countermeasures to employ should the problem occur.

Hoshin Kanri Planning: Method

Though it comes from Japan, Hoshin Kanri features and steps will be familiar to American planners. There is nothing radical, or even truly new, about Hoshin Kanri, other than the fact that it provides a well-organized and comprehensive set of steps which, if followed, lead to a well-defined strategy that takes into account the views and has the endorsement of everyone responsible for the plan's implementation.

There are six discrete steps to the Hoshin planning method. The first three are planning steps, and the last three deal with execution.

Step 1- The Five-Year Vision and Strategy: As noted earlier, the Hoshin process begins with development of a corporate vision, followed by development of a corporate-level strategy. The strategy is designed to achieve the vision, and should include plans for overcoming any obstacles seen to achievement of the vision.

Responsibility for preparation of the draft vision and strategy belongs to the CEO and his or her immediate staff. It is not something that is delegated to a planning office.

Though responsibility for developing the corporate vision and strategy belongs to the top corporate officers, they will want to reach into the organization for ideas. Upon having developed a draft vision and strategy for the corporation, the corporate officers submit their draft to the next level down in the organization for comment. By taking into account comments from operating units, the final corporate vision and strategy should emerge as a consensus document, and should have passed the *realism* test.

Step 2 - The One-Year Corporate Strategy: This, too, is developed by the top corporate officers. Again, they seek department-level input, subject their first draft to review and comment, and take those comments into account in the final one-year corporate strategy.

The one-year strategy is, of course, more detailed than the 3-5 year plan developed in step 1, and prescribes a course of action for the coming year that takes into account such things as obstacles to achievement of the five-year vision, customer requirements, market trends, and last year's performance.

Step 3 - Deployment to Departments: When the step 1 and step 2 plans are completed in final form, they are deployed to the company's operating units. On the basis of the corporate five-year and one-year strategies, each operating unit will prepare its own one-year plan. These department-level plans are greatly more detailed than their corporate-level predecessors. In the tradition of empowerment, the departments coordinate their plans with one another (without top-level involvement) to dovetail planned actions, to resolve overlaps, and to make sure that every requirement stated in the corporate documents is picked up by one of the departments.

Larger organizations generally have a several-tiered hierarchy. In keeping with the cascade principle earlier described, the plans of the next-higher unit provide the basis for preparation of one-year plans for the lower-level units.

Step 4 - Execution: Detailed project management documentation is prepared at the performing levels. To achieve departmental operating goals, Hoshin specifies detailed documentation of responsibilities, means, resources, and timetables.

Step 5 - Monthly Diagnosis: The Hoshin process requires monthly review of work status, at which time adjustments are made as needed to assignments or to the plan itself. The monthly diagnosis is conducted strictly at the work-unit level, without involvement of higher-level management except as solicited.

Step 6 - President's Annual Diagnosis: Once each year, the Hoshin process provides for top-level review of work status. Its avowed purpose is to help each manager perform to full potential. The review is intended to result in strategy (means) adjustments as needed to bring departmental performance up to levels specified in the plan.

Hoshin Policy Deployment

The Hoshin planning method calls for annual *policy deployment.* Its purpose is to identify the most important goals for the coming year, and to develop a strategy for their achievement. We are all familiar with the temptation to strive for parallel achievement of a substantial number of goals. Often, when we aim to accomplish too much in a short time, our attention and resources are scattered, and nothing gets done despite our good intentions.

By forcing the organization to specify and concentrate on a limited set of goals, the likelihood is that, because distractions will be fewer and resources more focused, our narrowed effort will achieve better results. Three to five policy deployment goals is about the right number. Remember, the Hoshin approach mandates that goals must always be supported by a means, a strategy that will achieve the goal.

Texas Instruments Defense Systems and AT&T Transmission Systems (both 1992 Baldrige winners) provide good examples which are reported in the next chapter under the section titled "Benchmarks for the Seven Baldrige Categories." Texas Instruments Defense Systems identified three Policy Deployment goals for 1992: improve customer satisfaction, improve the reward system, and reduce the supplier base. AT&T Transmission Systems identified four: improve customer satisfaction, improve the reward systems, increase employee involvement, and provide TQM training. In both cases, these few policy deployment goals became top goals for every part of the organization; cross-functional teams developed strategies for their achievement, assignments were made, and metrics were established.

The Corporate Vision

For corporations, as for individuals, the vision they hold of themselves is a factor in how they conduct their lives and in what they aim to become. Many years ago, Ted Levitt, a Professor at Harvard Business School, pointed out that, had railroads in the 1920's envisioned themselves as being in the transportation business, they might today be owners and operators of airlines.

William S. Paley, in 1928, took over a small radio network on the edge of failure. His vision was not merely expansion of the network; instead, it was that because he had a radio network, he had something to offer, even to give away. His vision was that CBS-developed radio entertainment programs, made available to affiliates, would attract affiliates to the network; affiliates with programs would attract audiences; audiences would attract sponsors; and advertising income would attract more and better programs. Paley's vision set the course not only for CBS's success, but for decades of development for radio and (much later) television.

The Saturn Mission and Philosophy

As noted earlier, the Saturn Corporation has implemented one of the strongest and most successful TQM strategies in the United States. In 1985, before the company was fully formed, a Saturn team visited 49 GM plants and 60 benchmark companies all over the world to determine best practices. They observed the following commonalties in successful companies:

1. Quality was a top priority.

2. Customers, both internal and external, were number one.

3. Everyone had ownership of the company's successes and failures.

4. Equality was practiced, not just preached.

5. There were no barriers to doing a good job.

6. Total trust was a must.

7. Union and management were partners.

8. People had authority to do the job.

Based on these observations, the Saturn founding team developed a statement of corporate philosophy:

> We, the Saturn Team, in concert with the UAW and General Motors, believe that meeting the needs of Saturn customers, members, suppliers, dealers, and neighbors is fundamental to our mission.
> To meet our customers' needs, our products and services must be world leaders in value and satisfaction.
> To meet our members' needs, we will create a sense of belonging in an environment of mutual trust, respect and dignity. We believe that all people want to be involved in decisions that affect them. We will develop the tools, training and education that each member needs. Creative, motivated, responsible team members who understand that change is critical to success are Saturn's most important asset.
> To meet our suppliers' and dealer's needs, we will create real partnerships with these organizations. We will strive for openness, fairness, trust, and respect with them, and we will work with them to help them feel ownership of Saturn's mission and philosophy.
> To meet our community neighbors' needs, we will be a good citizen and protect the environment, and we will seek to cooperate with government at all levels.

The Census Bureau Vision
The United States Census Bureau has assembled a vision statement that is a benchmark of excellence for beauty, for clarity, for brevity, and as a statement of social service:

> In its best interests, a civilized nation counts and profiles

its peoples and institutions. Doing so ably and objectively is the abiding mission of the United States Census Bureau.

We honor privacy, invite scrutiny, shun partisanship, and share our expertise locally. Striving to excel, we chronicle the nation's past, describe its present, and illuminate its future.

A Draft TQM Vision

The following paragraphs set forth a vision statement for a TQM strategy. It is written to be generically applicable:

> Implementation of TQM will result in measurable improvement to our operations within one year, and in profound improvement within three.
>
> Our TQM vision has several aspects that we wish to highlight:
>
> TQM has a single purpose: to improve business performance. It is a means to that end, and not an end in itself. Its most relevant measure of success is improvement of our organization's business fundamentals, not the details of the TQM strategy itself.
>
> TQM seeks to build bridges across hierarchical and departmental moats, forming a seamless web of corporate partnerships. We are an organization in which every member is both a corporate partner and manager of his or her part of the corporate whole.
>
> TQM will lead to better products and services, delighted customers, a more interested, involved, and dedicated work force, leaner and more focused management, more efficient use of resources, more effective suppliers, and improved quality and productivity.
>
> TQM is not a program. It is a strategy, a way of doing business, a way of managing the organization and its activities. It must not be allowed to develop its own bureaucracy.
>
> TQM, by providing a coherent and integrated management strategy, with its focus on people, customers, products, processes, and plans, brings about a shift in focus from vertical to horizontal management. Day-to-day problems, because of the TQM emphasis on business fundamentals, are dealt with in ways that confront and correct root causes as well as surface effects.

Corporate visions, when thoughtful and well written, strengthen peoples' bonds to one another and to their organization, are powerful guides to action, and can even be inspirational. When the corporate vision is perceived to have social value, members are transformed. They become partners in a creative and useful venture. They are affiliated with an endeavor in which they can take pride. An organization with social value confers status and dignity upon its members. When peoples' work becomes their passion, professional involvement, creativity, and productivity climb to new highs.

17

Strategic Planning

Overview

This chapter will bring together everything from the preceding chapters by developing the framework for a strategic plan for a TQM organization. Consider these recommendations:

• Use the seven Baldrige categories as the outline for your corporate strategic plan. There will be a section of your plan for each of these seven categories. Suggested content for each of the sections is provided below.

• For each of the seven Baldrige categories, study the achievements of Baldrige winners and use them as benchmarks when developing your own winning strategy.

For your guidance, representative Baldrige-winning strategies for each of the seven Baldrige categories are summarized below following the suggested plan outline.

• When developing your corporate strategic plan, use a proven planning method. There are any number of good methods, but the one I like is Hoshin Kanri, described in the previous chapter.

Baldrige As a Basis for Planning

A good way to interleave business plans with TQM principles is to use the seven Baldrige categories as the outline. The resulting strategic plan will provide a roadmap that speaks not only to company goals for products, markets, and resources, but equally (and simultaneously) to the means (the seven Baldrige categories) by which the company's strategic goals will be achieved. The Baldrige categories are:

1. Leadership
2. Information and Analysis
3. Strategic Quality Planning
4. Human Resource Development and Management
5. Management of Process Quality
6. Quality and Operational Results
7. Customer Focus and Satisfaction.

Correlation of Planning With Performance

The reader will have discerned that use of the Baldrige-based outline for the corporate strategic plan effectively results in an internal audit of every aspect of company operations while, at the same time, prescribing plans for improvement at every step. Use of the Baldrige criteria as the basis for the audit and as the outline for the company's strategic plan provides several additional advantages.

The first is that the Baldrige criteria are an excellent guide to good management. They were assembled by experts in quality management and have been improved every year since 1988 by taking into account the comments of Baldrige examiners and of the hundreds of companies that have undertaken the experience of a Baldrige audit as entrants into the annual award competition.

Second, the Baldrige criteria have become the common language of TQM companies worldwide. Each year, the Baldrige winners state the strategy they have employed to win the award; their statements describe best practices in each of the seven Baldrige categories. Companies employing these same Baldrige categories as the framework for their own management strategies are thereby annually presented with ready benchmarks from world-class TQM practitioners (see below).

Third, companies contemplating application for the Baldrige award will be stronger contenders after several years of experience with annual self-audits against the Baldrige criteria and by benchmarking previous Baldrige winners.

Company strategic plans should cover a period of no less than 3-5 years. They must be reviewed annually for updating or revision as dictated by changing circumstances. Only rarely will a 3-5 year strategic plan remain wholly credible one year after it is written. Separate plans may be required for different divisions or elements of the corporate hierarchy.

Outline for a Corporate Strategic Plan Based on the Seven Baldrige Categories

The seven-section outline spelled out below follows the seven Baldrige categories exactly. However, the detailed content suggested for each of the seven sections varies from the Baldrige criteria whenever warranted. Readers who decide to use this proposed outline for their corporate strategic plans will doubtless feel free to invent additional variations to bring about a plan outline consistent with their needs.

As you prepare your corporate strategic plan, refer to the chapters of this book that are appropriate to the topic at hand. For example, when developing your leadership strategy (Section 1 of the Plan), you will want refer to chapter 8 and this chapter for suggestions about leadership and vision, respectively. When developing your human resources strategy (Section 4 of the Plan) you will want to refer to chapters 3 (Listening), 4 (Empowerment), 5 (Teaming), 6 (Reward Systems), and 7 (Training). And so forth.

Section 1.0 of the Plan: Leadership

1.1. Statement of the Company's Vision. Development and articulation of the company's vision is one of the paramount responsibilities of leadership. Some ideas on how the vision should be developed (involving inputs and interaction with the empowered work force) will be described later in this chapter in the discussion of Hoshin Planning. Samples of some representative (and excellent) corporate visions are set forth in chapter 16, Hoshin Kanri Planning.

1.2. Statement of the Strategy to be Employed to Achieve the Vision. The vision, as important as it is, is meaningless fluff without a description of the strategy to be employed in achieving the vision. The strategy must be developed jointly by senior management and those at the operating level (possibly including suppliers) responsible for its implementation. Without full involvement and concurrence of the people who must make it happen, the strategy has not been tested for realism, and will not receive the full level of *buy-in* and informed support that every strategy requires to ensure successful implementation.

1.3. Senior Executive Leadership. Describe specific actions to be taken by senior executives to develop and sustain an environment for TQM excellence. Consider executive visibility, involvement, communication, and betterment. Include a description of the TQM management infrastructure and how it serves to facilitate TQM implementation.

1.4. Management for Quality. Discuss how the company's vision, strategy, and values will be deployed to lower-level management and to the work force. Describe how the company's customer focus and quality values will be integrated into day-to-day leadership of all company units and levels. Define and state the roles and responsibilities of subordinate managers and of the work force with respect to the company's vision, strategy, and values. Describe key indicators for evaluation and improvement of quality values among senior executives, managers, and supervisors.

1.5. Statement of the Company's Values. Discuss the company's commitment to workforce empowerment, customer focus, and continuous improvement of products, services, and processes. Include a statement of ethics and integrity as it applies to the company, its officers and the work force.

1.6. Public Responsibilities and Corporate Citizenship. The company's statement of values should include discussion of its commitment to public responsibility and corporate citizenship. Consider and describe the company's social purpose, environmental commitments, and community interests and commitments. Consider and describe how the company will lead as a corporate citizen of the community or communities in which it has facilities or otherwise does business. How will the company promulgate the quality philosophy and its quality practices among those with whom it does business and within its community?

Section 2.0 of the Plan: Information and Analysis

2.1. Scope and Management. Identify the set of processes, product and service parameters, and company functions on which data need to be gathered for ongoing improvement analysis. TQM is a fact-based management method, and data are needed as a basis for objective analysis leading to continuous improvement of every aspect of the company's endeavors. Comprehensive data sets also improve the company's ability to perform strategic planning, day-to-day management, and evaluation of quality and operational performance.

For each designated data category, responsibilities need to be assigned in the strategic plan to specific individuals and departments for collection and analysis.

2.2. Competitive Comparisons and Benchmarking. Specify benchmark goals and methods for the company's information and analysis effort, including at least the following categories: (1) customer-related; (2) product and service quality; (3) internal operations and performance, including business processes, support services, and employee-related; and (4) supplier performance.

Baldrige category 2.2 specifies that benchmarking these four data categories is intended to provide a basis for improved understanding of processes, encouragement of breakthrough approaches, and for the setting of *stretch* objectives. Section 2.2 of the strategic plan should state how this intention will be met.

2.3. Analysis and Uses of Company-Level Data. Describe: (1) how customer-related data will be aggregated with other key data to develop actionable information leading to prompt solutions to customer-related problems, and to identify customer-related trends to support planning; (2) how operational data will be translated into operational improvements, including cycle-time, productivity, and waste reduction; and (3) how the company plans to identify changes in overall financial performance and correlate those changes with improvements in product/service quality and operational performance.

Section 3.0 of the Plan: Strategic Quality Planning

3.1. Strategic Quality and Company Performance Planning Process. Develop the company's business plan in detail, including: (1) customer requirements and the expected evolution of those requirements; (2) projections of the competitive environment; (3) risks, including financial, market and societal; (4) company capabilities, including human resource development, and research and development to address key new requirements or technology leadership opportunities; and (5) supplier capabilities. The business plan should include plans for process improvement and reengineering.

3.2. Quality and Performance Plans. State the company's quality and operational performance goals for the short term (1-2 years) and the long term (3-5 years). Include key requirements and key operational performance indicators for deployment to work units and suppliers, and a description of resource requirements and commitments for key needs, such as capital equipment, facilities, education and training, and personnel.

Section 4.0 of the Plan: Human Resource Development and Management

4.1. Human Resource Planning and Management. Describe the company's overall human resource plans, including how they are integrated with its quality and operational performance goals. Address fully the needs and plans for development of the work force, including: (1) education, training, and empowerment; (2) planned changes in work organization, processes, or work schedules; (3) reward, recognition, benefits, and compensation; and (4) recruitment, including possible changes in work force diversity. Discuss planned improvements to human resource processes, such as recruitment, hiring, personnel actions, and services to employees. Identify employee-related data, to include at least absenteeism, turnover, grievances, and accidents, and how these data are used to improve human resource functions.

4.2. Employee Involvement. Describe plans for bringing about and/or sustaining high levels of involvement and how this will improve employee contributions to the company's quality and operational performance goals. Include consideration of employee feedback mechanisms and define key indicators of the extent and effectiveness of involvement (and how data will be gathered) for the various categories of employees.

4.3. Employee Education and Training. Set forth a plan for determining employee education and training needs, including ways to seek and use employee input to the plan. Training and education should relate both to job-skill enhancement and to problem solving, waste reduction, and process improvement. Show its relevance to company plans and to employee growth. Include a plan for measuring the effectiveness of education and training, including measurement of its effect on employee involvement (both the effectiveness and the extent of involvement) for each category of employee. The plan should address how training and education are to be delivered, including (1) classroom training, (2) on-the-job training, and (3) orientation of new employees.

4.4. Employee Performance and Recognition. Consider and describe plans for changes to the company's employee recognition, performance, compensation, reward, and feedback approaches (including for managers) aimed at improving employee and corporate performance. Include ways for involving employees in the development and implementation of these plans. Describe metrics to be used to evaluate performance and recognition systems, including: (1) effect on employee involvement, (2) effect on employee satisfaction, and (3) effect on employee and company performance.

4.5. Employee Well-Being and Satisfaction. State plans for improvement of health, safety, and ergonomics, including preventive methods and how root causes are determined for health and safety-related problems. Include goals and metrics for each element. Develop and state plans for special services (e.g. day care), facilities, and opportunities the company plans to make available to employees. Include plans for determining level of employee satisfaction for each employee category. State plans for benchmarking employee satisfaction results.

Section 5.0 of the Plan: Management of Process Quality

5.1. Design and Introduction of Quality Products and Services. Set forth how designs of products, services, and processes are developed so that: (1) customer requirements are translated into product and service design requirements; (2) all product and service quality requirements are addressed early in the overall design process by appropriate company units; (3) designs are coordinated and integrated to include all phases of production and delivery; and (4) key process performance characteristics are selected and measurement systems are developed to track them.

5.2. Process Management: Product and Service Production and Delivery Processes. State the company's plan for bringing about and/or sustaining the quality of production and delivery processes. Include: (1) a description of key processes and their requirements; (2) key indicators of quality and operational performance; and (3) how quality and operational performance are determined and maintained. Address the need for root cause determination for out-of-control variations in process output, and how processes are improved using: (1) process analysis/simplification, (2) benchmarking information, (3) process research and testing, (4) use of alternative technology (reengineering), (5) information from customers of the processes, and (6) challenge goals.

5.3. Process Management Business Processes and Support Services. State the company's plan for bringing about and/or sustaining the quality of key business and support service processes. Include the same information specified in 5.2.

5.4. Supplier Quality. Present a plan for defining and communicating quality and response time requirements to suppliers. Define required feedback and metrics for evaluation.

5.5. Quality Assessment. Present a plan for company assessment of the quality and performance of its systems, processes, and practices, and the quality of its products and services. This part of the plan pertains to all unit activities covered in 5.1, 5.2, 5.3, and 5.4.

Section 6.0 of the Plan: Quality and Operational Results

6.1. Product and Service Quality Results. Summarize trends for all key measures of product and service quality. Compare these data with principal competitors in key markets, industry averages, industry leaders, and appropriate benchmarks. Use factors most directly linked to customer satisfaction, such as accuracy, reliability, timeliness, performance, behavior, delivery, after-sale service, documentation, appearance, and effective management of complaints and inquiries. Plans for improvement should be specified.

6.2. Company Operational Results. Summarize trends for key measures of company performance. Compare with that of competitors, industry averages, industry leaders, and key benchmarks. Key metrics include those most closely linked to productivity, efficiency, and effectiveness, such as manpower, materials, energy, capital and assets, cycle time reduction, and environmental improvement. Trends in financial indicators should be included, and should be linked to quality and operational performance improvement activities of the company. Plans for improvement should be specified.

6.3. Business Process and Support Service Results. Summarize trends for key measures of quality and operational performance of business processes and support services. Compare with those of competitors, industry averages, industry leaders, and appropriate benchmarks. Key measures should include quality, productivity, cycle time, and cost for business and support service processes. Plans for improvement should be specified.

6.4. Supplier Quality Results. Summarize trends for key indicators of supplier quality. Compare with competitors and/or benchmarks. The results summarized in 6.4 derive from quality improvement activities described in 5.4. Plans for further improvement should be specified.

Section 7.0 of the Plan: Customer Focus and Satisfaction

7.1. Customer Expectations: Current and Future. Describe how the company determines near-term and longer-term requirements and expectations of customers.

7.2. Customer Relationship Management. Describe how the company provides effective management of its interactions and relationships with its customers and uses information gained from customers to improve customer relationship management processes.

7.3. Commitment to Customers. Describe the company's commitments to customers regarding its products/services and how these commitments are evaluated and improved.

7.4. Customer Satisfaction Determination. Describe how the company determines customer satisfaction, customer repurchase intentions, and customer satisfaction relative to competitors; describe how these determination processes are evaluated and improved.

7.5. Customer Satisfaction Results. Summarize trends in the company's customer satisfaction and in key indicators of customer dissatisfaction.

7.6. Customer Satisfaction Comparison. Compare the company's customer satisfaction results with those of competitors.

Benchmarks for The Seven Baldrige Categories[1]

There are as many different TQM implementation strategies as there are different organizations. The winning practices summarized below for each of the seven Baldrige categories will provide a basis for the development of a world-class quality strategy to meet the unique needs of your own organization.

Benchmarks for Baldrige Category 1.0: Leadership

Granite Rock Company

• Establish a set of "permanent" Corporate Objectives. For Granite Rock, there are nine: customer satisfaction, people, product quality, profit, management, community commitment, growth, productivity, and safety.

• Set annual Baseline Goals for each of the nine Corporate Objectives. There are 57 Baseline Goals, roughly evenly split among the nine Corporate Objectives.

• Communicate the Baseline Goals and strategies for achieving them throughout the organization. They become the basis for that year's strategic focus.

• Base executive compensation in key part on achievement of the Baseline Goals.

• Senior executives teach or facilitate courses and seminars for employees. This obliges executives to learn enough to teach, and results in bonding between employees and executives.

• Conduct an annual "recognition day" at each branch location for senior executives to receive reports of outstanding accomplishments, and to express appreciation in a festive atmosphere.

• Emphasize integrity. This applies even to customers. For Granite Rock, contractors who fail to meet standards of integrity do not qualify as customers.

• Develop a leadership culture in which executives and managers are coaches and teachers. Managers are rotated to stimulate interdepartmental cooperation and reduce parochialism.

AT&T Universal Card Services

• Develop and annually update a list of the "Ten Most Wanted Improvements." AT&T UCS's current list is: (1) analysis of customer feedback, (2) program management process, (3) empowerment of management, (4) quality metrics data base, (5) strategic planning process, (6) involvement of senior executives in quality improvement, (7) benchmarking, (8) supplier management, (9) employee opinion survey results, and (10) training commitment.

• Develop and communicate a set of corporate values. For AT&T UCS, they are: customer delight, commitment, teamwork, continuous improvement, trust and integrity, mutual respect, and a sense of urgency.

• Develop and communicate a basis for world-class service: meetings with customers, listening to customer's calls, daily review of metrics, meet with suppliers, benchmark, act upon customer feedback, team rallies, town-hall meetings with staff, and staff focus groups.

AT&T Transmission Systems

• Identify the corporate mission, vision, values, and share them with all the employees.

• Identify a responsible senior executive for each of the seven Baldrige criteria.

• Provide TQM training to senior executives, and asked them to lead implementation.

• Form a quality council, chaired by the CEO, and staffed by his direct reports. Meet bi-weekly.

Benchmarks for Baldrige Category 2.0: Information and Analysis

Granite Rock Company

• Granite Rock's "management by fact" system is based on constant measurement and feedback for the nine Corporate Objectives, and for the 57 Baseline Goals. Analysis of these data are the basis for continuous improvement.

• In addition to the Corporate Objectives and Baseline Goals, there are Branch Goals, unique to each branch (different locations). Data are locally accumulated and analyzed for improvement ideas.

• Analysis of delivery time led Granite Rock to search for a benchmark. They were unable to find another cement company that had a comparable data base; none was measuring delivery time. So Granite Rock turned to Domino's Pizza, a worldwide leader in on-time delivery of a rapidly perishable product. Domino's vast data base and extensive analysis provided the basis for a continuing benchmark relationship (since 1990) between these two very different companies, each of whom has a very similar and very central operating challenge.

AT&T Universal Credit Card Services
• The following data are accumulated and analyzed: customer satisfaction, customer attrition, employee opinion surveys, ten most wanted status, financial, quality, development time, and on-time delivery.

AT&T Transmission Systems
• The following data are accumulated and analyzed: product quality, process quality, customer satisfaction, customers won and lost, market share, complaints, internal operations, supplier performance, employee turnover, employee satisfaction, and productivity.
• Analysis strategies include: continuous analysis, assignment of improvement teams, identification of root causes for anomalies, development of improvement plans, and implementation of improvements.

Ritz-Carlton Hotel
• The following example typifies Ritz-Carlton's strategy for meeting the requirements of category 2.0:
Customers complained about time taken to provide room service at breakfast time. Analysis showed that the root cause was busy elevators, partly because linen was being carried to floors during breakfast hours. Solution: pre-stock linen on each floor during night hours. Though done to improve room service, linen pre-stock led to 5% reduction in room make-up time which, in turn, led to savings in maid time, earlier room availability, and increased customer satisfaction.
• The frequent ripple effect of quality improvement is amply demonstrated by this example.

Benchmarks for Baldrige Category 3.0: Strategic Planning

Granite Rock Company
• Quality plans and business plans are not separated. They are one and the same. The nine Corporate Objectives define focus areas which combine to bound a quality program.
• Annual Baseline Goals grow directly from Corporate Objectives. These goals are measurable, and become the responsibility of division managers.

• Granite Rock has created a planning chart called the "Quality by Design Timeline," By tracing all nine Corporate Objectives from the year they were first defined (1985) to the farthest projection point (three years hence), the timeline chart is both an historical and a forecasting tool. Trends are readily apparent.

• Planning is both top-down and bottom-up. Customer requirements drive the plan.

AT&T Universal Card Services

• Development of at strategic plan yields far more than a business tool. Its chief result is to bond together the many parts of the organization.

• The strategic plan is developed by 15 cross-functional teams. The teams draw ideas from everyone in the organization. To be useful, the strategic plan must be a consensus product of the entire organization, not just a few planners.

• Establish a *Customer Listening Post*. The Listening Post is a team comprised of senior managers. It meets monthly to consider ideas from customers and people. Its purpose is to find ways to improve customer *delight*.

• Suppliers are required to participate in the planning process.

• Employ Policy Deployment.

Texas Instruments Defense Systems

Policy Deployment examples:
• reduce the management hierarchy to five levels
• increase training
• reduce the supplier base.

AT&T Transmission Systems

•Policy Deployment aligns and engages the company's people in their quest for excellence.

• Policy Deployment examples:
    - improve customer satisfaction
    - improve the reward system
    - increase employee involvement
    - provide TQM training.

• Use *catch-ball* (relentless and continuous vertical/lateral communication) to develop strategies for each of the Policy Deployment objectives.

• Employ benchmarking to identify improvement ideas for each of the Policy Deployment objectives.

Benchmarks for Baldrige Category 4.0: Human Resource Development and Management

Granite Rock Company

• The Individual Professional Development Plan (prepared annually) is the basic people-development tool. It links the company's business/quality plans with human development.

• The company pays for requested outside education and training, whether work-related or not.

• People are empowered to satisfy customers: "do what is necessary; decide as though you owned the business."

• Open books: people are given complete information about the company: products, finances, prospects, plans, and competition.

• Promotions from within.

• People are involved in procurement of costly equipment. Procurement decisions on such costly items as cement mixer trucks and bulldozers are made by teams of managers, drivers, and mechanics.

• Such major procurement decisions were formerly the province of a vice-president. Now that actual users of the equipment are involved, questions are being asked and requirements are being specified that the vice-president alone would never have thought about. Moreover, people are *more* frugal with company resources than managers. "We are getting better decisions."

• A primary role of the manager is to bring a flood of information into the company. The company sponsors seminars on diverse topics: law, teamwork, leadership, quality, safety, suppliers, conducted by outside speakers and by company executives. The seminars are done on company time; attendance is voluntary. Seminars are generally attended by 50-70 people (out of a 400-person work force).

• An annual recognition day is held at each branch.

• People are involved in the hiring of new employees.

• Any employee thinking about applying to transfer or for promotion is entitled to try any job for a day.

• There are weekly and quarterly company publications to provide a constant stream of information about the company.

• Human resource metrics are as follows: numbers attending seminars, amount of cross-training, numbers attending company social functions, satisfaction with company benefits, time required to process insurance claims, absenteeism, turnover, number requesting education and training, and results of exit interviews.

Texas Instruments Defense Systems
• Emphasis on teamwork, empowerment, flattening the number of management levels from eight to four, increasing the span of control from less than 8:1 to greater than 10:1.

• People development, brought about by: training, job enhancement, and education reimbursement.

• Employee well-being enhanced by: safety, health, fitness center, recreational clubs, family events, counseling for personal problems, child care, and retirement planning.

• To provide a basis for improvement of human resource management, an employee survey is conducted annually, focus groups are convened, and other organizations are benchmarked.

• Self-directed work teams are responsible for team member work assignments, production planning, overtime scheduling, customer interface, training, and hiring.

• The manager's role is to listen. To do this well requires frequent informal meetings with people. Management listens for good ideas and promulgates them across the organization.

AT&T Universal Card Services
• Emphasis on orientation of new employees.
• Provide training in the corporate vision and values. At AT&T UCS, this is known as "Passport to Excellence" training.

Benchmarks for Baldrige Categories 5.0: Management of Process Quality, and 6.0: Quality and Operational Results

Because of their close relationship, benchmarks for categories 5.0 and 6.0 are dealt with together. Category 5.0 speaks to process improvement methods, and 6.0 speaks to process improvement results.

Texas Instruments Defense Systems
• Steps to six-sigma for manufactured products (recall from chapter 12 that six-sigma is a very high quality standard: defect rate is about 3 parts per million):

1. Identify the product characteristics that are critical to satisfy both the physical and functional requirements of the customer and the requirements of relevant regulatory agencies.

2. Determine the specific product's elements that contribute to achieving these critical characteristics.

3. According to product elements, determine the process step or process choice that controls each critical characteristic.

4. Determine a nominal design value and the maximum (real) allowable tolerance for each critical characteristic which still guarantees required performance.

5. Determine the capability for parts and process elements that control critical characteristics.

6. If Cp is < 2 or Cpk < 1.5, then change the design of the product and/or process to achieve results of at least these levels.

• Steps to six-sigma for office and administrative areas:

1. Identify the product you create or the service you provide.

2. Identify the customer(s) for your product or service, and determine what they consider important.

3. Identify your needs (what input you require to provide products/services that satisfy the customer).

4. Define the process for doing the work.

5. Mistake-proof the process and eliminate wasted effort.

6. Ensure continuous improvement by measuring, analyzing, and controlling the improved process.

• Benchmark all processes, administrative as well as manufacturing.

• Process design and improvement should be done by cross-functional teams who are most familiar with the process at the performance level.

AT&T Transmission Systems

• AT&T conducts quality audits at the corporate level for all divisions, based on the Baldrige criteria.

• Established nine expert *breakthrough* teams, called Achieving Process Excellence (APEX) teams. Their function is to identify process improvements needed to enable the company to develop and deploy new products more rapidly.

• Metrics tracked for category 6.0 are: productivity, quality, cost, timeliness, cycle time, revenue per employee, supplier performance, and reduction in the supplier base (number of suppliers).

Granite Rock Company

• Product/service discrepancy reports are generated both internally and by customers to document and explain complaints. The reports become a valuable basis for root cause analysis and product/process improvement.

• Business (administrative) processes are given emphasis equal to product/service processes.

Benchmarks for Baldrige Category 7.0: Customer Focus and Satisfaction

Granite Rock Company

• Place equal emphasis on immediate customers (contractors) and end customers (e.g. home owners).

• Establish partnering relationships with customers. For example, Granite Rock has partnering arrangements with contractors that provides for specification compliance certification, field testing, customer service technicians, and training.

• Commitment to customers is provided with a guarantee policy called "Short Pay". When customers are displeased with any aspect of service, they can withhold pay for that part of the service. This customer action leads to immediate resolution of the difficulty through root cause determination and improvement.

• Customer contact personnel are promoted from within. This policy is known as "TEC Hiring" (Traits, Experience/Education, Chemistry). TECs are schooled in the nine Corporate Objectives, Baseline Goals, and ethics.

• Annual customer surveys are performed, supplemented by customer focus groups. Customers are asked to rate competitors as well. Matrix analysis is performed to identify any gaps between competitor performance and company performance, and to devise strategies to regain competitive advantage. (This simple matrix analysis method is described in chapter 13).

• Metrics used for category 7.0 are: lost customers, Product/Service Discrepancies (PSDs), Short Pay, focus group results, and customer contact feedback.

• New ideas are communicated to customers via frequent seminars, demonstrations, customer contact, and company publications.

• Customer surveys disclosed customer concern about turnaround time while trucks were being loaded with cement. This led to establishment of "Granite Express" cards: after the driver inserts the card, the truck is automatically loaded to reduce truck waiting time.

Texas Instruments Defense Systems

• Field offices, staffed with skilled engineers, have been established near customers.

• A "key customer contact list" is maintained to promote communications between TI executives and customer counterparts.

• Senior executives frequently visit customers to seek feedback.

• TI seeks to "place itself in the customer's shoes" by working closely with customer maintenance personnel and end-users.

• Complaints are used as a basis for improvement.

• Guarantees and warranties are employed and scrupulously honored.

AT&T Transmission Systems

• Customer feedback is facilitated by the use of customer-initiated "report cards." The format of the card and the questions asked on the card were developed in partnership with customers.

• Report cards are used to develop better understanding of customer requirements, rate performance in key areas, and create a basis for improvement.

• Customers are assured of "risk-free" purchase, with a five-year warranty.

• Customers are provided with 24-hour technical support.

The von Moltke Rule

Prussian Field Marshall von Moltke, known as a superior strategist, once said, "A plan is only valid until the opponent makes his first move." In this, the last paragraph of the chapter on Strategic Planning, I thought it might be useful to elevate von Moltke's statement to the status of a planning *rule*. My purpose in doing so is that it affords me the opportunity to make two closing points. First, plans need to be flexible enough to accommodate changing circumstances. And second, I have observed a tendency among some to become obsessed with the planning process itself, perhaps because it can be both interesting and challenging; but planning must not become an excuse for inaction while we prolong the hunt for elusive "perfect" solutions.

18

Some Concluding Thoughts

One of the main purposes in writing this book was to provide readers with an in-depth discussion of TQM concepts, and to provide proven ideas on how to implement them. The best practices of recent Baldrige winners summarized in the preceding chapter enable you to integrate those practices with the material from earlier chapters. World-class business strategies tailored to the needs of your own organization should emerge from the synthesis.

What follows summarizes some of the most important ideas conveyed in this book. The ideas are listed in no special order and are intended as the basis for discussion (and debate) in your organizations.

• Management methods make a difference; remember George Washington's observations on the subject.

• The term *quality*, as it is used in TQM, has been transformed. Whereas quality once dealt with measurable things, such as voltages, dimensions, and defect rates, it now includes not only product excellence, but the means by which that excellence is achieved: empowerment, process improvement, customer focus, and strategic planning. Thus, broadly defined, TQM is what general management is all about. It is, indeed, *Total* Quality Control.

• TQM is simple and, in a sense, there is nothing new about it because its concepts and practices are the timeless principles of good management.

TQM integrates these principles into a cohesive whole, and provides methodology for their expeditious and successful accomplishment.

• The simplicity of TQM might be compared to the *simplicity* of the Golden Rule. While both are simple, each is endlessly profound, challenging, and rewarding.

• Benchmark everything you do. Consider especially the best practices of Baldrige winners.

• The Baldrige and President's Award Criteria provide a proven roadmap to successful implementation of your quality strategy. Their wide use provides a common language by which TQM practitioners can exchange best-practice ideas.

• Read everything you can get your hands on. Ideas come from the strangest places and at times when you would least expect them. They rarely come from board meetings.

• TQM is not a program, it is a strategy for conducting your business. It is a way of doing business. Its only purpose is to improve the performance of your business. It is a means to that end, not an end in itself.

• TQM must not be allowed to become merely another set of things to do, and added layer of bureaucracy. TQM is, by definition, anti-bureaucratic.

• The people who manage (lead) TQM are the very same people who manage (lead) the organization. Thus, your TQM management infrastructure is already in place. By wearing the two hats (business management and TQM management) your managers will be required to invest some of their time on business fundamentals (people, processes, customers, strategy) in the context of dealing with operational issues.

• TQM requires a cultural transformation.

• The "red-bead" experiment demonstrates the futility of blaming workers for poor results. The process is king.

• Process reengineering is vital to corporate transformation, but so is kaizen. Use both.

• Remember the rules of reengineering:
  - Rule 1: Consolidation
  - Rule 2: Flexibility
  - Rule 3: Employ technology
  - Rule 4: Begin with the customer
  - Rule 5: Lead from the top
  - Rule 6: Simplify

• Quality and productivity bear a non-zero-sum relationship to one another. Improvements in quality lead directly to corresponding improvements in productivity.

• TQM principles apply equally to product and service industries, to private and public sector organizations, and to small as well as to large organizations.

• CEO-level involvement in TQM implementation is vital to success. Top corporate officers should seek a profound understanding of TQM concepts and Baldrige best-practices.

• Drive out fear. Improvement entails risk, and people are willing to try something new only when they are relieved of fear from failure.

• Eliminate micro-management. Practice horizontal management.

• Listening to people is a vital first step. Remember the Xerox story; always ask people what they think. Its people are every organization's most important untapped resource.

• Empowerment does not imply abrogation of managerial responsibility, nor is it an absence of discipline.

• Matsushita was wrong: the industrial west is not going to "lose out."

• Fallows is right: we need to become "more like us."

• A number of things must be done to bring empowerment about:
  - Practice "open book" management.
  - Discretionary effort can make the difference between average and great performance. Remember the millwright.
  - Jobs need to be enriched, vertically and horizontally.

- Span of control should rarely be less than 20.
- People should be empowered to select new teammates.

• Leadership is very different from management. Leaders are made, not born. TQM requires leaders; people can and should manage themselves. Characteristics of successful leaders include:
- Knowledge
- Stature in the organization
- Participative
- Part of an effective network
- Listener and scholar
- Integrity
- Confidence
- Teacher
- Egalitarian

• Consider the Leadership Audit conducted by Deming Prize examiners. Leaders are encouraged to administer this test to themselves. Good leaders provide strong answers to these questions:
- What is your job? Not your title, but your job.
- What are the eight most important things you do?
- How do you measure your performance?
- Based on these requirements, how are you doing?
- Where do you want the company to be next year? In five years? How do you propose to get there?

• Self-directed teams are more effective than groups of coordinated and managed individuals. Team behavior is brought about with the following:
- Establish a clear charter for team members.
- Bring about a sense of commitment.
- Convey ownership of the task at hand to the team.
- Members need to feel a realistic sense of potency.
- Interdependence among members.
- Loyalty between members.
- Team-based reward system.
- Recognition of team performance.
- Team self-confidence.
- Wide responsibility, both horizontal and vertical.
- Self-direction.
- Information of the kind that managers get.
- Training, both in technical functions and in teambuilding.

• Corporate resources spent on training are good investments. While this is especially true for job-related training, it is also true for education that may be peripheral to the persons function.

• For repetitive processes, whether in the factory or in the office, employ statistical process control as a basis for process improvement and defect prevention. Strive for six-sigma quality levels.

• Remember the Taguchi loss function. Any deviation from the design parameters results in "loss to society."

• CARE: Customers are really everything. Put yourself in their shoes to get a profound understanding of their requirements and expectations.

• Employ the kansei approach: find ways to go beyond mere satisfaction of customers to customer delight and excitement.

• Study the Hoshin Planning process, and employ it or some near variant for development of your corporate strategic plan. Its most important features include:
  - Vision
  - Long-term emphasis
  - Targets are linked to means
  - There is a consensus among corporate players, achieved by involving as many as possible in the planning process
  - Policy deployment used to focus the entire organization on the few most important objectives for the coming performance period

• Use the seven Baldrige criteria as the outline for your corporate strategic plan, one section for each of the Baldrige categories.

• Remember the von Moltke rule.

The author welcomes comments and questions raised by the material presented in this book, and will make every effort to respond to inquiries. Please address any correspondence to the publisher, or directly to the author at: Eric Anschutz Associates, 4801 Hampden Lane, Suite 301, Bethesda, Maryland, 20814 USA. Telephone: 301-656-5578.

Notes

Chapter 1: TQM Overview

1. *GE Annual Report,* 1988.

2. *Reengineering the Corporation,* Michael Hammer and James Champy, Harper Business, New York, 1993.

3. *Prophets in the Dark,* David T. Kearns and David A. Nadler, Harper Collins, New York, 1992.

4. *Made in America (Report of the MIT Commission on Industrial Productivity)* , Dertouzos, Lester, and Solow, MIT Press, Cambridge, 1989.

5. *A Better Idea: Redefining the Way Americans Work,* Donald Petersen, Houghton Mifflin, Boston, 1991.

6. *Thriving on Chaos,* Tom Peters, Harper and Row, New York, 1987.

7. *Auto Week,* April 27, 1987.

8. *The Washington Post,* October 27, 1992, "School Tries Borrowing From Business," Maria E. Odum.

9. *GE Annual Report,* 1990.

10. *Business Week,* October 18, 1993, "Betting to Win on the Baldie Winners."

Chapter 2: Deming and His Fourteen Points

1. *Out of the Crisis,* W. Edwards Deming, MIT Press, Cambridge, 1987.

2. *The Man Who Discovered Quality,* Andrea Gabor, Random House, New York, 1990.

3. *A Better Idea: Redefining the Way Americans Work,* Donald Petersen, Houghton Mifflin, Boston, 1991.

Chapter 3: Listening is the First Step

1. *Prophets in the Dark*, David T. Kearns and David A. Nadler, Harper Collins, New York, 1992.

2. *Manufacturing Engineering*, "A Secret is Shared," February, 1988.

3. *GE Annual Report*, 1993.

4. *More Like Us (Making America Great Again)*, James Fallows, Houghton Mifflin, Boston, 1989.

5. *Harvard Business Review*, November/December, 1990, "How I Learned to Let My Workers Lead," Ralph Stayer.

Chapter 4: Empowerment: How to Make it Happen

1. *Fortune*, February 22, 1993, "The Non-Manager Managers," Brian Dumaine.

2. *Fortune*, April 19, 1993, "What Chief Executives Return to Shareholders per Square Foot of Office Space."

3. *Leadership is An Art*, Max DePree, Doubleday, New York, 1989.

4. *The Washington Post*, March 29, 1992, "Skills and Schools; Is Education Reform Just a Business Excuse?" Jonathan Weisman.

5. *The New York Times*, February 8, 1992, "Japan Studies U.S. Workers (AP)."

6. *The Washington Post*, February 8, 1992, "Tokyo: U.S. Workers Outproduce Japanese," T.R. Reid.

7. *The New York Times*, April 28, 1991.

8. *Fortune*, September 20, 1993, "The Real Key to Creating Wealth," by Shawn Tully.

Chapter 5: Teaming

1. *Fortune*, March 22, 1993, "Companies That Train Best," Ronald Henkoff.

2. *The New York Times*, May 18,1991.

3. *Inc.*, February, 1993, "Training Gets Physical," Alex Prud'Homme.

4. *Business Week*, May 4, 1992, "Putting a Damper on That Old Team Spirit," Aaron Bernstein.

5. *Inc.*, May, 1993, "Team Penalty," by M.P.C.

6. *Business Week*, January 25, 1993, "Making Teamwork Work and Appeasing Uncle Sam," Aaron Bernstein.

7. *In The Rings of Saturn*, Joe Sherman, Oxford University Press, 1994, New York.

8. *MIT Management*, Spring 1992, "Managerial and Technological Innovation at Saturn Corporation," Richard G. LeFauve and Arnold C. Hax.

9. *The New York Times*, January 23, 1990, "GM's Saturn Plant Starts to Make Friends and Impress Critics," Dorin P. Levin.

10. *A Better Idea: Redefining the Way Americans Work*, Donald Petersen, Houghton Mifflin, Boston, 1991.

11. *The New York Times*, "Where the Cadre Sets the Pattern," Claudia H. Deutsch.

12. *Business Week*, November 15, 1993, "A Case Study in Change at Harvard," Lori Bongiorno.

13. *Newsweek*, May 10, 1993, "The Group Classroom," Barbara Kantrowitz and Carey Monserrate.

14. Letter to the author, dated July 9, 1994, from Motorola's Director of Corporate Supply Management.

15. *Harvard Business Review*, January-February, 1994, "Why My Former Employees Still Work For Me," Ricardo Semler.

16. *Adventures of a Bystander*, Peter Drucker, HarperCollins, New York, 1991.

17. *Business Week*, April 26, 1993, "Executive Pay: The Party Ain't Over Yet," John Byrne and Chuck Hawkins.

Chapter 6: TQM Reward Systems

1. *The Washington Post*, March 21, 1993, "Job Performance Being Evaluated From Some New Angles," Frank Swoboda.

2. *Inc.*, August, 1993, "Gainsharing," Tom Eherenfeld.

3. *Adventures of a Bystander*, Peter Drucker, HarperCollins, New York, 1991.

4. *Fortune*, April 19, 1993, "Deal Those Workers In," John Labate.

5. Newsweek, February 20, 1993, "A Generation Topped Out," Jane Bryant Quinn.

6. *The New York Times*, June 6, 1993, "It's What You Can Do That Counts," Mary Rowland.

7. *Harvard Business Review*, November/December, 1990, "How I Learned to Let My Workers Lead," Ralph Stayer.

8. *The Washington Post*, November 29, 1989, "Ben and Jerry," Howard Kurtz.

9. *Newsweek*, February 1, 1993, "What Made You Mad Today?," Annette Miller.

10. *Inc.*, February, 1993, "Managing People."

Chapter 7: Training and Education

1. The Washington Post, August 17, 1990, "American Firms Must Come To See the Importance of Intellectual Capital," Michael Schrage.

2. *The New York Times*, January 18, 1993, "Old Mill Pioneers Workers' Education," Fox Butterfield.

3. *The Washington Post*, January 19, 1992, "Recession or Not, Training Remains an Essential Expense," Carol Kleiman.

4. *The Washington Post*, March 24, 1993, "Reeducating for Profit," Gary Lee.

5. *The New York Times*, January 18, 1993, "Old Mill Pioneers Workers' Education," Fox Butterfield.

6. *Proceedings of the Quest for Excellence Conference*, held in Washington, D.C., February 1993.

7. *The New York Times*, March 30, 1993, "Back to School for Honda Workers," Doron P. Levin.

8. *The New York Times*, March 31, 1993, "Ritz-Carlton's Keys to Good Service," Edwin McDowell.

9. *Fortune*, March 22, 1993. "Companies That Train Best," Ronald Henkoff.

10. *Business Week*, February 22, 1993, "How Much Good Will Training Do?" Aaron Bernstein with Paul Magnusson.

11. Ibid.

12. *Prophets in the Dark*, David T. Kearns and David A. Nadler, Harper Collins, New York, 1992.

13. *Inc.*, February 1993, "Ground-Zero Training," Martha Mangelsdorf.

14. *Quality Without Tears*, Phil Crosby, Penguin Books, New York, 1984.

15. *MIT Management*, Winter, 1992, "The State of the School," Dean Lester Thurow.

16. *Pacesetter*, The Philadelphia Area Council for Excellence, Fall 1990, "Academia Enters the TQM Arena."

17. *Business Week*, April 26, 1993, "From High Schools to High Skills," Christina DelValle.

Chapter 8: Leadership in a TQM Organization

1. *Leadership is an Art*, Max DePree, Doubleday, New York, 1989.

2. *GE Annual Report*, 1991.

3. *Leadership is an Art*, Max DePree, Doubleday, New York, 1989.

4. *Made in America: My Story*, Sam Walton, Doubleday, New York, 1992.

5. Notes from a presentation made by John Hudiberg in Caracas, Venezuela, June, 1992.

6. *MIT Management*, Winter 1989, "On Having What It Takes," Akio Morita.

7. *Harvard Business Review*, November-December, 1992, "The Work of the Leader," Lt. General William Pagonis.

Chapter 9: TQM Management Infrastructure
No notes for Chapter 9.

Chapter 10: Kaizen and Reengineering
1. *Kaizen*, Masaaki Imai, McGraw Hill, New York, 1986.

2. *Washington Post Magazine*, April 18, 1993, "The Many Crusades of Ira Magaziner," Steven Perlstein.

3. *Chicago Tribune*, January 7, 1990, "Ford Sets the Pace in Productivity for Auto Firms," Tom Hundley.

4. *The New York Times*, June 3, 1990.

5. *The Washington Post*, October 1, 1993, "Health-Violence Tie Prompts Gun Tax Talk," by Dana Priest,

6. *Wall Street Journal*, January 11, 1991.

7. *Reengineering the Corporation*, Michael Hammer and James Champy, Harper Business, New York, 1993.

8. *The New York Times*, April 19, 1992, "Ardent Preacher of Radical Change," Glen Rifkin.

9. *Modern Office Technology*, January 1993, "Reengineering - The Frantic Discovery of the Obvious," Michael Thomas.

10. *Business Week*, May 24, 1993, "Reengineering, Beyond the Buzzword," John A, Byrne.

11. *Fortune*, May 3, 1993, "The Promise of Reengineering" (a review of *Reengineering the Corporation*).

12. *Fortune*, August 23, 1993, "Reengineering, The Hot New Management Tool," James A. Stewart.

13. *Competing Against Time*, George Salk and Tom Hout, The Free Press, New York, 1990.

14. *The Washington Post*, June 6, 1993, "Slips and the Lisp," Elizabeth Austin.

Chapter 11: Process Improvement Methods
1. *Benchmarking*, Robert C. Camp, ASQC Quality Press, Milwaukee, 1989.

2. *Fortune*, August 12, 1991, "GE Keeps Those Ideas Coming," Thomas A. Stewart.

Chapter 12: SPC, Six-Sigma, and All That

1. *Out of the Crisis*, W. Edwards Deming, MIT Press, Cambridge, 1987.

2. *SPC Simplified*, Amsden, Butler, and Amsden, Kraus, New York, 1986.

Chapter 13: Customer Obsession

1. *The New York Times*, February 5, 1993, "Posing as a Welfare Recipient, Agency Head Finds Indignity," Allison Mitchell.

2. *A Passion for Excellence*, Tom Peters and Nancy Austin, Random House, New York, 1985.

3. *Vision in Action*, Tregoe, Zimmerman, Smith, and Tobia, Simon and Schuster, New York, 1989.

4. *Harvard Business Review*, July-August 1991, "Corporate Imagination and Expeditionary Marketing," Gary Hamel and C.K. Prahalad.

5. *A Better Idea: Redefining the Way Americans Work*, Houghton Mifflin, Boston, 1991.

Chapter 14: The Public Sector Challenge

1. *Report of the National Performance Review - Creating A Government That Works Better and Costs Less*, Vice President Al Gore, 1993.

2. *Reinventing Government*, David Osborne and Ted Gaebler, Addison-Wesley, Reading, Massachusetts, 1992.

3. *Newsweek*, August 16, 1993, "The Vice President's Ashtray," Joe Klein.

4. *Washington Post*, September 1, 1993, "Government at its Worst," Robert Samuelson.

5. *Washington Post*, May 18, 1993, "Gore's Chat With Interior Staff May Set Babbit Back By $38," Stephen Barr.

6. *Washington Post*, July 21, 1993, "Al Gore's Quality Revolution," David S. Broder.

Chapter 15: ISO: The Link With International Trade

1. *ISO 9000*, Greg Hutchins, Oliver Wight Publications, Inc., Essex Junction, Vermont, 1993.

2. *The ISO 9000 Book*, John Rabbitt and Peter Bergh, Quality Resources, White Plains, New York, 1993.

Chapter 16: The Hoshin Planning Process

1. *Hoshin Planning. The Developmental Approach*, Bob King, GOAL/QPC, Methuen, Massachusetts, 1991.

Chapter 17: Strategic Planning

1. The material presented in this section was taken from notes from the proceedings of the 1993 "Quest for Excellence" Conference, held in Washington, D.C., February, 1993.

Chapter 18: Some Concluding Thoughts

No notes for chapter 18.

Recommended Readings

The following TQM-related books belong in the library of any serious student or practitioner of the subject.

A Better Idea: Redesigning the Way Americans Work, Donald Petersen, Houghton-Mifflin, Boston, 1991.

Deming Management at Work, Mary Walton, Putnam, New York, 1990.

Deming's Road to Continual Improvement, William W. Scherkenbach, SPC Press, Knoxville, Tennessee, 1991.

Dr. Deming: The American Who Taught the Japanese About Quality, Rafeal Aguayo, Simon and Schuster, New York, 1990.

Juran on Planning for Quality, Joseph M. Juran, Macmillan, New York, 1988.

Leadership is an Art, Max DePress, Doubleday, New York, 1989.

Made in America, Dertouzos, Lester, and Solow, MIT Press, Cambridge, 1989.

Managing for the Future, Peter F. Drucker, Dutton, New York, 1992.

More Like Us, James Fallows, Houghton-Mifflin, Boston, 1989.

Out of the Crisis, W. Edward Deming, MIT Press, Cambridge, 1987.

Prophets in the Dark, David T. Kearns and David A. Nadler, Harper Collins, New York, 1992.

Quality is Free, Philip B. Crosby, McGraw-Hill, New York, 1978.

Quality or Else, Lloyd Dobbins & Clare Crawford-Mason, Houghton Mifflin, Boston, 1991.

Quality Without Tears, Phil Crosby, Penguin Books, New York, 1984.

Reengineering the Corporation, Michael Hammer and James Champy, Harper Business, New York, 1993.

Self-Directed Work Teams, Jack D. Orsburn, Linda Moran, Ed Musselwhite, Jon H. Zenger, Business One Irwin, Homewood, Illinois, 1990.

The Deming Management Method, Mary Walton, Putnam, New York, 1986.

The Frontiers of Management, Peter F. Drucker, Harper & Row, New York, 1986.

The Man Who Discovered Quality, Andrea Gabor, Random House, New York, 1990.

Thriving on Chaos - Handbook for a Management Revolution, Thomas J. Peters, Alfred A. Knopf, New York, 1987.

Why Work? - Leading the New Generation, Michael Maccoby, Simon & Schuster, New York, 1988.

Index

A

A Better Idea, 5, 16, 41
administrivia, 3, 132
Adventures of a Bystander, 80, 88
Aetna Life and Casualty, reengineering at, 134, 137
Air Force Logistics Commnd, 9
Alcoa, 96
American Cyanamid, 86
American Express, 169
Andersen Consulting, training at, 97
Apple Computer, 111
appraisal factors, 87
apprentice programs, 108-109
AT&T, 33, 55, 131
AT&T Credit, 73-74
AT&T Transmission Systems, benchmarks, 200-207
policy deployment goals, 186-187
AT&T Universal Card Service, 9, 173
benchmarks, 199-204
Austin, Elizabeth, 138-139
Australia, training requirements in, 97

B

Baldrige Award, 41, 64, 76, 160
Baldrige categories, 191-207
benchmarks for, 199-207
Baldrige criteria, 167
Baxter Healthcare, 78
Ben & Jerry's Homemade Ice Cream, 93
benchmarking, 141-147, 168
benchmarks, 199-207
benefits of training, 99
Bergh, Peter, 181
Beth Isreal Hospital, 89
Biojector, 169
Blockbuster, reengineering at, 133
Boeing, 81
Brennen, Supreme Court Justice William, 115
Briggs & Stratton, 55
Burr, Richard E., 70

C

Carnavale, Anthony, 96-97, 109
Carter, President, 174
Caterpillar, 81

C *continued*

CBS, 187
Champy, James, 3, 23, 124-125, 133
Chevron Corporation, training, 100
Chiles, Governor Lawton, 179
Chrysler, 9
Clinton,
  Hillary, 131
  President Bill, 42
Coca-Cola, 55
committment to customers, 166
communication, 25
Competing Against Time, 133
computers, use of in processes, 137
Conference on the Future of the American Workplace, 42
Corning, training at, 97, 102-103
corporate privacy, protecting, 44
corporate vision, 44, 187-190
  sample vision statement, 189-190
cost of capital, 55-56
cost of quality, 7
costs,
  employee health care, 30
  warranty, 30
Crate and Barrel, training at, 107
Crosby, Phil, 107
CSX Intermodal, 55, 56-57
cultural, transformation, 35
customer, 168
  expectations, 161
  involvement, 53
  obsession, 1, 3, 159-172
  relationship management, 164-166
  satisfaction, 198
  satisfaction index, 90

customer satisfaction,
  benchmarking, 168-169
  measuring, 163, 166
  reengineering for, 137-138
customer segmentation, 161
customers, internal, 171-172

D

Dana, 5
Dartmouth, 75
day-care, company-sponsored, 94
Deming Prize, 119
Deming, W. Edwards, 15-30, 83, 86, 168
  red bead experiment, 128-130
Department of Defense, 77
DePree, Max, 46, 111, 117
Desert Storm, 120
Digital Equipment, 81
dissatisfaction, customer, 168
diversity of teams, 68
Dodge/Plymouth, 169
Domino's Pizza, 200
Donahue, Dennis, 100
Dow Chemical, determining customer needs, 162
downsizing, 18, 20
Drexel University, TQM training , 108
Drexler, Alan, 64
Drucker, Peter, 37, 80, 88, 89, 132
DuPont, 89
  reengineering at, 134, 137

E

Eastern Realty Investments, 9
economic value added, 54-57
education, 95-109
  benefits of, 103
egalitarianism, 20

Electromation, Inc., 68
employee,
    classes, 45
    evaluation of supervisors, 88
    health care costs, 30
    selection, work force role in, 53
empowerment, 1, 2, 5, 32, 33, 36-39, 41-57, 87, 89, 179
    stages of, 37-38
evaluation of supervisors by employees, 88
expectations, customer, 161

F

Fallows, James, 33-34
Federal Express, 9
    training at, 97
Federal Quality Institute, 11-12
FelPro, 93
Fetterolf, C. Fred, 96
Fletcher Music Centers, 170
flexibility of processes, 135
Florida Power and Light, 119
Florida, 9
Ford Motor Co., 5, 9, 16, 24, 51, 70, 72-73, 77, 81, 86, 130-131, 134
    loss function, 157
    Task Force, 5, 6
Fourteen Points, Deming's, 17-30
Fowler, Robert, 101
France, training requirements in, 97

G

Gaebler, Ted, 175
gain sharing, 88-90
Galvin, Robert, 24, 41-42
Gardener's Supply Company, 93

General Electric, 3, 5, 13-14, 24, 33, 51, 65, 81, 84, 132
    leadership characteristics, 112-113
    Work-Out, 148
General Motors, 80-81, 86, 88, 96, 130-131
General Motors Powertrain Division, 86
George Washington University, 9
Germany, 15
    postal service of, 43
    training in, 97
Gore, Vice President Al, 132, 174-179
government, reinventing, 174-176
Granite Rock Company, 9
    benchmarks, 199-206
    training, 101, 107
Great Plains Software, 169
Griffeth Rubber Mills, training, 101
groups, organizational, 45
Grove, Andrew, 46

H

Hamel, Gary, 170
Hammer, Michael, 3, 23, 124-125, 133
Hampolen Papers, training, 100
Hampton, VA, 9
Harvard Business School, 75-76
Herman Miller Furniture Company, 46
Hewlett-Packard, 5
    adaptation of Hoshin planning, 183
Honda, training, 101
horizontal management, 50-52

H *continued*

Hoshin Kanri, 3-4
  deployment of, 186-187
  features of, 183-184
  methods, 184-186
  planning, 183-190
Hoult, Tom, 133
Hudibergm John, 119
human resource development, 195-196
Hurt, William, 160
Hutchins, Greg, 181

I

IBM, 5, 77, 96
  reengineering, 133
IBM Credit, reengineering at, 133-134, 137
infrastructure, TQM management, 121-125
inspection, mass, 21
Intel, 46
internal customers, 171-172
Internal Revenue Service, 9
International Organization of Standardization, 181-182
ISO 9000, 181
ITT Sheraton, rengineering at, 134

J

Japan, 5, 15-16, 33
  Labor Ministry, 49
  networking in, 113
  postal service of, 43
Japanese Union of Scientists and Engineers Code of Standards, 78
job enrichment, 48-50
Jobs, Steve, 42

Johnson's Wax, 93
Johnsville Foods, 38, 92
just-in-time delivery, 78

K

kaizen, 23, 96, 130-131, 140, 141
Kansei, 3, 169
Kearns, David, 3, 24, 31, 39, 112
Kodak, 49
Kruse, Douglas, 88-89

L

Lands' End, 93, 170
Lawler, Prof. Edward, 93
leaders, role of, 115
leadership, 23-24
  audit, 212
  characteristics, 111-115
  in reengineering, 138
Leadership is an Art, 46, 111
Lettuce Entertain You Enterprises, training at, 107
Levin, Henry, 49
Levitt, Ted, 187
Lexus U.S., 162
Lincoln Electric, 52
listening to employees, 31
listening, art of, 66
LTV Steel, 81

M

Made in America, 4
Made in America: My Story, 118
Madison, WI, 9
Maier, General James, 33
Malcolm Baldrige National Quality Award, 9-11, 14, 106, 181
Management by Objectives (MBO), 26, 83-85

management by strategy, 84-85
Mangelsdorf, Martha, 106-107
Marlow Industries, 9
Marriot, 93
matrix ranking of customer satisfaction, 164
Matsushita Company, training, 100
Matsushita, Kosusuke, 32
measuring customer satisfaction, 163, 166
Merck, 89
Metropolitan Life Insurance, 81
micro-management, 117
Microsoft, 89
Midwest Medical, 36
Milliken, 9, 159
MIT Commission on Industrial Productivity, 4-5, 6
MIT Sloan School of Management, 9, 108
More Like Us, 33
Morita, Akio, 119
Motorola, 9, 24, 41, 64, 65, 76-77, 86, 109, 162
    six-sigma process described, 155-156
    training expenditure at, 97
Motorola University, 102

N

Nandler, David, 3
National Broadcasting Company, 17
National Commission for Employment Policy, 97
National Institute for Standards and Technology, 11
National Labor Relations Board, 68-69

Naval Air Systems Command, 9, 106
Naval Weapons Support Center, 67
Navy, 68
newsletters, functions of, 44
Next Computer, 42
NLRB Act of 1935, 69
Northwestern University, 75
Nucleus of Technological Innovation, 79
Nucor Corporation, 46, 81
numerical goals, 83-85

O

obsession, customer, 1, 3
Oregon, 9
orientation training, 103-104
Osborne, David, 175
outward bound teambuilding, 67-67

P

Pagonis, Lt. Gen. William, 120
Paley, William S., 187
Panasonic, 32
performance appraisal, 85-88
Peters, Tom, 6, 159
Petersen, Don, 5, 16, 24, 41, 51, 70, 171
Philadelphia Area Council for Excellence, 108
Phoenix Design, reengineering at, 134, 137
planning, strategic, 191-207
Plumley Companies, Inc., training, 101
Polaroid Corporation, 92-93
Pomperaug High School, 75-76
Prahalad, C.K., 170

P *continued*

Presidential Award for Quality, 11-12
Print and Copy Factory, employee improvement at, 107
Pro Fasteners, training at, 107
process
  capability, 154-155
  design, 127
  improvement, 1, 2, 23
  improvement teams, 124-125, 148-149
  quality, 197
  reengineering, 179
Proctor and Gamble, 81
profit sharing, 88-90
promotion,
  of employees, 91-92
  two-track, 52
Prophets in the Dark, 3
public sector TQM, 173

Q

Quad Graphics, training at, 107
Quaker Oats, 55
quality
  council, 121-123
  management board, 121, 123-124, 149
  planning, 195
Quality System Reviews, 77
Quality Without Tears, 107
questionnaires, customer, 163, 16

R

Rabbitt, John, 181
red bead experiment, 128-130
Reebok, 169

reengineering, 23, 96, 131-140, 141
  rules of, 211
reengineering the corporation, 3, 23
Reinventing Government, 175
reward systems, 83-94
rewards, non-monetary, 93
Ritz-Carlton Hotel
  benchmarks, 201
  training, 102

S

Salk, George, 133
Sarah MacAuliffe Elementary School, 9
Saturn Corporation, 71-72, 78, 169
  benchmarking GM, 187-188
Schrage, Michael, 96
Sculley, John, 111
segmentation, customer, 161
self improvement, 26
Semco S/A, 79
Semmler, Roberto, 80
shared information, 41-45
six-sigma quality, 22, 155-156
  vs. three-sigma, 155
skill-based pay, 92-93
slogans, eliminating, 25
Smith, Adam, 25, 135
Smith-Kline-Beecham Pharmaceuticals, 169
Sobel, Barbara, 159
Southern Audio Services, 170
span of control, 52
specialization in workplace, 135
Springfield ReManufacturing, 89
stages of empowerment, 37-38
Standards and Poor's 500, 14

statistical process control, 150-154
Stayer, Ralph, 38, 92
Steelcase Furniture, 93
Stern, Joel M., 55
Stewart, G. Bennett, 55
stock option plans, 89
strategic planning, 1, 191-207
supervisor evaluation by employees, 88
supplier involvement, 53
suppliers
    as team members, 76-77
    reducing number of, 77-78
    selecting, 22
Syntex Corporation, 89

T

Taguchi loss function, 156-158
Taguchi, Genichi, 156
Tandem Computers, 89, 93
Taylor, Frederick, 25, 48, 135
team
    building, 65-67
    development, stages of, 63-65
    effectiveness, characteristics for, 60-63
teaming, 58-82
teams, process improvement, 124-125, 148-149
Teamsters Union, 68
teamwork, 5
Terry, Richard, 93
Texas Instruments Defense Systems
    benchmarks, 202, 204-206
    policy deployment goals, 186-187
The Doctors, 160
The ISO 9000 Book, 181

Thinkodrome, 80
3M, 5
three-sigma quality level, 21
Thurow, Lester, 108
Tom's of Maine, 93-94
Total Quality Control, 17
Toyota, 78
training, 20, 23, 95-109
    benefits of, 99
    expenditures, corporate, 97
    TQM, 104-106
        class size for, 106
        length of, 105
    types of, 98-99
transformation, cultural, 35
TRW, 5
two-track promotion, 91-92, 52

U

unions, 68-71
United Auto Workers Union, 70, 71-72, 130
United States Census Bureau, corporate vision, 188-189
United Technologies, 77
Universal National Bank and Trust Co., 74-75
universality of TQM, 9
University of Akron, 100
University of Tennessee, 75
University of Wisconsin, 9, 68
U.S. Navy Aviation Depot, 89
U.S. Postal Service, 43

V

valuing, 36
Vermont, 9
Vision in Action, 161
Volvo, training, 100
von Moltke rule, 207

W

wages for CEO's, 81-82
Wagner, Richard, 67
Wal-Mart, 118
Walton, Sam, leadership rules, 118
warranty costs, 30
Welch, Jack, 24, 51, 112
Westinghouse, 52
Will-Burt Company, benefits of training at, 99-100
work force empowerment, 1
Wyatt Company, 86

X

Xerox, 3, 9, 24, 31, 39, 65, 78, 86, 106
    training, 106
    expenditure, 97

Y

Yokich, Steve, 70

Z

zero sum relationships, 6-7

About the Author

Eric E. Anschutz is founder and president of Eric Anschutz Associates, an international resource center for the implementation of Total Quality Management. Anschutz is also a faculty member of the George Washington University Center for Organizational Effectiveness. He holds a Bachelors degrees from the Massachusetts Institute of Technology and a Masters degree from George Washington University.

Prior to forming his TQM consulting and training practice, Anschutz held senior executive positions in both industry and government, and contributed to the development and implementation of a presidential-award-winning TQM strategy for the Naval Air Systems Command.